Miracle in the Andes

Miracle
in the Andes

72 Days on the Mountain and

My Long Trek Home

Nando Parrado with Vince Rause

CROWN PUBLISHERS · NEW YORK

Copyright © 2006 by Nando Parrado

Published in the United States by Crown Publishers, an imprint of the
Crown Publishing Group, a division of Random House, Inc., New York.
www.crownpublishing.com

Library of Congress Cataloging-in-Publication Data

Parrado, Nando
Miracle in the Andes : 72 days on the mountain and my long trek home /
by Nando Parrado with Vince Rause.—1st ed.
p. cm.
1. Survival after airplane accidents, shipwrecks, etc.   2. Aircraft accidents—
Andes Region.   3. Cannibalism—Andes Region. 4. Parrado, Nando, 1949-
5. Aircraft accident victims—Uruguay—Biography.   I. Rause, Vince.
II. Title.
TL553.9.P37 2006
982′.6—dc22   2005021629

ISBN-13 978-1-4000-9767-8
ISBN-10 1-4000-9767-3

Printed in the United States of America

Design by Lauren Dong

*Map on page x–xi by Mapping Specialists, Ltd., Madison, WI;
maps on pages 47and 239 by David Cain*

10 9 8 7 6 5 4 3 2 1

First Edition

To Veronique, Veronica, and Cecilia.

It was all worth it. I would do it all again for you.

Contents

Miracle in the Andes

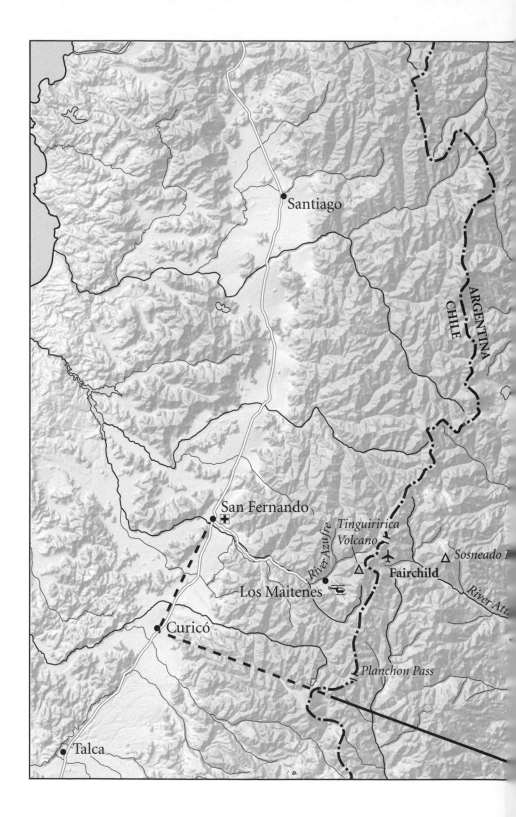

Santiago

ARGENTINA
CHILE

San Fernando

Tinguiririca
Volcano

River Azufre

△ Sosneado

Fairchild

Los Maitenes

River Atu

Curicó

Planchon Pass

Talca

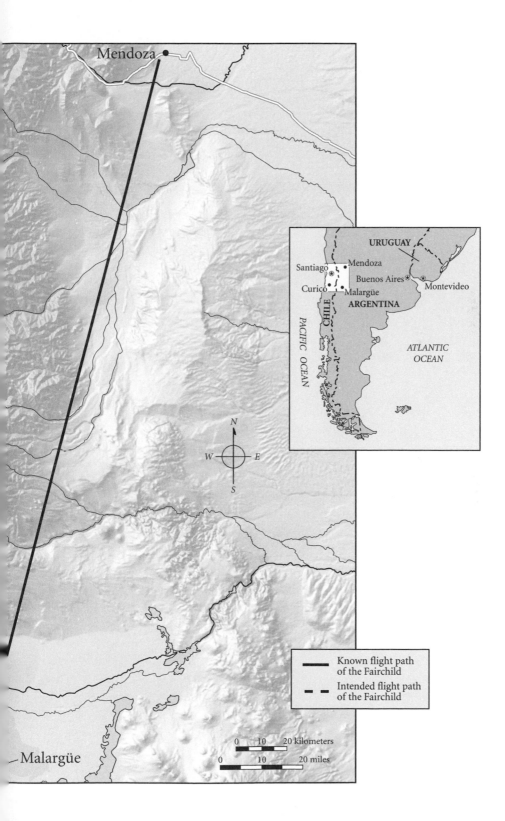

Mendoza

Malargüe

URUGUAY

Santiago
Curico
ARGENTINA

Mendoza
Buenos Aires
Malargüe
Montevideo

CHILE

PACIFIC OCEAN

ATLANTIC OCEAN

N
W · E
S

Known flight path
of the Fairchild

Intended flight path
of the Fairchild

0   10   20 kilometers
0   10   20 miles

Prologue

IN THE FIRST HOURS there was nothing, no fear or sadness, no sense of the passage of time, not even the glimmer of a thought or a memory, just a black and perfect silence. Then light appeared, a thin gray smear of daylight, and I rose to it out of the darkness like a diver swimming slowly to the surface. Consciousness seeped through my brain like a slow bleed and I woke, with great difficulty, into a twilight world halfway between dreaming and awareness. I heard voices and sensed motion all around me, but my thoughts were murky and my vision was blurred. I could see only dark silhouettes and pools of light and shadow. As I stared at those vague shapes in confusion, I saw that some of the shadows were moving, and finally I realized that one of them was hovering over me.

"*Nando, podés oírme?* Can you hear me? Are you okay?"

The shadow drew closer to me, and as I stared at it dumbly, it gathered itself into a human face. I saw a ragged tangle of dark hair and a pair of deep brown eyes. There was kindness in the eyes— this was someone who knew me—but behind the kindness was something else, a wildness, a hardness, a sense of desperation held in check.

"Come on, Nando, wake up!"

Why am I so cold? Why does my head hurt so badly? I tried desperately to speak these thoughts, but my lips could not form the words, and the effort quickly drained my strength. I closed my eyes and let myself drift back into the shadows. But soon I heard other voices, and when I opened my eyes, more faces were floating above me.

"Is he awake? Can he hear you?"

"Say something, Nando!"

"Don't give up, Nando. We are here with you. Wake up!"

I tried again to speak, but all I could manage was a hoarse whisper. Then someone bent down close to me and spoke very slowly in my ear.

"*Nando, el avión se estrelló! Caímos en las montañas.*"

We crashed, he said. The airplane crashed. We fell into the mountains.

"Do you understand me, Nando?"

I did not. I understood, from the quiet urgency with which these words were spoken, that this was news of great importance. But I could not fathom their meaning, or seize the fact that they had anything to do with me. Reality seemed distant and muffled, as if I were trapped in a dream and could not force myself to wake. I hovered in this haze for hours, but at last my senses began to clear and I was able to survey my surroundings. Since my first bleary moments of awareness, I had been puzzled by a row of soft circular lights floating above me. Now I recognized these lights as the small rounded windows of an airplane. I realized that I was lying on the floor of the passenger cabin of a commercial aircraft, but as I looked forward to the cockpit, I saw that nothing about this aircraft seemed right. The fuselage had rolled to the side, so that my back and head were resting against the lower wall of the plane's right side, while my legs stretched out into the upward-slanting aisle. Most of the plane's seats were missing. Wires and pipes dangled from the damaged ceiling, and torn flaps of insulation hung like filthy rags from holes in the battered walls. The floor around me was strewn with chunks of shattered plastic, twisted scraps of metal, and other loose debris. It was daylight. The air was very cold, and even in my dazed state, the ferocity of the cold astonished me. I had lived all my life in Uruguay, a warm country, where even the winters are mild. My only real taste of winter had come when I was sixteen years old and was living as an exchange student in Saginaw, Michigan. I hadn't brought any warm clothing with me to Saginaw, and I remember my first taste of a true Midwestern winter blast, how the wind cut through my thin spring jacket, and my feet turned to ice inside my lightweight moccasins. But never had I imagined anything like the bitter subzero gusts that blew through the fuselage. This was a savage, bone-crushing cold that scalded my skin like acid. I felt the pain in every cell of my body, and as I shivered spastically in its grip, each moment seemed to last an eternity.

Lying on the drafty floor of the airplane, there was no way to warm myself. But the cold was not my only concern. There was also a throbbing pain in my head, a pounding so raw and ferocious it seemed that a wild animal had been trapped inside my skull and was clawing desperately to get out. Carefully I reached up to touch the crown of my head. Clots of dried blood were matted in my hair, and three bloody wounds formed a jagged triangle about four inches above my right ear. I felt rough ridges of broken bone beneath the congealed blood, and when I pressed down lightly I felt a spongy sense of give. My stomach heaved as I realized what this meant—I was pressing shattered pieces of my skull against the surface of my brain. My heart knocked against my chest. My breath came in shallow gasps. Just as I was about to panic, I saw those brown eyes above me, and at last I recognized the face of my friend Roberto Canessa.

"What happened?" I asked him. "Where are we?"

Roberto frowned as he bent down to examine the wounds on my head. He had always been a serious character, strong willed and intense, and as I looked into his eyes I saw all the toughness and confidence he was known for. But there was something new in his face, something shadowy and troubling that I hadn't seen before. It was the haunted look of a man struggling to believe something unbelievable, of someone reeling from a staggering surprise.

"You have been unconscious for three days," he said, with no emotion in his voice. "We had given up on you."

These words made no sense. "What happened to me?" I asked, "Why is it so cold?"

"Do you understand me, Nando?" said Roberto. "We crashed into the mountains. The airplane crashed. We are stranded here."

I shook my head feebly in confusion, or denial, but I could not deny for long what was happening around me. I heard soft moans and sudden cries of pain, and I began to understand that these were the sounds of other people suffering. I saw the injured lying in makeshift beds and hammocks throughout the fuselage, and other figures bending down to help them, speaking softly to each other as they moved with quiet purpose back and forth through the cabin. I noticed, for the first time, that the front of my shirt was coated with a damp brown crust. The crust was sticky and clotted when I touched it with the tip of a finger, and I realized that this sad mess was my own drying blood.

"Do you understand, Nando?" Roberto asked again. "Do you remember, we were in the plane . . . going to Chile . . ." I closed my eyes and nodded. I was out of the shadows now; my confusion could no longer shield me from the truth. I understood, and as Roberto gently washed the crusted blood from my face, I began to remember.

Chapter One

Before

It was Friday, the thirteenth of October. We joked about that—flying over the Andes on such an unlucky day, but young men make those kinds of jokes so easily. Our flight had originated one day earlier in Montevideo, my hometown, its destination Santiago, Chile. It was a chartered flight on a Fairchild twin-engine turbo-prop carrying my rugby team—the Old Christians Rugby Club—to play an exhibition match against a top Chilean squad. There were forty-five people aboard, including four crew members—pilot, copilot, mechanic, and steward. Most of the passengers were my teammates, but we were also accompanied by friends, family members, and other supporters of the team, including my mother, Eugenia, and my younger sister, Susy, who were sitting across the aisle and one row in front of me. Our original itinerary was to fly nonstop to Santiago, a trip of about three and a half hours. But after just a few hours of flying, reports of bad weather in the mountains ahead forced the Fairchild's pilot, Julio Ferradas, to put the plane down in the old Spanish colonial town of Mendoza, which lies just east of the Andean foothills.

We landed in Mendoza at lunchtime with hopes that we would be back in the air in a few hours. But the weather reports were not encouraging, and it was soon clear that we would have to stay the night. None of us liked the idea of losing a day from our trip, but Mendoza was a charming place, so we decided to make the best of our time there. Some of the guys relaxed in sidewalk cafés along Mendoza's broad, tree-lined boulevards or went sightseeing in the city's historic neighborhoods. I spent the afternoon with some friends watching an auto race at a track outside of town. In the evening we went to a movie, while some of the others went dancing with some Argentinean girls they had met. My mother and Susy spent their time exploring Mendoza's quaint gift shops, buying presents for friends in Chile and souvenirs for the people at home. My mother was especially pleased to find a pair of red baby shoes in a small boutique, which she thought would make the perfect gift for my sister Graciela's new baby boy.

Most of us slept late the next morning, and when we woke we were anxious to leave, but there was still no word about our departure, so we all went our separate ways to see a little more of Mendoza. Finally we received word to gather at the airport at 1:00 p.m. sharp, but we arrived only to discover that Ferradas and his copilot, Dante Lagurara, had not yet decided whether or not we would fly. We reacted to this news with frustration and anger, but none of us understood the difficult decision confronting the pilots. The weather reports that morning warned of some turbulence along our flight path, but after speaking with the pilot of a cargo plane that had just flown in from Santiago, Ferradas was confident the Fairchild could fly safely above the weather. The more troubling problem was the time of day. It was already early afternoon. By the time the passengers were boarded and all the necessary arrangements were made with airport officials, it would be well past two o'clock. In the afternoon, warm air rises from the Argentine foothills and meets the frigid air above the snowline to create treacherous instability in the atmosphere above the mountains. Our pilots knew that this was the most dangerous time to fly across the Andes. There was no way to predict where these swirling currents might strike, and if they got hold of us, our plane would be tossed around like a toy.

On the other hand, we couldn't stay put in Mendoza. Our aircraft was a Fairchild F-227 that we had leased from the Uruguayan air force. The laws of Argentina forbade a foreign military aircraft to stay on Argentine soil longer than twenty-four hours. Since our time was almost up, Ferradas and Lagurara had to make a fast decision: should they take off for Santiago and brave the afternoon skies, or fly the Fairchild back to Montevideo and put an end to our vacation?

As the pilots pondered the options, our impatience grew. We had already lost a day of our Chilean trip, and we were frustrated by the thought of losing more. We were bold young men, fearless and full of ourselves, and it angered us that our vacation was slipping away because of what we regarded as the timidity of our pilots. We did not hide these feelings. When we saw the pilots at the airport, we jeered and whistled at them. We teased them and questioned their competence. "We hired you to take us to Chile," someone shouted, "and that's what we want you to do!" There is no way to know whether or not our behavior influenced their decision—it did seem to unsettle them—but finally, after one last consultation with Lagurara, Ferradas glanced around at the crowd waiting restlessly for an answer, and announced that the flight to Santiago would continue. We greeted this news with a rowdy cheer.

The Fairchild finally departed from Mendoza Airport at eighteen minutes after two o'clock, local time. As we climbed, the plane banked steeply into a left turn and soon we were flying south, with the Argentine Andes rising to our right on the western horizon. Through the windows on the right side of the fuselage, I gazed at the mountains, which thundered up from the dry plateau below us like a black mirage, so bleak and majestic, so astonishingly vast and huge, that the simple sight of them made my heart race. Rooted in massive swells of bedrock with colossal bases that spread for miles, their black ridges soared up from the flatlands, one peak crowding the next, so that they seemed to form a colossal fortress wall. I was not a poetically inclined young man, but there seemed to be a warning in the great authority with which these mountains held their ground, and it was impossible not to think of them as living things, with minds and hearts and an old brooding awareness. No wonder the ancients thought of these mountains as holy places, as the doorstep to heaven, and as the dwelling place of the gods.

Uruguay is a low-lying country, and like most of my friends on the plane, my knowledge of the Andes, or of any mountains at all, was limited to what I had read in books. In school we learned that the Andes range was the most extensive mountain system in the world, running the length of South America from Venezuela in the north to the southern tip of the continent in Tierra del Fuego. I also knew that the Andes are the second-highest mountain range on the planet; in terms of average elevation, only the Himalayas are higher.

I had heard people refer to the Andes as one of the earth's great geological wonders, and the view from the airplane gave me a visceral understanding of what that meant. To the north, south, and west, the mountains sprawled as far as the eye could see, and even though they were many miles away, their height and mass made them seem impassable. In fact, as far as we were concerned, they were. Our destination, Santiago, lies almost exactly due west of Mendoza, but the region of the Andes that separates the two cities is one of the highest sections of the entire chain, and home to some of the tallest mountains in the world. Somewhere out there, for example, was Aconcagua, the highest mountain in the Western Hemisphere and one of the seven tallest on the planet. With a summit of 22,831 feet, it stands just 6,200 feet shy of Everest, and it has giants for neighbors, including the 22,000-foot Mount Mercedario, and Mount Tupongato, which stands 21,555 feet tall. Surrounding these behemoths are other great peaks with elevations of between 16,000 and 20,000 feet, which no one in those wild reaches had ever bothered to name.

With such towering summits rising along the way, there was no chance that the Fairchild, with its maximum cruising altitude of 22,500 feet, could fly a direct east-west route to Santiago. Instead, the pilots had charted a course that would take us about one hundred miles south of Mendoza to Planchón Pass, a narrow corridor through the mountains with ridges low enough for the plane to clear. We would fly south along the eastern foothills of the Andes with the mountains always on our right, until we reached the pass. Then we'd turn west and weave our way through the mountains. When we had cleared the mountains on the Chilean side, we would turn right and fly north to Santiago. The flight should take about an hour and a half. We would be in Santiago before dark.

On this first leg of the trip, the skies were calm, and in less than an hour we had reached the vicinity of Planchón Pass. I didn't know the name of the pass, of course, or any of the flight details. But I couldn't help noticing that after flying for miles with the mountains always off in the western distance, we had banked to the west and were now flying directly into the heart of the cordillera. I was sitting in a window seat on the left side of the plane, and as I watched, the flat, featureless landscape below seemed to leap up from the earth, first to form rugged foothills, then heaving and buckling up into the awesome convolutions of true mountains. Shark-finned ridges raised themselves up like soaring black sails. Menacing peaks pushed up like gigantic spearheads or the broken blades of hatchets. Narrow glacial valleys gashed the steep slopes, forming rows of deep, winding, snow-packed corridors that stacked and folded one upon the other to create a wild, endless maze of ice and rock. In the Southern Hemisphere, winter had given way to early spring, but in the Andes, temperatures still routinely dipped to 35 degrees below zero Fahrenheit, and the air was as dry as a desert. I knew that avalanches, blizzards, and killing gale-force winds were common in these mountains, and that the previous winter had been one of the most severe on record, with snowfalls, in some places, of several hundred feet. I saw no color at all in the mountains, just muted patches of black and gray. There was no softness, no life, only rock and snow and ice and as I looked down into all that rugged wildness, I had to laugh at the arrogance of anyone who had ever thought that human beings have conquered the earth.

Watching out the window, I noticed that wisps of fog were gathering, then I felt a hand on my shoulder.

"Switch seats with me, Nando. I want to look at the mountains."

It was my friend Panchito, who was sitting in the aisle seat beside me. I nodded and rose from my seat. When I stood to change places someone yelled, "Think fast, Nando!" and I turned just in time to catch a rugby ball someone had tossed from the rear of the cabin. I passed the ball forward, and then sank into my seat. All around us there was laughing and talking, people were moving from seat to seat, visiting friends up and down the aisle. Some friends, including my oldest amigo, Guido Magri, were in the back of the plane playing cards with some crew members, including the flight steward, but when the ball began bouncing around the cabin, the steward stepped forward and tried to calm things down. "Put the ball away," he shouted. "Settle down, and please take your seats!" But we were young rugby players traveling with our friends, and we did not want to settle down. Our team, the Old Christians from Montevideo, was one of the best rugby teams in Uruguay, and we took our regular matches seriously. But in Chile we would be playing an exhibition match only, so this trip was really a holiday for us, and on the plane there was the feeling that the holiday had already begun.

It was a fine thing to be traveling with my friends, these friends especially. We had been through so much together—all the years of learning and training, the heartbreaking losses, the hard-fought wins. We had grown up as teammates, drawing from each other's strengths, learning to trust one another when the pressure was on. But the game of rugby had not only shaped our friendships, it had shaped our characters, and brought us together as brothers.

Many of us on the Old Christians had known each other for

more than ten years, since our days as schoolboy ruggers playing under the guidance of the Irish Christian Brothers at the Stella Maris School. The Christian Brothers had come to Uruguay from Ireland in the early 1950s, at the invitation of a group of Catholic parents who wanted them to found a private Catholic school in Montevideo. Five Irish Brothers answered the call, and in 1955 they created the Stella Maris College, a private school for boys between the ages of nine and sixteen, located in the Carrasco neighborhood, where most of the students lived.

For the Christian Brothers, the first goal of a Catholic education was to build character, not intellect, and their teaching methods stressed discipline, piety, selflessness, and respect. To promote these values outside the classroom, the Brothers discouraged our natural South American passion for soccer—a game that, in their view, fostered selfishness and egotism—and steered us toward the rougher, earthier game of rugby. For generations, rugby had been an Irish passion, but it was virtually unknown in our country. At first the game seemed strange to us—so brutal and painful to play, so much pushing and shoving and so little of soccer's wide-open flair. But the Christian Brothers firmly believed that the qualities required to master the sport were the same characteristics one needed to live a decent Catholic life—humility, tenacity, self-discipline, and devotion to others—and they were determined that we would play the game and play it well. It did not take us long to learn that once the Christian Brothers set their minds to a purpose, there was little that could sway them. So we set aside our soccer balls and acquainted ourselves with the fat, pointed pigskin used in rugby.

In long, tough practices on the fields behind the school, the Brothers started from scratch, drilling us in all the rugged intricacies of the game—mucks and rauls, scrumdowns and lineouts, how to kick and pass and tackle. We learned that rugby players wore no pads or helmets, but still we were expected to play aggressively and with great physical courage. But rugby was more than a game of brute strength; it required sound strategy, quick thinking, and agility. Most of all the game demanded that teammates develop an unshakeable sense of trust. They explained that when one of our teammates falls or is knocked to the ground, he "becomes grass." This was their way of saying that a downed player can be stomped on and trampled by the opposition as if he were part of the turf. One of the first things they taught us was how to behave when a teammate becomes grass. "You must become his protector. You must sacrifice yourself to shield him. He must know he can count on you."

To the Christian Brothers, rugby was more than a game, it was sport raised to the level of a moral discipline. At its heart was the ironclad belief that no other sport taught so devoutly the importance of striving, suffering, and sacrificing in the pursuit of a common goal. They were so passionate on this point that we had no choice but to believe them, and as we grew to understand the game more deeply, we saw for ourselves that the Brothers were right.

In simplest terms, the object of rugby is to gain control of the ball—usually through the combined use of cunning, speed, and brute force—and then, by passing it deftly from one sprinting teammate to another, advance the ball across the the goal or "try line" for a score. Rugby can be a game of dazzling speed and agility, a game of pinpoint passes and brilliant evasive maneuvers. But for me the essence of the game can only be found in the brutal, controlled melee known as the scrum, the signature formation of rugby. In a scrummage, each team forms a tight huddle, three rows deep, with the crouching players shoulder to shoulder and their arms interlocked to form a tightly woven human wedge. The two scrums square off, and the first row of one scrum butts shoulders with the first row of the opposition to form a rough closed circle. At the official's signal, the ball is rolled into this circle and each team's scrum tries to push the other far enough off the ball so that one of its own front-row players can kick it back through the legs of his teammates to the rear of the scrum, where his scrum half is waiting to pluck it free and pass it to a back who will start the attack.

The play inside the scrum is ferocious—knees knock against temples, elbows rock jaws, shins are constantly bloodied by kicks from heavy cleated shoes. It is raw, hard labor, but everything changes to lightning once the scrum half clears the ball and the attack begins. The first pass might be back to the agile fly half, who will dodge the oncoming defenders, buying time for the players behind him to find open field. Just as he is about to be dragged down, the fly half fires the ball back to the inside center, who sidesteps one tackler but is tripped up by the next, and as he stumbles forward he passes off to the trailing winger. Now the ball moves crisply from one back to the next—flanker to winger to center and back to the winger again, each man slashing, spinning, diving, or bulling his way forward, before tacklers drag them to the ground. Ball carriers will be mauled along the way, rucks will form when the ball falls free, every inch will be a battle, but then one of our men will find an angle, a small window of daylight and, with a final burst of effort, dash past the last defenders and dive across the try line for a score. Just like that, all the plodding grunt work of the scrum has turned to a brilliant dance. And no single man can claim the credit. The try was scored inch by inch, through an accumulation of individual effort, and no matter who finally carried the ball across the try line, the glory belongs to us all.

My job in the scrum was to line up behind the crouching first row, my head wedged between their hips, my shoulders butting their thighs, and my arms spread over their backsides. When play began, I would surge forward with all my might and try to push the scrum forward. I remember the feeling so well: at first the weight of the opposing scrum seems immense and impossible to budge. Still, you dig at the turf, you endure the stalemate, you refuse to quit. I remember, in moments of extreme exertion, straining forward until my legs were completely extended, with my body low and straight and parallel to the ground, pushing hopelessly against what seemed like a solid stone wall. Sometimes the stalemate seemed to last forever, but if we held our positions and each man did his job, the resistance would soften and, miraculously, the immovable object would slowly begin to budge. The remarkable thing is this: at the very moment of success you cannot isolate your own individual effort from the effort of the entire scrum. You cannot tell where your strength ends and the efforts of the others begin. In a sense, you no longer exist as an individual human being. For a brief moment you forget yourself. You become part of something larger and more powerful than you yourself could be. Your effort and your will vanishes into the collective will of the team, and if this will is unified and focused, the team surges forward and the scrum magically begins to move.

To me, this is the essence of rugby. No other sport gives you such an intense sense of selflessness and unified purpose. I believe this is why rugby players all over the world feel such a passion for the game and such a feeling of brotherhood. As a young man, of course, I could not put these things into words, but I knew, and my teammates knew, that there was something special about the game, and under the guidance of the Christian Brothers we developed a passionate love for the sport that shaped our friendships and our lives. For eight years we played our hearts out for the Christian Brothers—a brotherhood of young boys with Latin names, playing a game with deep Anglo roots under Uruguay's sunny skies, and proudly wearing the bright green shamrock on our uniforms. The game became so much a part of our lives, in fact, that when we graduated from Stella Maris at the age of sixteen, many of us could not bear the thought that our playing days were over. Our salvation came in the form of the Old Christians Club, a private rugby team formed in 1965 by previous alumni of the Stella Maris rugby program to give Stella Maris ruggers a chance to continue playing the game after our school years ended.

When the Christian Brothers first arrived in Uruguay, few people had ever seen a rugby match, but by the late 1960s the game was gaining in popularity, and there were plenty of good teams for the Old Christians to challenge. In 1965 we joined the National Rugby League, and soon we had established ourselves as one of the country's top teams, winning the national championship in 1968 and 1970. Encouraged by our success, we began to schedule matches in Argentina, and we quickly discovered that we could hold our own with the best teams that country had to offer. In 1971 we traveled to Chile, where we fared well in matches against tough competition, including the Chilean national team. The trip was such a success that it was decided we would return again this year, in 1972. I had been looking forward to the trip for months, and as I glanced around the passenger cabin there was no doubt my teammates felt the same. We had been through so much together. I knew that the friendships I'd made on the rugby team would last a lifetime, and I was happy that so many of my friends were on the phone with me. There was Coco Nicholich, our lock forward, and one of the biggest and strongest players on the team. Enrique Platero, serious and steady, was a prop—one of the burly guys who helped anchor the line in the scrum. Roy Harley was a wing forward, who used his speed to sidestep tacklers and leave them clutching air. Roberto Canessa was a wing, and one of the strongest and toughest players on the squad. Arturo Nogueira was our fly half, a great long passer and the best kicker on the team. You could tell by looking at Antonio Vizintin, with his broad back and thick neck, that he was one of the front line forwards who bore most of the weight in the scrum. Gustavo Zerbino—whose guts and determination I always admired—was a versatile player who manned many positions. And Marcelo Perez del Castillo, another wing forward, was very fast, very brave, a great ball carrier and a ferocious tackler. Marcelo was also our team captain, a leader we would trust with our lives. It was Marcelo's idea to return to Chile, and he had worked hard to make it all possible; he had leased the plane, hired the pilots, arranged the games in Chile, and created tremendous excitement about the trip.

There were others—Alexis Hounie, Gastón Costemalle, Daniel Shaw—all of them great players and all of them my friends. But my oldest friend was Guido Magri. He and I had met on my first day at the Stella Maris School—I was eight years old and Guido was one year older—and we had been inseparable ever since. Guido and I grew up together, playing soccer and sharing a love of motorcycles, cars, and auto racing. When I was fifteen we both had mopeds that we had modified in silly ways—removing the mufflers, turn signals, and fenders—and we would ride them to Las Delicias, a famous ice cream parlor in our neighborhood, where we would drool over the girls from the nearby School Sagrado Corazón, hoping to impress them with our souped-up scooters. Guido was a dependable friend, with a good sense of humor and an easy laugh. He was also an outstanding scrum half, as quick and smart as a fox, with good hands and great courage. Under the guidance of the Christian Brothers, both of us grew to love the game of rugby with a consuming passion. As seasons passed we worked hard to improve our skills, and by the time I was fifteen we had each earned a spot on the Stella Maris First XV, the team's starting lineup. After graduation, both of us went on to join the Old Christians and spent several happy seasons pursuing the high-octane social life of young rugby players. That rowdiness came to an abrupt end for Guido in 1969, when he met and fell in love with the beautiful daughter of a Chilean diplomat. She was now his fiancée, and he was happy to behave himself for her sake.

After Guido's engagement I saw less of him, and I began spending more time with my other great friend Panchito Abal. Panchito was a year younger than I, and although he was a graduate of Stella

Maris and a former member of the school's First XV, we had met only a few years earlier when Panchito joined the Old Christians. We became instant friends and, in the years since, had grown as close as brothers, enjoying a strong camaraderie and a deep *simpatía* between us, though to many we must have seemed an unlikely pair. Panchito was our winger, a position that requires a combination of speed, power, intelligence, agility, and lightning-quick reactions. If there is a glamour position on a rugby team, winger is it, and Panchito was perfect for the role. Long-legged and broad-shouldered, with blazing speed and the agility of a cheetah, he played the game with such natural grace that even his most brilliant moves seemed effortless. But everything seemed that way for Panchito, especially his other great passion—chasing pretty girls. It didn't hurt, of course, that he had the blond good looks of a movie star, or that he was rich, a fine athlete, and blessed with the kind of natural charisma most of us can only dream of. I believed, in those days, that the woman did not exist who could resist Panchito once he'd set his sights on her. He had no trouble finding girls; they seemed to find their way to him, and he picked them up with such ease that it sometimes seemed like magic. Once, for example, at the halftime break of a rugby match he said to me, "I have dates for us after the game. Those two there in the first row."

I glanced to where the girls were sitting. We had never seen these girls before.

"But how did you manage this?" I asked him. "You never left the field!"

Panchito shrugged off the question, but I remembered that early in the game he had chased a ball out of bounds near where the girls were sitting. He only had time to smile at them and say a few words, but for Panchito that was enough.

For me it was different. Like Panchito, I also had a great passion for rugby, but the game was never effortless for me. As a small child I had broken both my legs in a fall from a balcony, and the injuries had left me with a slightly knock-kneed stride that robbed me of the nimbleness required to play rugby's more glamorous positions. But I was tall and tough and fast, so they made me a forward on the second line. We forwards were good foot soldiers, always butting shoulders in rucks and mauls, rumbling in the scrums and jumping high to claw for the ball in lineouts. Forwards are usually the largest and strongest players on the team, and while I was one of our tallest players, I was thin for my height. When the large bodies started flying, it was only through hard work and determination that I was able to hold my own.

For me, meeting girls also required great effort, but I never stopped trying. I was just as obsessed with pretty girls as Panchito was, but while I dreamed of being a natural ladies' man like him, I knew I wasn't in his class. A little shy, long-limbed and gangly, with thick horn-rimmed glasses and average looks, I had to face the fact that most girls did not find me extraordinary. It wasn't that I was unpopular—I had my share of dates—but it would be a lie to say that girls were waiting in line for Nando. I had to work hard to catch a girl's interest, but even when I did, things did not always go as I planned. Once, for example, I managed, after months of trying, to get a date with a girl I really liked. I took her to Las Delicias and she waited in the car while I bought us some ice cream. As I was returning to the car with a cone in each hand, I tripped over something on the sidewalk and lost my balance. Stumbling and weaving wildly toward the parked car, I fought to keep my balance and save the cones, but I didn't have a chance. I have often wondered how it looked to that girl inside the car: her date lurching toward her in a wide circle across the street, hunched over, his eyes like saucers, his mouth gaping. He staggers toward the car, then seems to dive at her, his cheek smashing flat against the driver's window, his head bouncing hard off the glass. He slips from view as he slumps to the ground, and all that remains are two dripping blobs of ice cream smeared across the window.

This was something that would not have happened to Panchito in five lifetimes. He was one of the gifted ones, and everyone envied him for the grace and ease with which he glided through life. But I knew him well, and I understood that life was not as easy for Panchito as it seemed. Beneath all the charm and confidence was a melancholy heart. He could be irritable and distant. He often sank into long dark moods and ill-tempered silences. And there was a devilish restlessness in him that sometimes disturbed me. He was always provoking me with reckless questions: *How far would you go, Nando? Would you cheat on a test? Would you rob a bank? Steal a car?*

I always laughed when he talked this way, but I could not ignore the hidden streak of anger and sadness that those questions revealed. I did not judge him for this, because I knew it was all the result of a broken heart. Panchito's parents had divorced when he was fourteen years old. It was a disaster that had wounded him in ways he could not heal and had left him with much resentment. He had two brothers, and a stepbrother from his father's previous marriage, but still, there was something missing for him. I believe he had a great hunger for the love and comforts of a family that was happy and whole. In any case, it did not take me long to realize that despite all the natural gifts he had been blessed with, all the things I envied him for, he envied me more for the one thing I had that he could only dream of—my sisters, my grandmother, my mother and father, all of us together in a close and happy home.

But to me, Panchito was more a brother than a friend, and my family felt the same about him. From the moment they met, my father and mother embraced Panchito as a son, and gave him no other choice but to think of our home as his own. Panchito warmly accepted this invitation, and soon he was a natural part of our world. He spent weekends with us, traveled with us, was a part of all our holidays and family celebrations. He shared, with my father and me, a love for cars and driving, and he loved going with us to auto races. To Susy, he was a second big brother. My mother had a special affection for him. I remember that he would boost himself up on the kitchen counter while she cooked, and they would talk for hours. Often she would tease him about his obsession with girls. "It's all you think about," she would say. "When are you going to grow up?"

"When I grow up I'm really going to chase them!" Panchito would reply. "I'm just eighteen, Mrs. Parrado! I'm only getting started."

I could see much strength and depth in Panchito, in his loyalty as a friend to me, in the fiercely protective way he watched out for Susy, in the quiet respect he showed my parents, even in the affection with which he treated the servants at his father's house, who loved him like a son. More than anything, though, I saw in him a man who wanted nothing more in life than the joys of a happy family. I knew his heart. I could see his future. He would meet the woman who would tame him. He would become a good husband and a loving father. I would marry, too. Our families would be like one; our children would grow up together. We never spoke of these things, of course—we were boys in our teens—but I think he knew I understood these things about him, and I think that knowledge strengthened the bonds of our friendship.

Still, we were young men and the future was just a distant rumor. Ambition and responsibility could wait. Like Panchito, I lived for the moment. There would be time to be serious later. I was young, now was the time to play, and play was definitely the focus of my life. It's not that I was lazy or self-centered. I thought of myself as a good son, a hard worker, a trustworthy friend, and an honest and decent person. I simply was in no hurry to grow up. Life for me was something that was happening *today*. I had no strong principles, no defining goals or drives. In those days, if you had asked me the purpose of life, I might have laughed and answered, "To have fun." It did not occur to me at the time that I could only afford the luxury of this carefree attitude because of the sacrifices of my father, who, from a very young age, had taken his life seriously, planned his goals carefully, and, through years of discipline and self-reliance, had given me the life of privilege, security, and leisure I so casually took for granted.

My father, Seler Parrado, was born at Estación Gonzales, a dusty outpost in Uruguay's rich agricultural interior, where vast cattle ranches, or *estancias,* produced the prized high-quality beef for which Uruguay is known. His own father was a poor peddler who traveled in a horse-drawn cart from one *estancia* to the next, selling saddles, bridles, boots, and other staples of farm life to the ranch owners themselves, or directly to the rugged gauchos who watched over their herds. It was a difficult life, full of hardship and uncertainty and very few comforts. (Whenever I grumbled about my life, my father would remind me that when he was a boy, his bathroom was a tin shed fifty feet from the house, and that he never saw a roll of toilet paper until he was eleven years old and his family moved to Montevideo.)

Life in the country allowed little time for rest or play. Each day my father walked the dirt roads back and forth to school, but still he was expected to do his part in his family's day-to-day struggle to survive. When he was six years old he was already working long hours at his family's small homestead—minding chickens and ducks, carrying water from the well, gathering firewood, and helping to tend his mother's vegetable garden. By the time he was eight he had become his father's assistant, spending long hours in the peddler's cart as they made their rounds from one ranch to another. His childhood was not carefree, but it showed him the value of hard work, and taught him that nothing would be handed to him, that his life would be only what he made of it.

When my father was eleven years old his family moved to Montevideo, where his father opened a shop selling the same goods he had peddled to ranchers and farmers in the countryside. Seler became an auto mechanic—he had had a passion for cars and engines since he was a very young boy—but when he was in his mid-twenties my grandfather decided to retire, and my father assumed ownership of the shop. Grandfather had located the shop wisely, near Montevideo's main railway station. In those days the railroad was the main method of travel from the country to the city, and when ranchers and gauchos came to town to buy supplies, they would step off the trains and walk directly past his door. But by the time Seler took control of the business, things had changed. Buses had replaced trains as the most popular form of transportation, and the bus station was nowhere near the shop. To make things worse, the machine age had reached the Uruguayan countryside. Trucks and tractors were rapidly reducing the farmer's dependence on horses and mules, and that meant a dramatic drop in demand for the saddles and bridles my father was selling. Sales lagged. It seemed the business would fail. Then Seler tried an experiment—he cleared the farm goods from half of his store's floor space and devoted that space to basic hardware—nuts and bolts, nails and screws, wire and hinges. Immediately his business began to thrive. Within months he had removed all the country goods and stocked the shelves with hardware. He was still living on the edge of poverty, and sleeping on the floor in a room above the shop, but as sales continued to rise, he knew that he had found his future.

In 1945 that future became richer when Seler married my mother, Eugenia. She was just as ambitious and independent as he was, and from the very start they were more than a married couple; they were a strong team who shared a bright vision of the future. Like my father, Eugenia had struggled through a difficult youth. In 1939, when she was sixteen years old, she had emigrated from the Ukraine, with her parents and grandmother, to escape the ravages of World War II. Her parents, beekeepers in the Ukraine, settled in the Uruguayan countryside and managed a modest living by raising bees and selling honey. It was a life of hard work and limited opportunity, so, when she was twenty, Eugenia moved to Montevideo, like my father, to seek a better future. She had a clerical job at a large medical laboratory in the city when she married my father, and at first she helped out at the hardware store only in her spare time. In the early days of their marriage, they struggled. Money was so tight that they could not afford furniture, and they began their lives together in an empty apartment. But eventually their hard work paid off, and the hardware store began to turn a profit. By the time my older sister, Graciela, was born in 1947, my mother was able to quit her job at the laboratory and work full-time with my father. I came along in 1949. Susy followed three years later. By then, Eugenia had become a major force in the family business, and her hard work and business savvy had helped to give us a very nice standard of living. But despite the importance of her work, the center of my mother's life was always her home and family. One day, when I was twelve, she announced that she had found the perfect house for us in Carrasco, one of Montevideo's finest residential districts. I'll never forget the look of happiness in her eyes as she described the house: it was a modern, two-story home near the beach, she said, with big windows and large bright rooms, broad lawns and a breezy veranda. The house had a beautiful view of the sea, and this more than anything made my mother love it. I still remember the delight in her voice when she told us, "We can watch the sunset over the water!" Her blue eyes were shining with tears. She had started out with so little, and now she had found her dream house, a place that would be home for a lifetime.

In Montevideo, a Carrasco address is a mark of prestige, and in this new house we found ourselves living among the upper crust of Uruguayan society. Our neighbors were the nation's most prominent industrialists, professionals, artists, and politicians. It was a place of status and power, a far cry from the humble world my mother had been born into, and she must have felt a great sense of satisfaction in earning a spot for us there. But she had her feet planted too firmly on the ground to be overly impressed with the neighborhood, or with herself for living there. No matter how successful we might have grown, my mother was not about to abandon the values she was raised on, or ever forget who she was.

One of the first things my mother did at the house was to help her own mother, Lina, who had lived with us since we were small, dig up a broad patch of lush, green lawn behind the house to make way for a huge vegetable garden. (Lina also raised a small flock of ducks and chickens in the yard, and it must have startled the neighbors when they realized that this blue-eyed, white-haired old woman, who dressed with the simplicity of a European peasant and wore her gardening tools on a leather belt slung on her hips, was running a small working farm in one of the city's most mannered and manicured neighborhoods.) Under Lina's loving attention, the garden was soon producing bumper crops of beans, peas, greens, peppers, squash, corn, tomatoes—far too much for us to eat, but my mother would not let any of it go to waste. She spent hours in the kitchen with Lina, canning the surplus produce in mason jars, and storing it all in the pantry so that we could enjoy the fruits of the garden all year round. My mother hated waste and pretense, valued frugality, and never lost her faith in the value of hard work. My father's business demanded much from her, and she labored long and hard to make it successful, but she was also very active in our lives, always there to send us off to school or welcome us home, never missing my soccer and rugby games, or my sisters' plays and recitals at school. She was a woman of great, quiet energy, full of encouragement and sage advice, with deep reserves of resourcefulness and good judgment that won her the respect of everyone who knew her and time and again she proved herself to be a woman worthy of their trust.

Once, for example, as part of a Rotary Club expedition, my mother escorted fifteen young children from Carrasco on a weekend visit to Buenos Aires. Hours after they arrived, a military coup erupted in that city, with the purpose of toppling the Argentine government. Chaos reigned in the streets, and the phone at our house rang off the hook with calls from worried parents wanting to know if their children were safe. Again and again I heard my father reassure them, with total confidence in his voice, saying, "They are with Xenia, they will be all right." And they were all right, thanks to the efforts of my mother. It was near midnight. Buenos Aires was no longer safe, and my mother knew the last ferry to Montevideo would be leaving in minutes, so she phoned the ferry company and persuaded the jittery pilots to hold the last departure until she arrived with the children. Then she gathered all the kids and their things and led them through the unsettled streets of Buenos Aires to the dark waterfront where the ferry was docked. They all boarded safely, and the ferry set off just after 3:00 a.m., three hours after its scheduled departure. She was a true tower of strength, but her strength was always based in warmth and love and because of her love and protection I grew up believing the world was a safe, familiar place.

By the time I was in high school my parents owned three large, thriving hardware stores in Uruguay. My father was also importing merchandise from all over the world and wholesaling it to smaller hardware stores across South America. The poor country boy from Estación Gonzales had come a long way in life, and I think this gave him a great sense of satisfaction, but there was never a doubt in my mind that he had done it all for us. He had given us a life of comfort and privilege such as his own father never could have imagined, he had provided for us and protected us in the best way he could, and though he was not an emotionally expressive man, he always showed his love for us subtly, quietly, and in ways that were true to the man he was. When I was small, he would take me to the hardware store, walk me along the shelves, and patiently share with me the secrets of all the shiny merchandise on which our family's prosperity had been founded: *This is a toggle bolt, Nando. You use this to fasten things to a hollow wall. This is a grommet—it reinforces a hole in a canvas tarp so you can thread a rope through it to tie it down. This is an anchor bolt. This is a carriage bolt. These are wing nuts. Here is where we keep the washers—split washers, lock washers, ring washers, and flat washers in every size. We have lag screws, Phillips head screws, slotted screws, machine screws, wood screws, self-tapping screws . . . there are common nails, finish nails, roofing nails, ring-shank nails, box nails, masonry nails, double-headed nails, more kinds of nails than you can imagine. . . .*

These were precious moments for me. I loved the gentle seriousness with which he shared his knowledge, and it made me feel close to him to know he thought I was a big enough boy to be trusted with this knowledge. In fact, he wasn't simply playing, he was teaching me the things I would need to know to help him at the store. But even as a kid I sensed he was teaching me a deeper lesson: that life is orderly, life makes sense. *See, Nando, for every job there is the right nut or bolt or hinge or tool.* Whether he intended it or not, he was teaching me the great lesson his years of struggle had taught him: Don't let your head get lost in the clouds. Pay attention to the details, to the nuts-and-bolts realities of things. You can't build a life on a foundation of dreams and wishes. A good life isn't plucked from the sky. You build a life up from the ground, with hard work and clear thinking. Things make sense. There are rules and realities that will not change to suit your needs. It's your job to understand those rules. If you do, and if you work hard and work smart, you will be all right.

This was the wisdom that had shaped my father's life, and he passed it along to me in so many ways. Cars were especially important to him, and he handed down this passion to me. He made sure I understood what was under the hood of a car, how each of the systems worked and what routine maintenance was required. He taught me to bleed the brakes, to change the oil, and to keep the engine in tune. A great fan of motorsports and an avid amateur racer, he spent hours teaching me how to drive well—with spirit, yes, but smoothly and safely and always with balance and control. From Seler I learned to double-clutch as I shifted, to save wear and tear on the gearbox. He taught me to listen to and understand the sound of the engine, so that I could accelerate and shift at just the right moments—to be in harmony with the car and coax from it the best performance. He showed me how to find the precise line to follow through a curve, and the correct way to take a curve at speed: you brake hard just before entering the curve, then down-shift and accelerate smoothly through the curve. Car enthusiasts call this technique "heel-and-toe" driving because of the footwork involved—as the left foot works the clutch, the right foot pivots on its heel back and forth from the brake pedal to the throttle. It is a style of driving that requires skill and concentration, but my father insisted I learn it because it was the *right* way to drive. It kept the car balanced and responsive, but, most important, it gave the driver the control he needed to resist the physical forces of weight and momentum which, if ignored, could toss the car off the road or send it fishtailing into disaster. If you are not driving this way, my father told me, your car is simply floating through curves. You are driving blind, relinquishing control to the forces acting against you, and trusting that the road ahead will hold no surprises.

My respect for my father was endless, as was my appreciation for the life he gave us. I wanted desperately to be like him, but by the time I reached high school I had to face the fact that we were very different men. I did not have his clear vision, or his pragmatic tenacity. We saw the world in starkly different ways. For my father, life was something you created out of hard work and careful plan-ning and sheer force of will. For me, the future was like a story that slowly unfolds, with plots and subplots that twist and turn so that you can never see too far down the road. Life was something to be discovered, something that arrived in its own time. I was not lazy or self-indulgent, but I was something of a dreamer. Most of my friends knew their future—they would work at family businesses or in the same professions their fathers had pursued. It was generally expected that I would do the same. But I could not imagine myself selling hardware all my life. I wanted to travel. I wanted adventure and excitement and creativity. More than anything, I dreamed of becoming a racing car driver like my idol Jackie Stewart, the three-time world champion and maybe the greatest driver of all time. Like Jackie, I knew that driving was about more than horsepower and raw speed, it was about balance and rhythm, there was poetry in the harmony between a driver and his car. I understood that a great driver is more than a daredevil, he is a virtuoso with the guts and the talent to push his cars to limits of its capabilities, defying danger and nudging the laws of physics as he streaks along a razor's edge between control and disaster. This is the magic of racing. This was the kind of driver I dreamed I would be. When I stared at the poster of Jackie Stewart that hung in my room, I was convinced that he would understand this. I even dreamed he would see in me a kindred soul.

But these dreams seemed unreachable, and so when it finally came time to choose a college, I decided to enroll in agricultural school, because that was where my closest friends were going. When my father heard the news, he shrugged and smiled. "Nando," he said, "your friends' families own farms and ranches. We have hardware stores." It was not hard for him to talk me into changing my mind. In the end I did what made sense: I entered business school with no serious thought about what school would mean for me or where this decision might lead. I would graduate or I would not. I would run the hardware stores or maybe I wouldn't. My life would present itself to me when it was ready. In the meantime I spent the summer being Nando: I played rugby, I chased girls with Panchito, I raced my little Renault along the beach roads at Punte del Este, I went to parties and lay in the sun, I lived for the moment, drifting with the tide, waiting for my future to reveal itself, always happy to let others lead the way.

I COULDN'T HELP thinking of my father as the Fairchild flew above the Andes. He had dropped us off at the airport in Montevideo when our trip first began. "Have fun," he said. "I will pick you up on Monday." He kissed my mother and my sister, gave me a warm embrace, and then turned to go back to the office, to the orderly, predictable world in which he thrived. While we had fun in Chile he would do what he always did: solve problems, take care of things, work hard, provide. Out of love for his family he had arranged in his mind a future that would keep us all safe, happy, and always together. He had planned well and paid attention to all the details. The Parrados would always be fortunate people. He believed in this so firmly, and our trust for him was so strong, how could we ever doubt him?

"Fasten your seat belts, please," the steward said. "There is going to be some turbulence ahead." We were making our way over Planchón Pass. Panchito was still at the window, but we were flying through thick fog and there wasn't much to see. I was thinking about the girls Panchito and I had met on our last trip to Chile. We had gone with them to the beach resort of Viña del Mar and stayed out so late we almost missed our rugby match the following morning. They had agreed to meet us this year and had offered to pick us up at the airport, but our layover in Mendoza had thrown us off schedule and I hoped we would be able to find them. I was about to mention this to Panchito when the plane suddenly dipped sideways. Then we felt four sharp bumps as the belly of the plane skipped hard over pockets of turbulence. Some of the guys whooped and cheered, as if they were on an amusement park ride.

I leaned forward and smiled reassuringly at Susy and my mother. My mother looked worried. She had put away the book she was reading, and was holding my sister's hand. I wanted to tell them not to worry, but before I could speak, the bottom seemed to fall out of the fuselage, and my stomach pitched as the plane dropped for what must have been several hundred feet.

Now the plane was bouncing and sliding in the turbulence. As the pilots fought to stabilize the Fairchild, I felt Panchito's elbow in my side.

"Look at this, Nando," he said. "Should we be so close to the mountains?"

I bent down to look out the small window. We were flying in thick cloud cover, but through breaks in the clouds I could see a massive wall of rock and snow flashing past. The Fairchild was bobbing roughly, and the swaying tip of the wing was no more than twenty-five feet from the black slopes of the mountain. For a second or so I stared in disbelief, then the plane's engines screamed as the pilots tried desperately to climb. The fuselage began to vibrate so violently I feared it would shake itself to pieces. My mother and sister turned to look at me over the seats. Our eyes met for an instant, then a powerful tremor rocked the plane. There was a terrible howl of metal grinding. Suddenly I saw open sky above me. Frigid air blasted my face and I noticed, with an odd calmness, that clouds were swirling in the aisle. There was no time to make sense of things, or to pray or feel fear. It all happened in a heartbeat. Then I was torn from my seat with incredible force and hurled forward into the darkness and silence.

Chapter Two

Everything Precious

"HERE, NANDO, ARE you thirsty?"

It was my teammate Gustavo Zerbino crouching beside me, pressing a ball of snow to my lips. The snow was cold and it burned my throat as I swallowed, but my body was so parched I gobbled it in lumps and begged for more. Several hours had passed since I woke from the coma. My mind was clearer now, and I was full of questions. When I finished with the snow, I motioned Gustavo closer.

"Where is my mother?" I asked. "Where is Susy? Are they all right?"

Gustavo's face betrayed no emotion. "Get some rest," he said. "You're still very weak." He walked away, and for a while the others kept their distance. Again and again I pleaded with them to give me some news of my loved ones, but my voice was just a whisper and it was easy for them to pretend they didn't hear.

I lay shivering on the cold floor of the fuselage as the others bustled around me, listening for the sound of my sister's voice and glancing about for a glimpse of my mother's face. How desperately I wanted to see my mother's warm smile, her deep blue eyes, to be swept up in her arms and told that we would be okay. Eugenia was the emotional heart of our family. Her wisdom, strength, and courage had been the foundation of our lives, and I needed her so badly now that missing her felt like a physical pain worse than the cold or the throbbing in my head.

When Gustavo came again with another ball of snow, I grabbed his sleeve.

"Where are they, Gustavo?" I insisted. "Please."

Gustavo looked into my eyes and must have seen that I was ready to have an answer. "Nando, you must be strong," he said. "Your mother is dead."

When I look back on this moment, I cannot say why this news did not destroy me. Never had I needed my mother's touch so badly, and now I was being told I would never feel that touch again. For a brief moment, grief and panic exploded in my heart so violently that I feared I would go mad, but then a thought formed in my head, in a voice so lucid and so detached from everything that I was feeling that it could have been someone whispering in my ear. The voice said, *Do not cry. Tears waste salt. You will need salt to survive.*

I was astounded at the calmness of this thought, and shocked at the cold-bloodedness of the voice that spoke it. Not cry for my mother? Not cry for the greatest loss of my life? I am stranded in the Andes, I am freezing, my skull is in pieces! I should not cry?

The voice spoke again. *Do not cry.*

"There is more," Gustavo told me. "Panchito is dead. Guido, too. And many others." I shook my head feebly in disbelief. How could this be happening? Sobs gathered in my throat, but before I could surrender to my grief and shock, the voice spoke again, and louder. *They are all gone. They are all a part of your past. Don't waste energy on things you can't control. Look forward. Think clearly. You will survive.*

Gustavo still knelt above me, and I wanted to grab him, shake him, make him tell me it was all a lie. Then I remembered my sister, and through no effort of my own, I did what the voice wanted; I let my grief for my mother and friends slip into the past, as my mind filled with a wild surge of fear for my sister's safety. I stared at Gustavo numbly for a moment as I gathered my courage for the question I had to ask.

"Gustavo, where is Susy?"

"She's over there," he said, pointing to the rear of the plane, "but she is hurt very badly." Suddenly, everything changed for me. My own suffering faded and I was filled with an urgent desire to reach my sister. Struggling to my feet, I tried to walk, but the pain in my head made me swoon and I slumped back roughly to the floor of the fuselage. I rested for a moment, then rolled onto my stomach and dragged myself on my elbows toward my sister. The floor all around me was littered with the sort of debris that called to mind the violent interruption of ordinary life—cracked plastic cups, splayed magazines, a scattering of playing cards and paperback books. Damaged seats from the plane were stacked in a tangled pile near the cockpit bulkhead, and as I crawled on my stomach I could see, on either side of the aisle, the broken metal brackets that had held those seats to the floor. For a moment I imagined the terrible force it would take to tear the seats loose from such sturdy anchors.

I inched slowly toward Susy, but I was very weak and my progress was slow. Soon my strength gave out. I let my head slump to the floor to rest, but then I felt arms lifting me and carrying me forward. Someone helped me to the rear of the plane and there, lying on her back, was Susy. At first glance she did not seem to be badly injured. There were traces of blood on her brow, but someone had obviously washed her face. Her hair had been smoothed back. Someone had comforted her. She was wearing the new coat she had purchased just for this trip—a beautiful coat made from antelope leather—and the soft fur collar of the coat moved against her cheek in the frigid breeze.

My friends helped me lie down beside her. I wrapped my arms around her and whispered in her ear. "I am here, Susy. It's Nando." She turned and looked at me with her soft, caramel-colored eyes, but her gaze was unfocused and I couldn't be sure she knew it was me. She rolled in my arms as if to move closer to me, but then she groaned softly and pulled away. It hurt her to lie that way, so I let her find a less painful position, then I embraced her again, wrapping my arms and legs around her to protect her, as well as I could, from the cold. I lay with her that way for hours. Mostly she was quiet. Sometimes she would sob or quietly moan. From time to time she would call out for our mother.

"Mamá, please," she would cry, "I am so cold, please, Mamá, let's go home." These words pierced my heart like arrows. Susy was my mother's baby, and the two of them had always shared a special tenderness. They were so similar in temperament, so gentle and patient and warm, so at ease in each other's company that I don't remember them ever having a fight. They would spend hours together, cooking, taking walks, or just talking. I remember them so many times sitting alone on the sofa, their heads together, whispering, nodding, laughing at some shared secret. I believe my sister told my mother everything. She trusted my mother's advice, and sought her counsel on the things that mattered to her—friendships, studies, clothes, ambitions, values, and, always, how to deal with men.

Susy had my mother's strong, soft Ukrainian features, and she loved hearing about our family's origins in Eastern Europe. I remember each day, when we would have our after-school *café con leche,* she would coax our grandmother Lina to tell stories about the rustic little village where she was born: how cold and snowy it was in winter, and how all the villagers had to share and work together to survive. She understood the sacrifices Lina had made to come here, and I think these stories made her feel closer to our family's past. Susy shared my mother's love for the closeness of family, but she was no stay-at-home girl. She had many friends, she loved music and dancing and parties, and as much as she adored our home life in Montevideo, she always dreamed of seeing other places. When she was sixteen she spent a year as an exchange student living with a family in Florida, an experience that taught her to love the U.S.A. "Anything is possible there," she would tell me. "You can dream anything and make it come true!" It was her dream to do her college studies in the States, and often she would suggest that she might end up staying there even longer. "Who knows?" she would say. "I might meet my husband there, and become an American for good!"

When Susy and I were small, we were each other's favorite playmates. As we grew older, I became a trusted confidant. She shared her secrets with me, told me her hopes and her worries. I remember that she was always concerned about her weight—she thought she was too heavy, but she was not. She had broad shoulders and wide hips, but she was tall and her body was trim and proportional. She had the strong, shapely build of a gymnast or a swimmer. But her true beauty was in her deep, clear caramel eyes, her fine skin, and the sweetness and strength that glowed in her strong, kind face. She was young, and had not yet had a serious boyfriend, and I knew she worried that boys would not find her attractive. But I saw nothing but beauty when I looked at her. How could I convince her that she was a treasure? My little sister Susy had been precious to me from the moment she was born, and the first time I held her in my arms I knew it would always be my job to protect her. As I lay with her on the floor of the fuselage, I remembered a day at the beach when we were both small. Susy was still a toddler; I was five or six years old. She was playing in the sand with the sun in her eyes. I was not swimming or playing. My eye was always on her, watching that she did not wander into the surf where the tide could snatch her, or stray into the dunes where some stranger could whisk her away. I never let her out of my sight. I stared down anyone who came near her. Even as a child I realized that the beach was full of dangers, and I had to be vigilant to keep her safe.

This sense of protectiveness only grew stronger as we grew older. I made a point of knowing her friends and her hangouts, and when I got old enough to drive, I became the regular chauffeur for Susy and her gang. I would take them to dances and parties and pick them up afterwards. I liked to do this. It was a satisfying thing, knowing they would be safe with me. I remember taking them to the big movie house in our neighborhood—a place where all our friends would meet on weekends. She would sit with her friends and I would sit with mine, but I would keep my eye on her in the dark, always checking to make sure she was all right, being sure she knew I was close enough if she should need me. Other girls might have hated a brother like this, but I think Susy liked it that I cared enough to watch over her, and in the end it drew us closer.

Now, as I held her in my arms, I felt a terrible pang of helplessness. Watching her suffer was an unspeakable anguish for me, but there was nothing I could do. All my life, I would have done anything to keep Susy safe, and spare her from pain. Even now, in the battered shell of this aircraft, I would have gladly given my own life to end her suffering and send her home to my father.

My father! In all the chaos and confusion, I had not had the time to consider what he must be going through. He would have heard the news three days ago, and for all that time he would have lived believing he had lost us all. I knew him well, I knew his deep practicality, and I knew he would not allow himself the luxury of false hope. To survive a plane crash in the Andes? At this time of year? Impossible. Now I saw him clearly, my strong, loving father tossing in his bed, staggered by his unimaginable loss. After all his concern for us, all his work and planning, all his trust in the orderliness of the world and the certainty of our happiness, how could he bear the brutal truth: *He could not protect us. He could not protect us.* My heart broke for him, and this heartbreak was more painful than the thirst, the cold, the grinding fear, and the shattering pain in my head. I imagined him grieving for me. *Grieving* for me! I could not stand the idea that he thought I was dead. I felt an urgent, almost violent longing to be with him, to comfort him, to tell him I was caring for my sister, to show him he had not lost us all.

"I am alive," I whispered to him. "I am alive."

How badly I needed my father's strength, his wisdom. Surely, if he were here, he would know how to get us home. But as the afternoon passed and it grew colder and darker, I sank into a mood of pure despair. I felt as far from my father as a soul in heaven. It seemed that we had fallen through a crack in the sky into some frozen hell from which no return to the ordinary world was even possible. Like other boys, I knew myths and legends in which heroes had fallen into an evil underworld, or had been lured into enchanted forests from which there was no escape. In their struggles to return to their homes, they had to suffer through many ordeals— they battled dragons and demons, matched wits with sorcerers, sailed across treacherous seas. But even those great heroes needed magical help to succeed—a wizard's guidance, a flying carpet, a secret charm, a magic sword. We were a group of untested boys who had never in our lives truly suffered. Few of us had ever seen snow. None of us had ever set foot in the mountains. Where would we find our hero? What magic would carry us home?

I buried my face in Susy's hair to keep myself from sobbing. Then, as if with a will of its own, an old memory began to glow in my mind, a story my father had told me countless times. When he was a young man, my father was one of Uruguay's top competitive rowers, and one summer he traveled to Argentina to compete in a race on the section of the Uruguay River known as the Delta del Tigre. Seler was a powerful rower, and he quickly pulled away from most of the field, but one Argentine racer stayed with him. They raced, neck and neck, the length of the course, both of them straining with all their might to gain the slightest advantage, but as the finish line approached, it was still too close to call. My father's lungs were burning and his legs were seized with cramps. All he wanted was to slump forward, gulp air into his lungs, and end his suffering. *There will be other races,* he told himself, as he eased his grip on the oars. But then he glanced at his competitor in the scull beside him, and saw pure agony in that man's face. "I realized he was suffering as much as I was," my father told me. "So I decided I would not quit after all. I decided I would suffer a little longer."

With new resolve, Seler dug the oars into the water and stroked with all the power he could muster. His heart pounded and his stomach pitched and his muscles felt as if they were being torn from the bone. But he forced himself to struggle, and when the racers reached the finish line, the prow of my father's scull got there first, by inches.

I was five years old the first time my father told me that story, and I was awestruck by this image of my father—hovering on the verge of surrender, then somehow finding the will to endure. As a boy, I asked him to tell me the story over and over again. I never grew tired of hearing it, and I never lost that heroic image of my father. Many years later, when I'd see him in the office at the hardware store, weary, working late, stooped over his desk and squinting through his thick glasses at stacks of invoices and order forms, I still saw that heroic young man on the river in Argentina, suffering, struggling, but refusing to give in, a man who knew where the finish line was, and who would do anything required to get there.

As I huddled in the plane with Susy, I thought of my father struggling on that Argentine river. I tried to find the same strength in myself, but all I felt was hopelessness and fear. I heard my father's voice, his old advice: *Be strong, Nando, be smart. Make your own luck. Take care of the people you love.* The words inspired nothing in me but a black sense of loss.

Susy groaned softly and shifted in my arms. "Don't worry," I whispered to her, "they will find us. They will bring us home." Whether I believed those words or not, I can't say. My only thought now was to comfort my sister. The sun was setting, and as the light in the fuselage dimmed, the frigid air took on an even sharper edge. The others, who had already lived through two long nights in the mountains, found their sleeping places and braced for the misery they knew lay ahead. Soon the darkness in the plane was absolute, and the cold closed on us like the jaws of a vise. The ferocity of the cold stole my breath away. It seemed to have a malice in it, a predatory will, but there was no way to fight off its attack except to huddle closer to my sister. Time itself seemed to have frozen solid. I lay on the cold floor of the fuselage, tormented by the icy gusts blowing in through every gap and crack, shivering uncontrollably for what seemed like hours, certain that dawn must be only moments away. Then someone with an illuminated watch would announce the time and I would realize that only minutes had passed. I suffered through the long night breath by frozen breath, from one shivering heartbeat to the next, and each moment was its own separate hell. When I thought I couldn't stand it any longer, I would draw Susy closer, and the thought that I was comforting her kept me sane. In the darkness, I couldn't see Susy's face; I could only hear her labored breathing. As I lay beside her, the sweetness of my love for her, for my lost friends and my family, for the suddenly fragile notion of my own life and future, swelled in my heart with an ache so profound it sapped all my strength, and for a moment I thought I would pass out. But I steadied myself and eased closer to Susy, wrapping my arms around her as gently as I could, mindful of her injuries and fighting the urge to squeeze her with all my might. I pressed my cheek against hers so I could feel her warm breath on my face, and held her that way all night, gently, but very close, never letting go, embracing her as if I were embracing all the love and peace and joy I had ever known and would ever know; as if by holding on tight I could keep everything precious from slipping away.

Chapter Three

A Promise

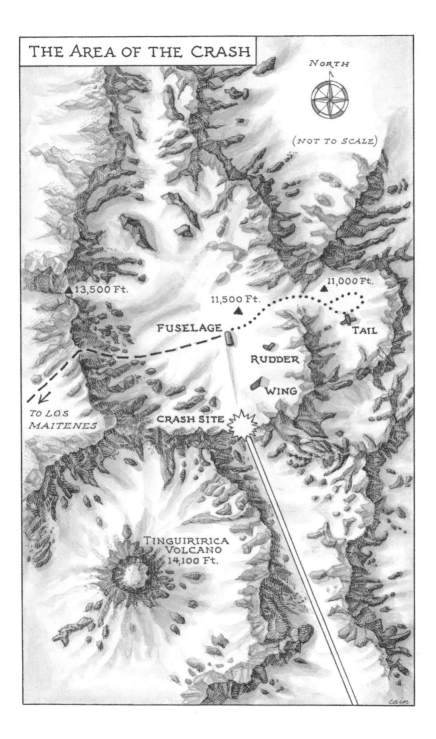

THE AREA OF THE CRASH

NORTH

(NOT TO SCALE)

▲ 13,500 Ft.

11,000 Ft. ▲

11,500 Ft. ▲

FUSELAGE

TAIL

RUDDER

WING

TO LOS MAITENES

CRASH SITE

TINGUIRIRICA VOLCANO 14,100 Ft.

cain

I slept very little that first night out of the coma, and as I lay awake in the frigid darkness, it seemed that dawn would never come. But at last a thin light slowly brightened the windows of the fuselage, and the others began to stir. My heart sank when I first saw them—their hair, eyebrows, and lips glistened with thick silver frost, and they moved stiffly and slowly, like old men. As I began to rise, I realized that my clothes had frozen stiff on my body, and frost had clumped on my brows and lashes. I forced myself to stand. The pain inside my skull still throbbed, but the bleeding had stopped, so I staggered outside the fuselage to take my first look at the strange white world into which we had fallen.

The morning sun lit the snow-covered slopes with a hard white glare, and I had to squint as I surveyed the landscape surrounding the crash site. The Fairchild's battered fuselage had come to rest on a snow-packed glacier flowing down the eastern slope of a massive, ice-crusted mountain. The plane sat with its crumpled nose pointing slightly down the mountainside. The glacier itself plunged down the mountain, then streamed off into a broad valley that wound for miles through the cordillera until it disappeared into a maze of snow-capped ridges marching off to the eastern horizon. East was the only direction in which we could see for any great distance. To the north, south, and west, the view was blocked by a stand of towering mountains. We knew we were high in the Andes, but the snowy slopes above us rose up even higher, so that I had to tilt my head back on my shoulders to see their summits. At the very top, the mountains broke through the snow cover in black peaks shaped like crude pyramids, colossal tents, or huge, broken molars. The ridges formed a ragged semicircle that ringed the crash site like the walls of a monstrous amphitheater, with the wreckage of the Fairchild lying at center stage.

As I surveyed our new world, I was so baffled by the dreamlike strangeness of the place that at first I struggled to convince myself it was real. The mountains were so huge, so pure and silent, and so profoundly removed from the reach of anything in my experience, that I simply could not find my bearings. I had lived all my life in Montevideo, a city of one and a half million people, and had never even considered the fact that cities are manufactured things, built with scales and frames of reference that had been designed to suit the uses and sensibilities of human beings. But the Andes had been thrust up from the earth's crust millions of years before human beings ever walked the planet. Nothing in this place welcomed human life, or even acknowledged its existence. The cold tormented us. The thin air starved our lungs. The unfiltered sun blinded us and blistered our lips and skin, and the snow was so deep that once the morning sun had melted the icy crust that formed on its surface each night, we could not venture far from the plane without sinking to our hips in the drifts. And in all the endless miles of frozen slopes and valleys that entrapped us, there was nothing that any living creature could use as food—not a bird, not an insect, not a single blade of grass. Our chances of survival would have been better if we'd been stranded in the open ocean, or lost in the Sahara. At least some sort of life survives in those places. During the cold months in the high Andes, there is no life at all. We were absurdly out of place here, like a seahorse in the desert, or a flower on the moon. A dread began to form in my mind, an unformed thought that I was not yet able to verbalize: *Life is an anomaly here, and the mountains will tolerate that anomaly for only so long.*

From my very first hours in the mountains, I felt, deep in my bones, the immediacy of the danger that surrounded us. There was never a moment I did not feel the realness and closeness of death, and never a moment in which I was not gripped by primal fear. Still, as I stood outside the Fairchild, I could not help myself from being swept away by the awesome grandeur all around us. There was incredible beauty here—in the hugeness and power of the mountains, in the windswept snowfields that glowed so perfectly white, and in the astounding beauty of the Andean sky. As I looked up now, the sky was cloudless, and it crackled with an iridescent shade of cold, deep blue. Its eerie beauty left me awestruck, but like everything else here, the vastness and emptiness of that endless sky made me feel small and lost and impossibly far from home. In this primeval world, with its crushing scale, its lifeless beauty and its strange silence, I felt awkwardly out of joint with reality in the most fundamental sense, and that scared me more than anything, because I knew in my gut that our survival here would depend on our ability to react to challenges and catastrophes we could not now even imagine. We were playing a game against an unknown and unforgiving opponent. The stakes were terrible—play well or die—but we didn't even know the ground rules. I knew that in order to save my life I would have to understand those rules, but the cold white world around me was offering up no clues.

In those early days of the ordeal, I might have felt more grounded in my new reality if I remembered more of the crash. Because I'd blacked out in the earliest stages of the accident, I had no recollection of anything until I came to my senses three days later. But most of the other survivors had been conscious for every second of the disaster, and as they recounted the details of the crash, and the desperate days that followed, I realized it was a miracle that any of us were alive.

I remembered the flight through Planchón Pass, where we traveled in cloud cover so heavy that visibility was nearly zero and the pilots were forced to fly on instruments. Severe turbulence was tossing the plane around, and at one point we hit an air pocket that forced the plane to drop several hundred feet. This rapid descent dropped us below the clouds, and that was probably the moment when the pilots first saw the black ridge rising dead ahead. Immediately they gunned the Fairchild's engines in a desperate effort to climb. This effort managed to raise the plane's nose a few degrees— preventing a head-on collision with the ridge, which, at a cruising speed of 230 miles per hour, would have reduced the Fairchild to shreds—but their actions were too late to lift the plane completely over the mountain. The Fairchild's belly slammed into the ridge at roughly the point where the wings met the body, and the damage was catastrophic. First the wings broke away. The right wing spiraled down into the pass. The left wing slammed back against the plane, where its propeller sliced through the Fairchild's hull before it, too, plunged into the mountains. A split second later the fuselage fractured along a line directly above my head, and the tail section fell away. Everyone sitting behind me was lost—the plane's navigator, the flight steward, and the three boys playing cards. One of those boys was Guido.

In that same instant, I felt myself lifted from my seat and hurled forward with indescribable force, as if some giant had scooped me up like a baseball and hurled me with all his might. I remember slamming into something, probably the bulkhead between the passenger cabin and the cockpit. I felt the wall flex, then I lost consciousness, and for me the crash was over. But the others still faced a terrifying ride as the fuselage, stripped of its wings, engines, and tail, sailed forward like an unguided missile. Here we were blessed with the first of many miracles. The plane did not wobble or spiral. Instead, whatever aerodynamic principles govern such things kept the remains of the Fairchild flying upright long enough to clear yet another black ridge. But the plane was losing momentum, and at last the nose dipped and it began to fall. Now the second miracle saved us, as the Fairchild's angle of descent matched almost exactly the steep slope of the mountain onto which we were falling. If this angle had been just a few degrees steeper or shallower, the plane would have cartwheeled on the mountain and slammed to pieces. But instead it landed on its belly and began to rocket down the snow-covered mountainside like a toboggan. Passengers screamed and prayed out loud as the fuselage raced down the slope at a speed of two hundred miles per hour for a distance of more than four hundred yards, finding a fortunate path between the boulders and rocky outcrops that studded the mountain before slamming into a huge snow berm and coming to a sudden, violent stop. The forces of the collision were huge. The Fairchild's nose was crumpled like a paper cup. In the passenger cabin, seats were ripped loose from the floor of the fuselage and hurled forward along with the people sitting in them, and dashed against the cockpit bulkhead. Several passengers were crushed instantly as the rows of seats closed on them like the folds of an accordion, then tumbled into a mangled heap that filled the front of the fuselage almost to the ceiling.

Coche Inciarte, one of the team's supporters, told me how he grasped the back of the seat in front of him as the plane streaked down the mountain, waiting to die at any second. After the impact, he said, the fuselage rolled slightly to the left, then settled heavily in the snow. For moments there was nothing but stunned silence, but soon the quiet was broken by soft moans, and then sharper cries of pain. Coche found himself lying in the tangle of seats, uninjured and amazed to be alive. There was blood everywhere, and the arms and legs of motionless bodies stuck out from under the compressed jumble of seats. In his confusion, his attention was drawn to his tie, which, he saw, had been shredded to threads by the force of the wind generated during the Fairchild's wild slide down the mountain. Alvaro Mangino remembered being forced beneath the seat in front of him at the final impact. As he lay trapped on the floor, he heard moaning and crying all around him, and he especially remembered being baffled by the appearance of Roy Harley, who seemed to have turned bright blue. Later he would realize that Roy had been soaked in airplane fuel.

Gustavo Zerbino was sitting next to Alvaro. He explained that in the first impact, when the plane hit the mountain ridge, he saw the seat in which Carlos Valeta was sitting rip loose from the floor and disappear into the sky. As the fuselage skidded down the slope, Gustavo stood and grabbed the luggage rack above his head. He closed his eyes and prayed. "Jesus, Jesus, I want to live!" he cried. He was certain he was about to die. Miraculously, he was still standing when the plane smashed into the snowbank and heaved to a sudden stop.

So it's true, he thought, *you are still thinking after you are dead.* Then he opened his eyes. When he saw the wreckage in front of him, he instinctively took a step backward, and immediately sank to his hips in snow. Looking up, he saw the ragged line of the fracture where the tail section had broken away from the fuselage, and he realized that everything and everyone behind him had disappeared. The floor of the fuselage was at the level of his chest now, and as he pulled himself back up into the plane, he was forced to climb over the motionless body of a middle-aged woman. Her face was bruised and covered with blood, but he recognized her as my mother. Gustavo, a first-year medical student, bent down and took her pulse, but she was already gone.

Gustavo moved forward in the fuselage toward the pile of seats. He pried one of the seats from the pile and found Roberto Canessa underneath. Canessa, also a medical student, was not injured, and within moments Roberto and Gustavo began pulling more seats from the pile and tending, as well as they could, to the injured passengers they freed.

At the same time, Marcelo Perez was pulling himself from the wreckage. Marcelo had hurt his side in the crash, and his face was bruised, but these injuries were minor, and as our longtime captain he immediately took control. His first action was to organize the uninjured boys and set them to work freeing the passengers who had been trapped under the heap of wrecked seats. This was laborious work. The force of the crash had crumpled the seats into an impossible tangle, with each seat interlocking with others in clusters too heavy to move. Many of the survivors were athletes, in top physical condition, but still, as they struggled to wrench and pry the seats apart; they found themselves gasping for breath in the thin mountain air.

As passengers were pulled, one by one, from the wrecked seats, Roberto Canessa and Gustavo Zerbino assessed their condition, and did their best to tend to their injuries, some of which were grisly. Both of Arturo Nogueira's legs had been broken in several places. Alvaro had a broken leg, and so did Pancho Delgado. A six-inch steel tube had impaled Enrique Platero's stomach like the point of a spear, and when Zerbino yanked the tube from his friend's gut, several inches of Platero's intestines came out with it. The injury to Rafael Echavarren's right leg was even more gruesome. His calf muscle had been ripped off the bone and twisted forward so that it hung in a slippery mass across his shin. When Zerbino found him Echavarren's leg bone was completely exposed. Zerbino, swallowing his revulsion, grabbed the loose muscle, pressed it back in place, and then bandaged the bloody leg with strips of someone's white shirt. He bandaged Platero's stomach, too, and then the quiet, stoic Platero immediately went to work freeing others who were trapped in the seats.

As more and more passengers were pulled from the wreckage, the "doctors" were amazed to see that most of the survivors had suffered only minor injuries. Canessa and Zerbino cleaned and bandaged their wounds. They sent others, with injuries to their arms and legs, out onto the glacier where they were able to dull their pain by cooling their limbs in the snow. Each uninjured survivor who was freed from the seats became another worker, and soon the workers had freed all of the trapped passengers except for one, a middle-aged woman named Señora Marinari. The señora was not traveling as part of our group. Instead, she was traveling to her daughter's wedding in Chile, and had purchased tickets on this flight directly from the air force as an inexpensive way to make the trip. In the crash, her seat back had collapsed forward, pressing her chest forward against her knees and pinning her legs back beneath her seat. Other seats had fallen on top of her, burying her beneath a pile so heavy and wickedly tangled that no amount of effort could free her. Both of her legs were broken, and she was screaming in agony, but there was nothing anyone could do for her.

And there was nothing to be done for Fernando Vasquez, one of the team's supporters. When Roberto checked on him in the first moments after the crash, he seemed dazed but unharmed, and Roberto moved on. When Roberto checked again, he found Vasquez dead in his seat. His leg had been severed below the knee by the plane's propeller when it slashed through the hull, and in the time Roberto was away from him, he had bled to death. Our team doctor, Francisco Nicola, and his wife, Esther, had been flung from their seats and were lying dead, side by side, at the front of the passenger cabin. Susy was lying beside my mother's body. She was conscious but incoherent, with blood streaming over her face. Roberto wiped the blood from Susy's eyes and saw that it was coming from a superficial scalp wound, but he suspected, correctly, that she had suffered much more serious internal injuries. A few feet away they found Panchito, bleeding from the head and rambling in semi-consciousness. Roberto knelt beside him and Panchito took Roberto's hand, begging him not to leave. Roberto cleaned the blood from Panchito's eyes, comforted him, then moved on. In the front of the plane he found me lying senseless, my face covered in blood and black bruises, my head already swollen to the size of a basketball. He checked my pulse and was surprised to see that my heart was still beating. But my injuries seemed so grave that he gave me no chance of surviving, so he and Zerbino moved on, saving their efforts for the ones they believed they could help.

There were moans coming from the cockpit, but the cockpit door was still hopelessly barricaded by the wall of toppled seats, so Canessa and Zerbino had to step outside the fuselage and struggle through the deep snow to the front of the plane, where they were able to climb up through the luggage compartment and into the cockpit. There they found Ferradas and Lagurara still strapped in their seats. The plane's final impact with the snowbank had crushed the Fairchild's nose and forced the instrument panel into their chests, pinning them against the backs of their seats. Ferradas was dead. Lagurara was conscious, but gravely injured and in terrible pain. Canessa and Zerbino tried to pry the instrumental panel off the copilot's chest, but it wouldn't budge. "We passed Curicó," Lagurara muttered, as the doctors tried to help him, "we passed Curicó." Canessa and Zerbino managed to remove the cushion of his seatback, and this relieved some of the pressure on his chest, but there was not much more they could do for him. They fed him some snow to ease his thirst, then they asked if they could use the Fairchild's radio. Lagurara told them how to set the dial for transmission, but when they tried to send a message, they found that the radio was dead. Lagurara begged for more snow, and the doctors fed it to him, then they turned to leave. As he realized the hopelessness of his situation, Lagurara pleaded with the boys to bring him the revolver he kept in his flight bag, but Canessa and Zerbino ignored him and headed back to the passenger cabin. As they climbed down from the cockpit, they heard Lagurara murmuring, "We passed Curicó, we passed Curicó . . ."

Back in the fuselage, Marcelo was working out some grim calculations in his head. We had crashed at three-thirty in the afternoon. He guessed it would be four o'clock before officials could confirm that the plane was missing. By the time they could organize a helicopter rescue, it would be five-thirty or six. The helicopters would not reach us until seven-thirty at the earliest, and since no pilot in his right mind would fly in the Andes at night, Marcelo knew no rescue would be launched until the following day. We would have to spend the night here. Daylight was already fading. The temperatures, which were already well below freezing when we crashed, were dropping fast. Marcelo knew we were not prepared to weather a subzero night in the Andes. We were dressed only in light summer clothing—some of us were wearing blazers or sports jackets, but most of us were in shirtsleeves. We had no warm coats, no blankets, nothing to protect us from the savage cold. Marcelo knew that unless we found a way to turn the fuselage into a decent shelter, none of us would last until morning, but the plane was so full of jumbled seats and loose debris that there wasn't enough clear floor space for the injured to lie down, let alone provide sleeping room for dozens of uninjured survivors.

Realizing that the clutter would have to be cleared from the fuselage, Marcelo set to work. First he gathered a crew of healthy survivors and gave them the task of removing the dead and injured from the fuselage. They began dragging the dead out into the open, using long nylon straps they'd found in the luggage compartment. The injured were carried out more gently, and once they were laid on the snow, Marcelo directed the survivors to clear as much floor space as they could. The workers labored valiantly to follow his orders, but the work was grueling and excruciatingly slow. They suffered from the frigid wind and gasped for breath in the thin air. By the time darkness fell, they had cleared just a small space near the gaping hole at the rear of the fuselage.

At six o'clock, Marcelo directed the others to move the injured back into the fuselage, then the healthy survivors filed in and prepared for the long night ahead. Once everyone was settled, Marcelo began to build a makeshift wall to seal off the huge opening at the rear of the fuselage where the tail section had broken away. With Roy Harley's help, he stacked suitcases, fragments of the aircraft, and loose seats in the opening, then he packed the gaps with snow. It was far from airtight, and the air temperature in the fuselage was still viciously frigid, but Marcelo hoped the wall would shield us from the worst of the subzero cold.

When the wall was finished, the survivors settled in for the night. Forty-five passengers and crew members had been on board the Fairchild. There were five known dead at the crash site. Eight were unaccounted for, although the survivors felt certain that one of them, Carlos Valeta, was dead. Zerbino had seen Valeta's seat fall from the plane, but, incredibly, he had survived his fall. In the moments just after the crash, a group of boys had spotted him staggering down the mountain slope a few hundred yards from the Fairchild. They called to him and he seemed to turn toward the crash site, but then he stumbled in the deep snow and tumbled down the slope and out of sight. This left thirty-two people alive at the crash site. Lagurara was still trapped in the cockpit. Some of the injured, along with Liliana Methol, the only uninjured woman survivor, were gathered in the shelter of the Fairchild's luggage compartment, which was the warmest part of the plane. The rest packed into a cramped space on the litter-strewn floor of the fuselage that measured no more than eight by ten feet square.

Because night had fallen so quickly, there hadn't been time to remove all the bodies, and the survivors were forced to hunker down among the dead, shoving and prodding the corpses of friends for a few more inches of space. It was a scene from a nightmare, but the fear and physical suffering the survivors were enduring overshadowed their horror. The tight quarters were intensely uncomfortable, and despite Marcelo's wall, the cold was unbearable. The survivors huddled together to share the warmth of their bodies. Some of them begged the boys near them to punch their arms and legs to keep the blood flowing in their veins.

At some point, Roberto realized that the cloth coverings of the seats could easily be unzipped and removed and used as blankets.

They were made of thin nylon and offered little protection against the cold, but Roberto understood the risks of hypothermia, and knew the survivors had to do everything they could to conserve as much body heat as possible. Even if the blankets would not prevent anyone from suffering in the cold, they might help them retain enough body heat to survive until morning.

They laid me beside Susy and Panchito at the base of Marcelo's wall. This was the coldest part of the cabin. Wind leaked through the makeshift wall, and the floor below us, which had been torn away in the crash, allowed cold air to stream up from below, but they placed us here because they had already given up hope that we would live very long, and they saved the warmer places for those who had a chance to survive. Susy and Panchito, who were still conscious, must have suffered terribly that first night, but I was still in a coma, and was spared that agony. In fact, the frigid air may have saved my life by reducing the swelling that would have destroyed my brain.

As the night grew deeper, the cold bore down on the survivors, chilling them bone-deep and crushing their spirits. Each moment was an eternity, and as the last light faded, it was as if the mountain darkness were seeping into the survivors' souls. All the purposeful work they had done in the aftermath of the crash had kept them from dwelling on their fears, and the physical activity had helped them keep warm. But now, as they lay helpless in the dark, there was nothing to protect them from the cold or, worse, from the despair. Survivors who had performed stoically in the daylight now wept and screamed in pain. There were savage bursts of anger as one boy shifted position in the cramped quarters and bumped the injured leg of another, or someone unintentionally kicked someone else as he tried to sleep. The moments crept by.

At some point, Diego Storm—another medical student in our group—saw something in my face that made him think I might live, so he dragged me away from Marcelo's wall to a warmer place in the fuselage, where the others kept me warm with their bodies. Some managed to sleep that night, but most simply endured, second by second, breath by breath, as sounds of suffering and delusion filled the darkness. In a thin voice, Panchito pleaded pathetically for help, and constantly muttered that he was freezing. Susy prayed, and called for our mother. Señora Mariani screamed and wailed in her agony. In the cockpit, the raving copilot begged for his gun, and insisted, over and over, "We passed Curicó, we passed Curicó . . ." "It was a nightmare, Nando," Coche told me. "It was Dante's Hell."

The survivors suffered through that first night, surrounded by chaos. The hours were endless, but at last morning came. Marcelo was the first on his feet. The others, still huddling on the floor of the fuselage to keep warm, were reluctant to rise, but Marcelo roused them. The night had shaken them deeply, but as they moved around in the daylight filtering into the cabin, their spirits began to rise. They had done the impossible—they had survived a frigid night in the Andes. Surely the rescue party would find them today. All through the terrible night, Marcelo had assured them that it would. Now they felt certain that they would be home soon, that the worst of their ordeal was over.

As the others prepared themselves for the day, Canessa and Zerbino moved through the fuselage, checking on the injured. Panchito was lying still and stiff. He had died during the night. In the cockpit, they found Lagurara's lifeless body. Señora Mariani was motionless, but when Canessa tried to move her, she screamed again in agony and he left her alone. When he returned to check on her again, she had died.

The doctors did what they could for the injured survivors. They cleaned wounds, changed dressings, and led the boys with broken bones out onto the glacier, where they could ease their pain by laying their shattered limbs in the snow. They found Susy lying beneath Panchito's body. She was conscious, but still delusional.

Roberto rubbed her feet, which were black with frostbite, then he wiped the blood from her eyes. Susy was lucid enough to thank him for his kindness.

While the doctors made their rounds, Marcelo and Roy Harley had knocked down part of the wall they'd built the night before, and the survivors began their second day on the mountain. All day long they searched the skies for signs of rescue. In late afternoon they heard a plane pass over, but the skies were overcast and they knew they hadn't been seen. In the fast-fading twilight, the survivors gathered in the fuselage to face another long night. With more time to work, Marcelo built a better, more windproof wall. The last of the dead bodies had been removed from the fuselage, and that, along with the absence of the others who had died, provided more sleeping space on the fuselage floor, but still the night was long and their suffering was grim.

In the afternoon of the third day, I finally woke from my coma, and as I slowly gathered my wits about me, I was staggered by the thought of the horrors my friends had already endured. The strain of what they had been through seemed to have aged them years. Their faces were drawn and pale from tension and lack of sleep. Physical exhaustion and the energy-sapping effects of the thin air made their movements slow and uncertain, so that many of them stooped and shuffled about the crash site as if they had grown decades older in the last thirty-six hours. There were twenty-nine survivors now, most of us young men between the ages of nineteen and twenty-one, but some were as young as seventeen. The oldest survivor now was thirty-eight-year-old Javier Methol, but he suffered so badly from the nausea and fatigue caused by severe altitude sickness that he could barely stand. Both pilots and most of the crew were dead. The only crew member to survive was Carlos Roque, the plane's mechanic, but the shock of the crash had rattled him so badly that all we could get from him was senseless raving. He couldn't even tell us where emergency supplies like flares and blankets might be kept. There was no one to help us, no one with any knowledge of mountains or airplanes or the techniques of survival. We lived constantly on the verge of hysteria, but we did not panic. Leaders emerged, and we responded in the way we'd been taught by the Christian Brothers—as a team.

Much of the credit for our survival in those critical early days must go to Marcelo Perez, whose decisive leadership saved many lives. From the very first moments of the ordeal, Marcelo responded to the staggering challenges before us with the same combination of courage, decisiveness, and foresight with which he had led us to so many victories on the rugby field. He instantly understood that the margin for error here was slim, and that the mountain would make us pay dearly for stupid mistakes. In a rugby match, hesitation, indecision, and confusion can cost you the game. Marcelo realized that in the Andes, these same mistakes would cost us our lives. His strong presence in the first hours after the crash prevented what could have been total panic. The rescue operation he quickly organized saved the lives of many people who were pulled from the tangled seats, and without the sheltering wall he built that first night, we all would have frozen to death by morning.

Marcelo's leadership was heroic. He slept at night in the coldest part of the fuselage, and he always asked all the other uninjured boys to do the same. He forced us to keep busy, when many among us simply wanted to huddle in the fuselage and wait to be saved. More than anything, he buoyed our spirits by convincing us that our suffering would be over soon. He was convinced that rescue was on its way, and he was very forceful in convincing others this was true. Still, he understood that surviving in the Andes, even for just a few days, would test us to our limits, and he made it his responsibility to take the measures that would give us the best chance of surviving that long. One of the first things he did was to gather everything edible that could be found in suitcases or scattered around the cabin. There wasn't much—a few chocolate bars and other candies, some nuts and crackers, some dried fruit, several small jars of jam, three bottles of wine, some whiskey, and a few bottles of liqueur. Despite his conviction that rescue was only hours away, some natural instinct for survival told him to err on the side of caution, and on the second day of the ordeal, Marcelo began to carefully ration the food—each meal was nothing more than a small square of chocolate or a dab of jam, washed down with a sip of wine from the cap of an aerosol can. It was not enough to satisfy anyone's hunger, but as a ritual, it gave us strength. Each time we gathered to receive our meager rations, we were making a statement, to each other and to ourselves, that we would do everything we could to survive.

In those early days we all believed that rescue was our only chance of survival, and we clung to that hope with an almost religious zeal. We had to believe this. The alternatives were simply too horrible. Marcelo made sure our faith in rescue remained strong. Even as days passed, and no rescue arrived, he would not let us doubt the fact that we all would be saved. Whether he truly believed this for himself, or if it was just a courageous ploy to keep us from losing heart, I cannot say. He professed this belief so firmly I never doubted him, but I didn't realize at the time the terrible burden he was carrying, and how deeply he blamed himself for taking us all on this doomed journey.

On the afternoon of the fourth day, a small prop-driven plane flew over the crash site, and several of the survivors who saw it were certain it had dipped its wings. This was taken as a signal that we had been sighted, and soon a sense of relief and jubilation spread through the group. We waited as the long shadows of late afternoon stretched down the mountains, but by nightfall no rescuers had arrived. Marcelo insisted that the pilots of the plane would send help soon, but others, wearied by the strain of waiting, were beginning to admit their doubts.

"Why is it taking so long for them to find us?" someone asked.

Marcelo answered this question in the same way he always did: perhaps helicopters cannot fly in the thin mountain air, he would say, so the rescue party might be coming on foot, and that will take time.

"But if they know where we are, why haven't they flown over to drop supplies?"

Impossible, Marcelo would say. Anything dropped from a plane would simply sink into the snow and be lost. The pilots would know this. Most of the boys accepted the logic of Marcelo's explanations. They also trusted heavily in the goodness of God. "God saved us from dying in the crash," they'd say. "Why would He do that just to leave us here to die?"

I listened to these discussions as I spent the long hours caring for Susy. I wanted so badly to trust in God as they did. But God had already taken my mother and Panchito and so many others. Why would He save us and not them? In the same way, I wanted to believe rescue was coming, but I could not chase away the gnawing sense that we were on our own. As I lay with Susy, I felt a terrible helplessness and sense of urgency. I knew she was dying, and that the only hope was to get her to a hospital soon. Each moment lost was an agony for me, and in every waking second I listened hard for the sound of rescuers approaching. I never stopped praying for their arrival, or for the intercession of God, but at the same time the cold-blooded voice that had urged me to save my tears was always whispering in the back of my mind: *No one will find us. We will die here. We must make a plan. We must save ourselves.* From my very first moments of consciousness, I was nagged by the sobering apprehension that we were on our own here, and it alarmed me that the others were placing so much trust in the hope that we would be saved. But soon I realized that others thought like me. The "realists," as I thought of them, included Canessa and Zerbino, Fito Strauch, a former member of the Old Christians who had come on the trip at the invitation of his cousin Eduardo, and

Carlitos Paez, whose father, Carlos Paez-Villaro, was a famous Uruguayan painter, adventurer, and friend of Picasso. For days this group had been discussing their plans to climb the mountain above us and see what lay beyond. We had reason to believe escape was possible. All of us knew the words our copilot had moaned as he lay dying: *We passed Curicó, we passed Curicó* . . . In the first few hours after the crash, someone had found sets of flight charts in the cockpit. Arturo Nogueira, whose shattered legs confined him to the fuselage, spent hours studying the complex charts, searching for the town of Curicó. Finally he found it, situated inside the Chilean border, well beyond the western slopes of the Andes. None of us were experts at reading these charts, but it seemed clear that if we had, in fact, traveled as far west as Curicó, there was no doubt that we had flown across the entire breadth of the cordillera. That meant the crash site must be somewhere in the western foothills of the Andes. We were encouraged in this belief by the reading on the Fairchild's altimeter, which showed our altitude to be seven thousand feet. If we were deep in the Andes, our altitude would be much higher than that. Surely we were in the foothills, and the tall ridges to our west were the last high peaks of the Andes range. We grew certain that beyond those western summits were the green fields of Chile. We would find a village there, or at least a shepherd's hut. Someone would be there to help us. We would all be saved. Until now, we had felt like victims of a shipwreck, lost in an ocean with no sense of where the nearest shore might be. Now we felt a small sense of control. We knew one fact at least: *To the west is Chile.* This phrase quickly became a rallying call for us, and we used it to bolster our hopes throughout our ordeal.

ON THE MORNING of October 17, our fifth day on the mountain, Carlitos, Roberto, Fito, and a twenty-four-year-old survivor named Numa Turcatti decided the time had come to climb. Numa was not an Old Christian—he had come on the trip as a guest of his friends Pancho Delgado and Gaston Costemalle—but he was as fit and sturdy as any of us, and had come through the crash with hardly a scratch. I did not yet know him well, but in the few difficult days we had spent together he had impressed me, and the others, with his calmness and his quiet strength. Numa never panicked or lost his temper. He never fell into self-pity or despair. There was something noble and selfless in Numa. Everybody saw it. He cared for the weaker ones and comforted the ones who wept or were afraid. He seemed to care about the welfare of the rest of us as much as he cared about himself, and we all drew strength from his example. From the first moments, I knew that if we would ever escape these mountains, Numa would have something to do with it, and I wasn't surprised for a second that he had volunteered to go on the climb.

And I was not surprised that Carlitos and Roberto had volunteered. Both of them had escaped injury in the crash and each, in his way, had made himself one of the more prominent personalities in our group: Roberto with his intelligence, medical knowledge, and sometimes belligerent nature; and Carlitos with his optimism and brave humor. Fito, a former player for the Old Christians, was a quiet, serious boy. He had suffered a mild concussion in the crash, but he had recovered fully now, and this was a good thing for us, for Fito would turn out to be one of the wisest and most resourceful of all the survivors. Shortly after the crash, when we were struggling to walk in the deep, soft snow surrounding the fuselage, Fito realized that if we tied the cushions of the Fairchild's seats to our feet with seat belts or lengths of wire cable, they would serve as makeshift snowshoes, and allow us to walk without sinking into the snow. The four climbers had Fito's snowshoes strapped to their boots now as they set off across the deep drifts toward the mountain. Their hope was to reach the summit and see what lay beyond. Along the way they would search for the Fairchild's missing tail section, which we all hoped would be filled with food and warm clothing. We even wondered if there could be other survivors living inside it. And Carlos Roque, the Fairchild's flight mechanic, who had slowly regained his senses, remembered the batteries that powered the Fairchild's radio were stored in a compartment in the tail. If we found them, he said, it was possible we could fix the radio and broadcast a call for help.

The weather was clear as they set off. I wished them well, then busied myself with caring for my sister. Afternoon shadows had fallen over the Fairchild by the time the climbers returned. I heard commotion in the fuselage as they arrived, and I looked up to see them stumble into the fuselage and sag to the floor. They were physically wasted and gasping for air. The others quickly surrounded them, badgering them with questions, eager for some promising news. I went to Numa and asked him how it was.

He shook his head and scowled. "It was damned hard, Nando," he said as he tried to catch his breath. "It is steep. Much steeper than it looks from here."

"There is not enough air," Canessa said. "You can't breathe. You can only move very slowly."

Numa nodded. "The snow is too deep, every step is agony. And there are crevasses under the snow. Fito almost fell into one."

"Did you see anything to the west?" I asked.

"We barely made it halfway up the slope," Numa said. "We couldn't see anything. The mountains block the view. They are much higher than they seem."

I turned to Canessa. "Roberto," I said, "what do you think? If we try again, can we climb it?"

"I don't know, man," he whispered, "I don't know . . ."

"We can't climb that mountain," muttered Numa. "We must find another route—if there is one."

That night, gloom hung in the air of the fuselage. The four who had climbed were the strongest and healthiest among us, and the mountain had defeated them with ease. But I did not accept this defeat. Perhaps, if I had been in an ordinary state of mind, I would have seen in their faces, and in the dark glances they exchanged, the grim revelation the climb had shown them: that we could not escape this place, that we were all already dead. Instead, I told myself that they were soft, they were afraid, they had quit too easily. The mountain did not seem so treacherous to me. I was certain that if we chose the right route and the right time, and we simply refused to give in to the cold and the exhaustion, we could surely reach the summit. I clung to this belief with the same blind faith that kept the others praying for rescue. What choice did I have? To me it seemed gruesomely simple: Life is not possible here. I must move toward a place where life exists. I must go west, to Chile. My mind was filled with so much doubt and confusion that I clung desperately to the one thing I knew for certain to be true: *To the west is Chile. To the west is Chile.* I let those words echo in my mind like a mantra. I knew that someday I would have to climb.

IN THE FIRST few days of our ordeal, I rarely left my sister's side. I spent all my time with her, rubbing her frozen feet, giving her sips of water I had melted, feeding her the little squares of chocolate that Marcelo would set aside. Mostly I tried to comfort her and keep her warm. I was never sure if she was aware of my presence. She was always semiconscious. Often she moaned. Her brow was constantly knit with worry and confusion, and there was always a forlorn sadness in her eyes. Sometimes she would pray, or sing a lullaby. Many times she would call for our mother. I would soothe her and whisper in her ear. Each moment with her was precious, even in this terrible place, and the softness of her warm breath on my cheek was a great comfort to me.

Late in the afternoon of the eighth day, I was lying with my arms around Susy when suddenly I felt her change. The worried look faded from her face. The tenseness eased from her body. Her breathing grew shallow and slow, and I felt her life slipping from my arms, but I could do nothing to stop it. Then her breathing stopped, and she was still.

"Susy?" I cried. "Oh God, Susy, please, no!"

I scrambled to my knees, rolled her on her back, and began to give her mouth-to-mouth resuscitation. I was not even sure how to do this, but I was desperate to save her. "Come on, Susy, please," I cried. "Don't leave me!" I worked over her until I fell, exhausted, to the floor. Roberto took my place, with no success. Then Carlitos tried, but it was no good. The others gathered around me in silence.

Roberto came to my side. "I'm sorry, Nando, she is gone," he said. "Stay with her tonight. We will bury her in the morning." I nodded and gathered my sister in my arms. Now at last I could embrace her with all my might, without the fear of hurting her. She was still warm. Her hair was soft against my face. But when I pressed my cheek against her lips, I no longer felt her warm breath on my skin. My Susy was gone. I tried to memorize this feeling of embracing her, the feel of her body, the smell of her hair. As I thought of all I was losing, the grief surged inside me, and my body was shaken by great, heaving sobs. But just as my sadness was about to overwhelm me, I heard, once again, that cool, disembodied voice whisper in my ear:

Tears waste salt.

I lay awake with her all night, my chest heaving with sobs, but I did not allow myself the luxury of tears.

IN THE MORNING we tied some long nylon luggage straps around Susy's torso and dragged her from the fuselage out into the snow. I watched as they pulled her to her gravesite. It seemed crude to treat her this way, but the others had learned from experience that dead bodies were heavy and limp and very hard to handle, and this was the most efficient way to move them, so I accepted it as normal.

We dragged Susy to a spot in the snow to the left of the fuselage where the other dead were buried. The frozen corpses were clearly visible, their faces obscured by only a few inches of ice and snow. I stood above one of the graves, and easily made out the hazy shape of my mother's blue dress. I dug a shallow grave for Susy next to my mother. I laid Susy on her side and brushed back her hair. Then I covered her slowly with handfuls of crystallized snow, leaving her face uncovered until the very end. She seemed peaceful, as if she were sleeping under a thick fleece blanket. I took one last look at her, my beautiful Susy, then I gently tossed handfuls of snow across her cheeks until her face had vanished beneath the sparkling crystals.

After we finished, the others walked back inside the fuselage. I turned and looked up the slope of the glacier, to the ridges of mountains blocking our path to the west. I could still see the wide path the Fairchild had cut into the snow as it skied down the slope after clipping the ridge. I followed this path up the mountain to the very spot where we had fallen from the sky into the madness that was now the only reality we knew. How could this happen? We were boys on our way to play a game! Suddenly I was struck by a sickening sense of emptiness. Since my first moments on the mountain I had spent all my time and energy caring for my sister. Comforting her had given me purpose and stability. It had filled my hours and distracted me from my own pain and fear. Now I was so terribly alone, with nothing to distance me from the awful circumstances that surrounded me. My mother was dead. My sister was dead. My best friends had fallen from the plane in flight, or were buried here beneath the snow. We were injured, hungry, and freezing. More than a week had passed, and still the rescuers had not found us. I felt the brute power of the mountains gathered around me, saw the complete absence of warmth or mercy or softness in the landscape. As I understood, with a stinging new clarity, how far we were from home, I sank into despair, and for the first time I knew with certainty I would die.

In fact, I was dead already. My life had been stolen from me. The future I had dreamed of was not to be. The woman I would have married would never know me. My children would not be born. I would never again enjoy the loving gaze of my grandmother, or feel the warm embrace of my sister Graciela. And I would never return to my father. In my mind I saw him again, in his suffering, and I felt such a violent longing to be with him that it almost drove me to my knees. I gagged on the impotent rage that rose in my throat, and I felt so beaten and trapped that for a moment I thought I would lose my mind. Then I saw my father on that river in Argentina, wasted, defeated, on the verge of surrender, and I remembered his words of defiance: *I decided I would not quit. I decided I would suffer a little longer.*

It was my favorite story, but now I realized it was more than that: it was a sign from my father, a gift of wisdom and strength. For a moment I felt him with me. An eerie calmness settled over me. I stared at the great mountains to the west, and imagined a path leading over them and back to my home. I felt my love for my father tugging at me like a lifeline, drawing me toward those barren slopes. Staring west, I made a silent vow to my father. *I will struggle. I will come home. I will not let the bond between us be broken. I promise you, I will not die here! I will not die here!*

Chapter Four

Breathe Once More

IN THE HOURS after we buried Susy, I sat alone in the dark fuselage, slumped against the Fairchild's tilting wall with my shattered skull cradled in my hands. Powerful emotions stormed my heart—disbelief, outrage, sorrow, and fear—and then, finally, a sense of weary acceptance washed over me like a sigh. I was too depressed and confused to see it at the time, but it seemed my mind was racing through the stages of grief at breakneck speed. In my old life, my ordinary life in Montevideo, the loss of my little sister would have brought my existence to a standstill and left me emotionally staggered for months. But nothing was ordinary anymore, and something primal in me understood that in this unforgiving place, I could not afford the luxury of grieving. Once again I heard that cold, steady voice in my head rise above the emotional chaos. *Look forward,* it said. *Save your strength for the things you can change. If you cling to the past, you will die.* I didn't want to let go of my sorrow. I missed having Susy with me in the fuselage, where I could comfort and care for her, and my sadness was my only connection to her now, but I seemed to have no say in the matter. As the long night passed and I struggled to fight the cold, the intensity of my emotions began to fade and my feelings for my sister simply dissolved, the way a dream dissolves as you wake. By morning all I felt was a sour, dull emptiness as my beloved Susy, like my mother and Panchito, drifted into my past, a past that was already beginning to feel distant and unreal. The mountains were forcing me to change. My mind was growing colder and simpler as it adjusted to my new reality. I began to see life as it must appear to an animal struggling to survive—as a simple game of win or lose, life or death, risk and opportunity. Basic instincts were taking hold, suppressing complex emotions and narrowing the focus of my mind until my entire existence seemed to revolve around the two new organizing principles of my life: the chilling apprehension that I was going to die, and the searing need to be with my father.

In the days after Susy died, my love for my father was the only thing that kept me sane, and time after time I would calm myself by reaffirming the promise I had made at Susy's grave: to return to him; to show him I had survived and to ease his suffering a little. My heart swelled with longing to be with him, and not a moment passed that I did not picture him in his anguish. Who was comforting him? How was he fighting off despair? I imagined him wandering at night from one empty room to another, or tossing until dawn in his bed. How it must torture him to feel so helpless. How betrayed he must feel—to have spent a lifetime protecting and providing for the family he cherished, only to have that family ripped away. He was the strongest man I knew, but was he strong enough to endure this kind of loss? Would he keep his sanity? Would he lose all hope and his will to live? Sometimes my imagination got the best of me, and I worried that he might harm himself, choosing to end his suffering and join his loved ones in death.

Thinking of my father this way always triggered in me a burst of love so radiant and urgent that it took my breath away. I couldn't stand the thought that he would suffer one second longer. In my desperation, I raged silently at the great peaks that loomed above the crash site, blocking the path to my father, and trapping me in this evil place where I could do nothing to ease his pain. That claustrophobic frustration gnawed at me until, like a man buried alive, I began to panic. Every moment that passed was filled with a visceral fear, as if the earth beneath my feet were a ticking bomb that might explode at any second; as if I stood blindfolded before a firing squad, waiting to feel the bullets slam into my chest. This terrifying sense of vulnerability—the certainty that doom was only moments away—never rested. It filled every moment of my time on the mountain. It became the backdrop for every thought and conversation. And it produced in me a manic urge to flee. I fought this fear the best I could, trying to calm myself and think clearly, but there were moments when animal instinct threatened to overcome reason, and it would take all my strength to keep from bolting off blindly into the cordillera.

At first, the only way I could quiet these fears was to picture in my mind the moment when rescuers would arrive to save us. In the early days of the ordeal, this was the hope we all clung to. Marcelo fed these hopes with his assurances, but as the days passed and the absence of the rescuers became harder to explain, Marcelo, a deeply devout Catholic, began to rely more and more upon the beliefs that had always shaped his life. "God loves us," he would say. "He would not ask us to endure such suffering only to turn his back on us and allow us to die meaningless deaths." It was not our place to ask why God was testing us so harshly, Marcelo insisted. Our duty—to God, to our families, and to each other—was to survive from one moment to the next, to accept our fears and suffering, and to be alive when the rescuers finally found us.

Marcelo's words had a powerful effect on the others, most of whom embraced his arguments without question. I wanted to believe in Marcelo so badly, but as time passed I could not silence the doubts that were growing in my mind. We had always assumed that the authorities knew roughly where our plane had gone down. They must have known our route through the mountains, we told ourselves, and surely the pilots had radioed along the way. It would simply be a matter of searching along the flight path, beginning at the point of the last radio contact. How hard could it be to spot the wreckage of a large airplane lying in plain view on an open glacier?

But surely, I thought, a concentrated search would have found us by now, and the fact that rescue hadn't come forced me to consider two grim conclusions: either they had a mistaken idea of where we had fallen, and were searching some other stretch of the cordillera, or, they had no idea at all where in the sprawling mountains we might be, and no efficient way to narrow their search. I remembered the wildness of the mountains as we flew through Planchón Pass, all those steep-walled ravines plunging thousands of feet along the slopes of so many black, winding ridges, and nothing but more slopes and ridges as far as the eye could see. These thoughts forced me to a grim conclusion: *They haven't found us yet because they have no idea where we are, and if they don't know even roughly where we are, they will never find us.*

At first I kept these thoughts to myself, telling myself I didn't want to dash the hopes of the others. But perhaps I had motives that were not so selfless. Perhaps I didn't want to speak my feelings out loud because I feared that would make them real. When hope is lost, the mind protects us with denial, and my denial protected me from facing what I knew. Despite all my doubts about the likelihood of rescue, I still wanted what the others wanted—for someone to come and lift me out of this hell, to take me home and give me back my life. No matter how forcefully my instincts told me to abandon wishful thinking, I could not allow myself to shut the door on the possibility of a miracle. Ignoring the hopelessness of our plight, my heart continued to hope just as naturally as it continued to beat. So I prayed every night with the others, beseeching God to speed the rescuers on their way. I listened for the fluttering drone of helicopters approaching. I nodded in agreement when Marcelo urged us all to keep faith. Still, my doubts would never rest, and in every quiet moment my mind would drift off to the west, to the massive ridges that penned us in, and a barrage of frightful questions would erupt in my brain. *What if we have to climb out of here on our own?* I wondered. *Do I have the strength to survive a trek through this wilderness? How steep are the slopes? How cold at night? Is the footing stable? What path should I follow? What would happen if I fell?* And always: *What lies to the west, beyond those black ridges?*

Deep down, I always knew we'd have to save ourselves. Eventually I began to express this belief to the others, and the more I spoke of it, the more the thought of climbing obsessed me. I examined the idea from every angle. I began to rehearse my escape so vividly and so often that my daydreams soon became as real as a movie playing in my head. I'd see myself climbing the white slopes toward those bleak summits, visualizing every fragile finger-hold in the snow, testing each rock for stability before I grasp it, studying each careful placement of my feet. I'd be lashed by freezing winds, gasping in the thin air, struggling through hip-deep snow. In my daydream, each step of the ascent is an agony, but I do not stop, I struggle upward until finally I reach the summit and look to the west. Spreading out before me is a broad valley sloping down toward the horizon. In the near distance I see the snowfields give way to a neat patchwork of browns and greens—the cultivated fields that blanket the valley floor. The fields are bisected by thin gray lines, and I know these lines are roads. I stumble down the westward side of the mountain and hike for hours over rocky terrain until I reach one of those roads, then I walk west on the smooth asphalt surface. Soon I hear the rumble of an approaching truck. I flag down the startled diver. He is wary of such a desperate stranger hiking in the middle of nowhere. I would have to make him understand, and I know exactly what to say:

Vengo de un avión que cayó en las montañas . . .

I come from a plane that fell in the mountains . . .

He understands, and lets me climb into the cab. We travel west through the green farmlands to the nearest town, where I find a phone. I dial my father's number, and in moments I hear his astonished sobs as he recognizes my voice. A day or two later we are together and I see the look in his eyes—a little joy now, shining through all the sadness. He says nothing, just my name. I feel him collapse against me when I take him into my arms . . .

Like a mantra, like my own personal myth, this dream soon became my touchstone, my lifeline, and I nurtured it and refined it until it sparkled in my mind like a jewel. Many of the others thought I was crazy, that climbing out of the cordillera was impossible, but as the fantasy of escape became more lucid, the promise I made to my father took on the power of a sacred calling. It focused my mind, turned my fears to motivation, and gave me a sense of direction and high purpose that lifted me out of the black well of helplessness in which I'd languished since the crash. I still prayed with Marcelo and the others, I still petitioned God for a miracle, I still strained my ears each night to hear the distant sound of helicopters weaving their way through the cordillera. But when none of those measures could calm me, when my fears grew so violent I thought they would drive me insane, I would close my eyes and think of my father. I would renew my promise to return to him, and, in my mind, I would climb.

AFTER SUSY'S DEATH, twenty-seven survivors remained. Most of us had suffered bruises and lacerations, but considering the forces unleashed in the accident, and the fact that we had experienced three severe impacts at very high speed, it was a miracle so few of us had been badly injured. Some of us had escaped with barely a scratch. Roberto and Gustavo had suffered only light injuries. Others, including Liliana, Javier, Pedro Algorta, Moncho Sabella, Daniel Shaw, Bobby François, and Juan Carlos Mendendez—a former student at Stella Maris and a friend of Pancho Delgado's—had also survived with only cuts and scrapes. Those with more serious injuries, like Delgado and Alvaro Mangino, who had broken his legs in the crash, were now on the mend, and able to hobble around the crash site. Antonio Vizintin, who had almost bled to death from a lacerated arm, was rapidly recovering his strength. Fito Strauch and his cousin Eduardo had been knocked senseless in the final impact, but they had recovered quickly. Only three of us, in fact, had suffered truly serious wounds. The damage to my head was one of the worst injuries suffered in the accident, but the shattered fragments of my skull were beginning to knit themselves together, which left only two of us with truly serious wounds: Arturo Nogueira, who suffered multiple fractures to both of his legs, and Rafael Echavarren, whose calf muscle had been ripped loose from the bone. Both boys were in severe and constant pain, and watching them in their agony was one of the greatest horrors we had to face.

We did what we could for them. Roberto fashioned beds for them, simple swinging hammocks, made from aluminum poles and sturdy nylon straps we'd salvaged from the luggage hold. Suspended in the hammocks, Rafael and Arturo were spared the agony of sleeping with the rest of us in that restless tangle of humanity on the fuselage floor, where the slightest bump or jostle caused them excruciating pain. In the swinging beds they no longer shared the warmth of our huddled bodies, and they suffered more intensely from the cold. But for them the cold, cruel as it was, was a smaller misery than the pain.

Rafael was not an Old Christian, but he had friends on the team who had invited him on the trip. I didn't know him before the flight, but I'd noticed him on the plane. He was laughing heartily with his friends, and he struck me as a friendly and openhearted guy. I liked him immediately, and only liked him better as I saw how he bore his suffering. Roberto kept a close eye on Rafael's wounds and treated them as best he could, but our medical supplies were pathetic and there was little he could do. Each day he would change the bloody bandages and bathe the wounds in some eau de cologne he had found, hoping that the alcohol content would keep the wounds from going septic. But Rafael's wounds were constantly oozing pus, and the skin of his leg was already turning black. Gustavo and Roberto suspected gangrene, but Rafael never allowed himself to sink into self-pity. Instead he kept his courage and humor, even as the poison flowed through his system and the flesh of his leg rotted before his eyes. "I am Rafael Echavarren!" he would shout every morning, "and I will not die here!" There was no surrender in Rafael, no matter how he suffered, and I felt stronger every time I heard him say those words.

Arturo, on the other hand, was a quieter, more serious boy. He was a teammate, a fly half for the Old Christians First XV. I hadn't been especially close to him before the crash, but the courage with which he bore his suffering drew me to him. Like Rafael, Arturo should have been in an intensive care ward, with specialists tending to him around the clock. But he was here in the Andes, swinging in a makeshift hammock, with no antibiotics or pain relievers, and only a couple of first-year medical students and a gang of inexperienced boys to care for him. Pedro Algorta, another of the team's supporters, was especially close to Arturo, and he spent many hours with his friend, bringing him food and water, and trying to distract him from his pain. The rest of us also took turns sitting with him, as we did with Rafael. I always looked forward to my conversations with Arturo. At first we talked mostly about rugby. Kicking is an important part of the game—a well-placed kick can change the course of a match—and Arturo was the strongest and most accurate kicker on our team. I would remind him of great kicks he had made at crucial moments in our matches, and ask him how he'd managed to boot the ball with such distance and precision. Arturo enjoyed these conversations, I think. He took pride in his kicking ability, and he often tried to teach me his techniques as he lay in his hammock. Sometimes he would forget himself and try to demonstrate a kick with one of his shattered legs, which would cause him to wince in pain, and remind us where we were.

But as I got to know Arturo, our conversations went much deeper than sports. Arturo was different from the rest of us. For one thing, he was a passionate socialist, and his uncompromising views of capitalism and the pursuit of personal wealth made him something of an oddball in the world of affluence and privilege in which most of us had been raised. Some of the guys thought he was simply posing—dressing in shabby clothes and reading Marxist philosophy just to be contrary. Arturo was not an easygoing person. He could be prickly and strident in his opinions, and this rubbed many of the guys the wrong way, but as I got to understand him a little, I began to admire his way of thinking. It wasn't his politics I was drawn to—at that age I barely had a political thought in my head. What fascinated me about Arturo was the seriousness with which he lived his life and the fierce passion with which he had learned to think for himself. Important things mattered to Arturo, matters of equality, justice, compassion, and fairness. He was not afraid to question any of the rules of conventional society, or to condemn our system of government and economics, which he believed served the powerful at the expense of the weak.

Arturo's strong opinions bothered many of the others, and often led to angry arguments at night concerning history or politics or current affairs, but I always wanted to hear what Arturo had to say, and I was especially intrigued by his thoughts about religion. Like most of the other survivors, I had been raised as a traditional Catholic, and though I was no one's idea of a devout practitioner, I never doubted the fundamental teachings of the Church. Talking with Arturo, however, forced me to confront my religious beliefs, and to examine principles and values I had never questioned.

"How can you be so sure that of all the sacred books in the world, the one you were taught to believe in is the only authentic word of God?" he would ask. "How do you know that your idea of God is the only one that's true? We are a Catholic country because the Spanish came and conquered the Indians here, then they replaced the God of the Indians with Jesus Christ. If the Moors had conquered South America, we would all be praying to Muhammad instead of Jesus."

Arturo's ideas disturbed me, but his thinking was compelling. And it fascinated me that despite all his religious skepticism, he was a very spiritual person, who sensed my anger at God, and urged me not to turn away from Him because of our suffering.

"What good is God to us?" I replied. "Why would he let my mother and sister die so senselessly? If he loves us so much, why does He leave us here to suffer?"

"You are angry at the God you were taught to believe in as a child," Arturo answered. "The God who is supposed to watch over you and protect you, who answers your prayers and forgives your sins. This God is just a story. Religions try to capture God, but God is beyond religion. The true God lies beyond our comprehension. We can't understand His will; He can't be explained in a book. He didn't abandon us and He will not save us. He has nothing to do with our being here. God does not change, He simply *is*. I don't pray to God for forgiveness or favors, I only pray to be closer to Him, and when I pray, I fill my heart with love. When I pray this way, I know that God *is* love. When I feel that love, I remember that we don't need angels or a heaven, because we are a part of God already."

I shook my head. "I have so many doubts," I said. "I feel I have earned the right to doubt."

"Trust your doubts," said Arturo. "If you have the balls to doubt God, and to question all the things you have been taught about Him, then you may find God for real. He is close to us, Nando. I feel Him all around us. Open your eyes and you will see Him, too."

I looked at Arturo, this ardent young *socialista* lying in his hammock with his legs broken like sticks and his eyes shining with faith and encouragement, and I felt a strong surge of affection for him.

His words moved me deeply. How did such a young man come to know himself so well? Talking with Arturo forced me to face the fact that I had never taken my own life seriously. I had taken so much for granted, spending my energy on girls and cars and parties, and coasting so casually through my days. After all, what was the hurry? It would all be there tomorrow for me to figure out. There was always tomorrow . . .

I laughed sadly to myself, thinking, *If there is a God, and if He wanted my attention, He certainly has it now.* Often I would lean over Arturo with my arm across his chest to keep him warm. As I listened to his rhythmic breathing, and felt his body tense periodically from the pain, I said to myself, *This is truly a man.*

There were others whose courage and selflessness also inspired me. Enrique Platero, whose abdomen had been impaled by a pipe in the final impact, was able to shrug off his injury as if it were a scratch and become one of our hardest workers, even though a week after the crash a portion of his intestine still protruded from the puncture wound in his gut. I had always liked Enrique. I admired the respect he showed for his parents, and the obvious affection he felt for his family, who attended all our games. Enrique, who played the prop position, was not a flashy player, but he was a steady and dependable presence on the field, always in position, holding nothing back in his effort to help us win. He was the same here on the mountain. He always did what was asked of him, and more; he never complained or openly despaired, and though he was a very quiet presence in the fuselage, we knew he would always do all he could to help us survive.

I was also impressed by the strength of Gustavo Nicholich, whom we called Coco. Coco was a third row forward for the Old Christians. Fast, strong, and an excellent tackler, he was a tough player, but he had a warm spirit and a fine sense of humor. Marcelo had put Coco in charge of the clean-up crew, which was made up mostly of the younger boys in our group—Alvaro Mangino, Coche

Inciarte, Bobby François, and the others. Their job was to keep the fuselage as tidy as possible, to air out the seat cushions we slept on every morning, and to arrange the cushions on the floor of the plane every night before we all went to sleep. Coco made sure his crew members took their responsibilities seriously, but he also knew that by keeping the young guys busy, he was keeping their minds off their fear. As he led the boys through their paces, he kept their spirits up by telling jokes and stories. During breaks, he would coax them to play charades and other games. Whenever anyone was laughing, it was usually Coco's doing. The sound of laughter in those mountains was like a miracle, and I admired Coco for his courage—lightening so many spirits when, like the rest of us, he was so weary and afraid.

And I was especially impressed with the strength and courage of Liliana Methol. Liliana, thirty-five years old, was the wife of Javier Methol, who, at the age of thirty-eight, was the oldest of all the survivors. Liliana and Javier were extremely close and affectionate with each other. They were both avid fans of the team, but for them this trip was also to be a short romantic getaway, a chance to enjoy a rare weekend alone together, away from the four young children they had left with grandparents at home. Immediately after the crash, Javier had been stricken by a severe case of altitude sickness, which left him in a constant state of nausea and profound fatigue. His thinking was slow and muddled, and he could do little more than stumble about the crash site in a semi-stupor. Liliana spent much of her time caring for him, but she also found time to serve as a tireless nurse for Roberto and Gustavo, and was a great help to them as they cared for the injured.

After Susy died, Liliana was the only woman survivor, and at first we treated her with deference, insisting that she sleep alongside the seriously injured in the Fairchild's luggage compartment, which was the warmest section of the plane. She did so for only a few nights, and then she told us she would no longer accept such special treatment. From that point on, she slept in the main section of the fuselage with the rest of us, where she would gather the youngest boys around her, doing her best to comfort them and keep them warm. "Keep your head covered, Coche," she would say, as we lay in the shadows at night, "you're coughing too much, the cold is irritating your throat. Bobby, are you warm enough? Do you want me to rub your feet?" She worried constantly about the children she had left at home, but still she had the courage and love to mother these frightened boys who were so far from their families. She became a second mother for all of us, and she was everything you would want a mother to be: strong, soft, loving, patient, and very brave.

But the mountains showed me there were many forms of bravery, and for me, even the quietest ones among us showed great courage simply by living from day to day. All of them contributed, by their simple presence and the force of their personalities, to the close sense of community and common purpose that gave us some protection from the brutality and ruthlessness that surrounded us. Coche Inciarte, for example, gave us his quick, irreverent wit and warm smile. Carlitos was a source of constant optimism and humor. Pedro Algorta, a close friend of Arturo's, was an unconventional thinker, highly opinionated, and very smart, and I enjoyed talking with him at night. I felt especially protective of Alvaro Mangino, an amiable, soft-spoken supporter of the team who was one of the youngest guys on the plane, and I often sought a sleeping space beside him. If not for Diego Storm, who had pulled me in from the cold while I still lay in a coma, I would certainly have frozen to death beside Panchito. Daniel Fernandez, another cousin of Fito's, was a steady, level-headed presence in the fuselage who helped ward off panic. Pancho Delgado, a sharp-witted, articulate law student and one of Marcelo's strongest supporters, helped keep our hopes alive with his eloquent assurances that rescue was on the way. And then there was Bobby François, whose forthright, unapologetic, almost cheerful refusal to fight for his life somehow charmed us all. Bobby seemed unable to care for himself in even the simplest ways—if his covers came off him at night, for example, he would not exert the effort to cover himself up again. So we all looked out for Bobby, doing our best to keep him from freezing, checking his feet for frostbite, making sure he rolled out of bed in the morning. All of these boys were a part of our family in the mountains, contributing, in whatever ways they could, to our common struggle.

But for all the different kinds of courage I saw around me, the blatant and the subtle, I knew that every one of us lived each moment in fear, and I saw each survivor deal with those fears in his or her own fashion. Some of them vented their fears through anger, raging at the fates for stranding us here, or at the authorities for being so slow in coming to save us. Others begged God for answers and pleaded for a miracle. And many were so incapacitated by their fears, by all the forces stacked so grimly against us, that they sank into despair. Those boys showed no initiative at all. They would work only if forced, and even then they could only be trusted to do the simplest chores. With each day that passed, they seemed to fade more deeply into the background, growing more depressed and listless until finally some of them grew so apathetic they would lie all day in the same spot where they had slept, waiting for rescue or death, whichever might come first. They dreamed of home and prayed for miracles, but as they languished in the shadows of the fuselage, tortured by fears of dying, with their eyes dull and hollow, they were becoming ghosts already.

Those of us who were strong enough to work were not always gentle with these boys. With all the pressures we were facing, it was hard at times not to think of them as cowards or parasites. Most of them were not seriously injured, and it angered us that they could not summon the will to join in our common fight to survive. "Move your ass!" we would shout at them. "Do something! You aren't dead yet!" This emotional rift between the workers and the lost boys created a potential fault line in our small community that could have led to conflict, cruelty, and even violence. But somehow that never happened. We never surrendered to recrimination and blame. Perhaps it was all the years together on the rugby field. Perhaps the Christian Brothers had taught us well. In any case, we were able to rein in our resentments and struggle as a team. Those who had the heart for it, and the physical strength, did what had to be done. The weaker ones, and the injured, simply endured. We tried to prod them into action, sometimes we bossed them, but we never despised them or abandoned them to their own fates. We understood, intuitively, that no one in this awful place could be judged by the standards of the ordinary world. The horrors we faced were overwhelming, and there was no telling how any one of us might react at any given time. In this place, even simple survival required heroic effort, and these boys were fighting their own private battles in the shadows. We knew it was useless to ask anyone to do more than he could. So we made sure they had enough to eat and warm clothes to wear. In the coldest hours of the night we massaged their feet to protect them from frostbite. We made sure they covered themselves well at night, and we melted water for them when they couldn't muster the optimism required to go outside and breathe fresh air. Above all, we remained comrades in our suffering. We had lost too many friends already. Every life was precious to us. We would do what we could to help all of our friends survive.

"Breathe once more," we would tell the weaker ones, when the cold, or their fears, or despair, would shove them to the edge of surrender. "Live for one more breath. As long as you breathe, you are fighting to survive." In fact, all of us on the mountain were living our lives one breath at a time, and struggling to find the will we needed to endure from one heartbeat to the next. We suffered each moment, and in many ways, but always the source of our greatest suffering was the cold. Our bodies never adjusted to the frigid temperatures—no human body could. It was early spring in the Andes, but very wintry still, and often blizzards raged around the clock, keeping us trapped inside the plane. But on clear days the strong mountain sun beat down and we spent as much time outside the fuselage as possible, soaking up the warming rays. We had even dragged some of the Fairchild's seats outside the plane and arranged them on the snow like lawn chairs so we could sit as we basked in the sun. But all too soon the sun would dip behind the ridges to the west, and in what seemed like seconds the crackling blue sky would fade to deep violet, stars would appear, and shadows would stream down the side of the mountain toward us like a tide. Without the sun to warm the thin air, temperatures would plummet, and we would retreat to the shelter of the fuselage to prepare for the misery of another night.

High-altitude cold is an aggressive and malevolent thing. It burns you and slashes you, it invades every cell of your body, it presses down on you with a force that seems strong enough to crack bone. The drafty fuselage shielded us from the winds that would have killed us, but still, the air inside the plane was viciously frigid. We had cigarette lighters, and could easily have lit a fire, but there was very little combustible material on the mountain. We burned all the paper money we had—almost $7,500 went up in smoke—and we found enough scrap wood in the plane to fuel two or three small fires, but these fires burned themselves out quickly, and the brief luxury of warmth only made the cold seem worse when the flames had died. For the most part, our best defense against the cold was to huddle together on the loose seat cushions we'd scattered over the aircraft's floor and draw our flimsy blankets around us, hoping to gather enough warmth from each other's bodies to survive another night. I would lie in the dark for hours, my teeth chattering violently, and my body shivering so hard that the muscles of my neck and shoulders were constantly in spasm.

We were all very careful about protecting our extremities from frostbite, so I always kept my hands tucked under my armpits as I slept, and my feet beneath someone's body. Still the cold made my fingers and toes feel as if they'd been struck by a mallet. Sometimes, when I feared that the blood was freezing in my veins, I would ask the others to punch my arms and legs to stimulate circulation. Always I slept with a blanket over my head to trap the warmth of my exhaled breath. Sometimes I would lie with my head close to the face of the boy next to me, to steal a little breath, a little warmth, from him. Some nights we talked, but it was difficult, since our teeth chattered and our jaws trembled in the frigid air. I often tried to distract myself from my misery by praying, or by picturing my father at home, but the cold could not be ignored for very long. Sometimes there was nothing you could do but surrender to the suffering and count the seconds until morning. Often, in those helpless moments, I was certain I was going mad.

The cold was always our greatest agony, but in the earliest days of the ordeal, the greatest threat we faced was thirst. At high altitude, the human body dehydrates five times faster than it does at sea level, primarily because of the low levels of oxygen in the atmosphere. To draw sufficient oxygen from the lean mountain air, the body forces itself to breathe very rapidly. This is an involuntary reaction; often you pant just standing still. Increased inhalations bring more oxygen into the bloodstream, but each time you breathe in you must also breathe out, and precious moisture is lost each time you exhale. A human being can survive at sea level for a week or longer without water. In the Andes the margin of safety is much slimmer, and each breath brings you closer to death.

There certainly was no lack of water in the mountains—we were sitting on a snow-packed glacier, surrounded by millions of tons of frozen H_2O. Our problem was making the snow drinkable. Well-equipped mountain climbers carry small gas stoves to melt

snow into drinking water, and they guzzle water constantly—
gallons every day—to keep themselves safely hydrated. We had no
stoves, and no efficient way to melt snow. At first we simply
scooped handfuls of snow into our mouths and tried to eat it, but
after only a few days our lips were so cracked, bloody, and raw from
the arid cold that forcing the icy clumps of snow into our mouths
became an unbearable agony. We found that if we packed the snow
into a ball and warmed the ball in our hands, we could suck drops
of water from the snowball as it melted. We also melted snow by
sloshing it around inside empty wine bottles, and we slurped it up
from every small puddle we could find. For example, the snow on
the top of the fuselage would melt in the sun, sending a trickle of
water down the aircraft's windshield, where it would collect in a
small aluminum channel that held the base of the windshield in
place. On sunny days we would line up and wait our turn to suck a
little water out of the channel, but it was never enough to satisfy
our cravings. In fact, none of our efforts to make drinkable water
were providing us with enough fluid to fight off dehydration. We
were weakening, growing lethargic and thickheaded as toxins accumulated in our blood. Surrounded by a frozen ocean, we were
slowly dying of thirst. We needed an efficient way to melt snow
quickly, and, thanks to Fito's inventiveness, we found one.

One sunny morning, as he sat outside the fuselage, craving
water like the rest of us, Fito noticed that the sun was melting the
thin crust of ice that formed every night on the snow. An idea came
to him. He quietly rummaged through a pile of wreckage that had
been dragged out of the fuselage and soon found, beneath the torn
upholstery of a battered seat, a small rectangular sheet of thin aluminum. He turned up the corners of the aluminum sheet to form a
shallow basin, and pinched one of the corners to form a spout.
Then he filled the basin with snow and set it in the bright sunshine.
In no time the snow was melting and water was trickling steadily

from the spout. Fito collected the water in a bottle, and when the others saw how well his contraption worked, they gathered more of the aluminum sheets—there was one in every seat—and fashioned them in the same way. Marcelo was so impressed with Fito's contraptions that he formed a crew of boys whose main responsibility was to tend them, making sure we had a constant supply of water. We could not produce as much as we really needed, and our thirst was never quenched, but Fito's ingenuity did give us enough hydration to keep us alive. We were holding our own. Through cleverness and cooperation, we had found ways to keep the cold and thirst from killing us, but soon we faced a problem that cleverness and teamwork alone could not resolve. Our food supplies were dwindling. We were beginning to starve.

In the early days of the ordeal, hunger was not a great concern for us. The cold and the mental shock we'd endured, along with the depression and fear we all were feeling, acted to curb our appetites, and since we were convinced that rescuers would find us soon, we were content to get by on the meager rations Marcelo doled out. But rescue did not come.

One morning near the end of our first week in the mountains, I found myself standing outside the fuselage, looking down at the single chocolate-covered peanut I cradled in my palm. Our supplies had been exhausted, this was the last morsel of food I would be given, and with a sad, almost miserly desperation I was determined to make it last. On the first day, I slowly sucked the chocolate off the peanut, then I slipped the peanut into the pocket of my slacks. On the second day I carefully separated the peanut halves, slipping one half back into my pocket and placing the other half in my mouth. I sucked gently on the peanut for hours, allowing myself only a tiny nibble now and then. I did the same on the third day, and when I'd finally nibbled the peanut down to nothing, there was no food left at all.

At high altitude, the body's caloric needs are astronomical. A climber scaling any of the mountains surrounding the crash site would have required as many as 15,000 calories a day simply to maintain his current body weight. We were not climbing, but even so, at such high altitude our caloric requirements were much higher than they would have been at home. Since the crash, even before our rations had run out, we had never consumed more than a few hundred calories a day. Now, for days, our intake was down to zero. When we boarded the plane in Montevideo, we were sturdy and vigorous young men, many of us athletes in peak physical condition. Now I saw the faces of my friends growing thin and drawn. Their movements were sluggish and uncertain, and there was a weary dullness in their eyes. We were starving in earnest, with no hope of finding food, but our hunger soon grew so voracious that we searched anyway. We became obsessed by the search for food, but what drove us was nothing like ordinary appetite. When the brain senses the onset of starvation—that is, when it realizes that the body has begun to break down its own flesh and tissue to use as fuel—it sets off an adrenaline surge of alarm just as jarring and powerful as the impulse that compels a hunted animal to flee from an attacking predator. Primal instincts had asserted themselves, and it was really fear more than hunger that compelled us to search so frantically for food. Again and again we scoured the fuselage in search of crumbs and morsels. We tried to eat strips of leather torn from pieces of luggage, though we knew that the chemicals they'd been treated with would do us more harm than good. We ripped open seat cushions hoping to find straw, but found only inedible upholstery foam. Even after I was convinced that there was not a scrap of anything edible to be found, my mind would not rest. I would spend hours compulsively racking my brain for any possible source of food. *Maybe there is a plant growing somewhere, or some insects under a rock. Maybe the pilots had snacks in the cockpit. Perhaps some food was thrown out by accident when we dragged the seats from the plane. We should check the trash pile again. Did we check all the pockets of the dead before they were buried?*

Again and again I came to the same conclusion: unless we wanted to eat the clothes we were wearing, there was nothing here but aluminum, plastic, ice, and rock. Sometimes I would rise from a long silence to shout out loud in my frustration: "There is *nothing* in this fucking place to *eat!*" But of course there was food on the mountain—there was meat, plenty of it, and all in easy reach. It was as near as the bodies of the dead lying outside the fuselage under a thin layer of frost. It puzzles me that despite my compulsive drive to find *anything* edible, I ignored for so long the obvious presence of the only edible objects within a hundred miles. There are some lines, I suppose, that the mind is very slow to cross, but when my mind did finally cross that line, it did so with an impulse so primitive it shocked me. It was late afternoon and we were lying in the fuselage, preparing for night. My gaze fell on the slowly healing leg wound of a boy lying near me. The center of the wound was moist and raw, and there was a crust of dried blood at the edges. I could not stop looking at that crust, and as I smelled the faint blood-scent in the air, I felt my appetite rising. Then I looked up and met the gaze of other boys who had also been staring at the wound. In shame, we read each other's thoughts and quickly glanced away, but for me something had happened that I couldn't deny: I had looked at human flesh and instinctively recognized it as food. Once that door had been opened, it couldn't be closed, and from that moment on my mind was never far from the frozen bodies under the snow. I knew those bodies represented our only chance for survival, but I was so horrified by what I was thinking that I kept my feelings quiet. But finally I couldn't stay silent any longer, and one night in the darkness of the fuselage, I decided to confide in Carlitos Paez, who was lying beside me in the dark.

"Carlitos," I whispered, "are you awake?"

"Yes," he muttered. "Who can sleep in this freezer?"

"Are you hungry?"

"*Puta carajo,*" he snapped. "What do you think? I haven't eaten in days."

"We are going to starve here," I said. "I don't think the rescuers will find us in time."

"You don't know that," Carlitos answered.

"I know it and you know it," I replied, "but I will not die here. I will make it home."

"Are you still thinking about climbing out of here?" he asked. "Nando, you are too weak."

"I am weak because I haven't eaten."

"But what can you do?" he said. "There is no food here."

"There is food," I answered. "You know what I mean."

Carlitos shifted in the darkness, but he said nothing.

"I will cut meat from the pilot," I whispered. "He's the one who put us here, maybe he will help us get out."

"*Fuck,* Nando," Carlitos whispered.

"There is plenty of food here," I said, "but you must think of it only as meat. Our friends don't need their bodies anymore."

Carlitos sat silently for a moment before speaking. "God help us," he said softly. "I have been thinking the very same thing . . ."

In the following days, Carlitos shared our conversation with some of the others. A few, like Carlitos, admitted to having had the same thoughts. Roberto, Gustavo, and Fito especially believed it was our only chance to survive. For a few days we discussed the subject among ourselves, then we decided to call a meeting and bring the issue out into the open. We all gathered inside the fuselage. It was late afternoon and the light was dim. Roberto began to speak.

"We are starving," he said simply. "Our bodies are consuming themselves. Unless we eat some protein soon, we will die, and the only protein here is in the bodies of our friends."

There was a heavy silence when Roberto paused. Finally,

someone spoke up. "What are you saying?" he cried. "That we eat the dead?"

"We don't know how long we will be trapped here," Roberto continued. "If we do not eat, we will die. It's that simple. If you want to see your families again, this is what you must do."

The faces of the others showed astonishment as Roberto's words sank in. Then Liliana spoke softly.

"I cannot do that," she said. "I could never do that."

"You won't do it for yourself," said Gustavo, "but you must do it for your children. You must survive and go home to them."

"But what will this do to our souls?" someone wondered. "Could God forgive such a thing?"

"If you don't eat, you are choosing to die," Roberto answered. "Would God forgive that? I believe God wants us to do whatever we can to survive."

I decided to speak. "We must believe it is only meat now," I told them. "The souls are gone. If rescue is coming, we must buy time, or we will be dead when they find us."

"And if we must escape on our own," said Fito, "we will need strength or we will die on the slopes."

"Fito is right," I said, "and if the bodies of our friends can help us to survive, then they haven't died for nothing."

The discussion continued all afternoon. Many of the survivors—Liliana, Javier, Numa Turcatti, and Coche Inciarte among others, refused to consider eating human flesh, but no one tried to talk the rest of us out of the idea. In the silence we realized we had reached a consensus. Now the grisly logistics had to be faced. "How will this be done?" asked Pancho Delgado. "Who is brave enough to cut the flesh from a friend?" The fuselage was dark now. I could see only dimly lit silhouettes, but after a long silence someone spoke. I recognized the voice as Roberto's.

"I will do it," he said.

Gustavo rose to his feet and said quietly, "I will help."

"But who will we cut first?" asked Fito. "How do we choose?"

We all glanced at Roberto.

"Gustavo and I will take care of that," he replied.

Fito got up. "I'll go with you," he said.

"I'll help, too," said Daniel Maspons, a wing forward for the Old Christians and a good friend of Coco's.

For a moment no one moved, then we all reached forward, joined hands, and pledged that if any of us died here, the rest would have permission to use our bodies for food. After the pledge, Roberto rose and rummaged in the fuselage until he found some shards of glass, then he led his three assistants out to the graves. I heard them speaking softly as they worked, but I had no interest in watching them. When they came back, they had small pieces of flesh in their hands. Gustavo offered me a piece and I took it. It was grayish white, as hard as wood and very cold. I reminded myself that this was no longer part of a human being; this person's soul had left his body. Still, I found myself slow to lift the meat to my lips. I avoided meeting anyone's gaze, but out of the corners of my eyes I saw the others around me. Some were sitting like me with the meat in their hands, summoning the strength to eat. Others were working their jaws grimly. Finally, I found my courage and slipped the flesh into my mouth. It had no taste. I chewed, once or twice, then forced myself to swallow. I felt no guilt or shame. I was doing what I had to do to survive. I understood the magnitude of the taboo we had just broken, but if I felt any strong emotion at all, it was a sense of resentment that fate had forced us to choose between this horror and the horror of certain death.

Eating the flesh did not satisfy my hunger, but it calmed my mind. I knew that my body would use the protein to strengthen itself and slow the process of starvation. That night, for the first time since we'd crashed, I felt a small flickering of hope. We had come to grips with our grim new reality, and found that we had the strength to face an unimaginable horror. Our courage gained us a small measure of control over our circumstances, and bought us precious time. There were no illusions now. We all knew our fight for survival would be uglier and more harrowing than we had imagined, but I felt, that as a group, we had made a declaration to the mountain that we would not surrender, and for myself, I knew that in a small, sad way, I had taken my first step back toward my father.

Chapter Five

Abandoned

EARLY THE NEXT MORNING, our eleventh day on the mountain, I stood outside the fuselage, leaning against the Fairchild's aluminum hull. It was a clear morning, about half past seven, and I was warming myself in the first rays of the sun, which had just risen above the mountains to the east. Marcelo and Coco Nicholich were with me, and so was Roy Harley, a tall, swift wing-forward for the Old Christians. At eighteen, Roy was one of the youngest passengers on the plane. He was also the closest thing we had to an electronics expert, having once helped a cousin install a complicated stereo system in his house. Just after the crash, Roy had found a battered transistor radio in the litter of the wreckage, and with a little tinkering he had coaxed it back to life. In the rocky cordillera, reception was very poor, but Roy fashioned an antenna from electrical wires he had stripped from the plane, and with a little effort we were able to tune in stations from Chile. Early each morning, Marcelo would wake Roy and lead him out onto the glacier, where he would manipulate the antenna while Roy worked the dial. Their hope was to hear news about the progress of rescue efforts, but so far they had managed only to pick up soccer scores, weather reports, and political propaganda from stations controlled by the Chilean government.

This morning, like all the others, the signal faded in and out, and even when reception was at its best, the radio's small speaker crackled with static. Roy did not want to waste the batteries, so, after fiddling with the dial for several minutes, he was about to turn the radio off when we heard, through all the buzzing and popping, the voice of an announcer reading the news. I don't recall the exact words he used, but I will never forget the tinny sound of his voice and the dispassionate tones with which he spoke: After ten days of fruitless searching, he said, Chilean authorities have called off all efforts to find the lost Uruguayan charter flight that disappeared over the Andes on October 13. Search efforts in the Andes are simply too dangerous, he said, and after so much time in the frigid mountains, there is no chance that anyone still survives.

After a moment of stunned silence, Roy cried out in disbelief, and then began to sob.

"What?" cried Marcelo. "What did he say?"

"*Suspendieron la búsqueda!*" Roy shouted. "They have canceled the search! They are abandoning us!" For a few seconds Marcelo stared at Roy with a look of irritation on his face, as if Roy had spoken gibberish, but when Roy's words sank in, Marcelo dropped to his knees and let out an anguished howl that echoed through the cordillera. Reeling from shock, I watched my friends' reactions with a silence and sense of detachment that an observer might have mistaken for composure, but in fact I was falling to pieces, as all the claustrophobic fears I'd been struggling to contain were now bursting free, like floodwaters over a crumbling dam, and I felt myself being swept toward the brink of hysteria. I pleaded with God. I cried out to my father. Driven more powerfully than ever by the animal urge to sprint off blindly into the cordillera, I manically scanned the horizon as if, after ten days on the mountain, I might suddenly spot an escape route I hadn't seen before. Then, slowly, I turned west and faced the tall ridges that blocked me from my home. With new clarity, I saw the terrible power of the mountains. What foolishness it had been to have thought that an untested boy like me could conquer such merciless slopes! Reality bared its teeth for me now, I saw that all my dreams of climbing were nothing more than a fantasy to keep my hopes alive. Out of terror and defiance, I knew what I had to do: I would run to a crevasse and leap into the green depths. I'd let the rocks smash all the life and fear and suffering from my body. But even as I pictured myself falling into silence and peace, my eye was on the western ridges, guessing at distances and trying to imagine the steepness of the slopes, and the cool voice of reason was whispering in my ear: *That gray line of rock might give some good footing. . . . There might be some shelter under that outcrop just below that ridge. . . .*

It was a kind of madness, really, clinging to hopes of escape even though I knew escape was impossible, but that inner voice gave me no other choice. Challenging the mountains was the only future this place would allow me, and so, with a sense of grim resolve that was now more ferociously entrenched than ever before, I accepted in my heart the simple truth that I would never stop fighting to leave this place, certain the effort would kill me, but frantic to start the climb.

Now, a frightened voice drew my attention. It was Coco Nicholich, standing at my side.

"Nando, please, tell me this is not true!" he stammered.

"It is true," I hissed. "*Carajo.* We are dead."

"They are killing us!" cried Nicholich. "They are leaving us here to die!"

"I have to leave this place, Coco," I cried softly. "I can't stay here another minute!"

Nicholich nodded toward the fuselage. "The others have heard us," he said. I turned and saw several of our friends emerging from the plane.

"What's the news?" someone called out. "Have they spotted us?"

"We have to tell them," whispered Nicholich.

We both glanced at Marcelo, who sat slumped in the snow. "I can't tell them," he mumbled. "I can't bear it."

The others were closer now.

"What's going on?" someone asked. "What did you hear?"

I tried to speak, but my words caught in my throat. Then

Nicholich stepped forward and spoke firmly, despite his own fear. "Let's go inside," he said, "and I'll explain." We all followed Coco back into the fuselage and gathered around him. "Listen, guys," he said, "we have heard some news. They have stopped looking for us." The others were stunned by Coco's words. Some of them cursed, and some began weeping, but most simply stared at him in disbelief.

"But don't worry," he continued, "this is good news."

"Are you crazy?" someone shouted. "This means we are stuck here forever!" I felt panic gathering in the group, but Coco kept his head and continued.

"We have to stay calm," he said. "Now we know what we have to do. We have to rely on ourselves. There's no reason to wait any longer. We can start making plans to get out on our own."

"I have made my plans," I snapped. "I am leaving this place *now!* I will not die here!"

"Calm down, Nando," said Gustavo.

"Fuck no, I will not calm down! Give me some meat to carry. Someone lend me another jacket. Who will come with me? I will go by myself if I have to. I will not stay here another second!"

Gustavo took my arm. "You're talking nonsense," he said.

"No, no, I can do it!" I pleaded. "I know I can. I will climb out of here, find help . . . but I have to go *now!*"

"If you go now, you will die," Gustavo replied.

"I am dead if I stay here!" I said. "This place is our graveyard! Death touches everything here. Can't you see it? I can feel its hands on me! I can smell its fucking breath!"

"Nando, shut up and listen!" shouted Gustavo. "You have no winter gear, you have no experience at climbing, you are weak, we don't even know where we are. It would be suicide to leave now. These mountains would kill you in a day."

"Gustavo is right," said Numa. "You are not strong enough yet. Your head is still cracked like an egg. You would be throwing your life away."

"We have to go!" I shouted. "They have given us a death sentence! Are you just going to wait here to die?" I was rummaging through the fuselage blindly, searching for anything—gloves, blankets, socks—that I thought would help me on the trek, when Marcelo spoke to me softly. "Whatever you do, Nando," he said, "you must think of the good of the others. Be smart. Don't waste yourself. We are still a team, and we need you." Marcelo's voice was steady, but there was a sadness in it now, a sense of wounded resignation. Something inside him had shattered when he heard that the search had been canceled, and it seemed that in moments he had lost the strength and confidence that had made him such a trusted leader. Leaning against the wall of the passenger cabin now, he seemed smaller, grayer, and I knew he was slipping rapidly into despair. But my respect for him was still very deep, and I could not deny the wisdom of his words, so, reluctantly, I nodded in agreement and found a place to sit beside the others on the fuselage floor.

"We all need to stay calm," said Gustavo, "but Nando is right. We will die if we stay here, and sooner or later we will have to climb. But we must do it in the smartest way. We must know what we're up against. I say two or three of us climb today. Maybe we can get a look at what lies beyond these mountains."

"It's a good idea," said Fito. "On the way, we can look for the tail section. There might be food and warm clothing inside. And if Roque is right, the batteries for the radio are there, too."

"Good," said Gustavo. "I will go. If we leave soon, we can be back before the sun goes down. Who is coming with me?"

"I am," said Numa, who had already survived the first attempt to climb the western slopes.

"Me too," said Daniel Maspons, one of the brave ones who helped cut the flesh.

Gustavo nodded. "Let's find the warmest clothes we can, and get started," he said. "Now that we know the score, there is no time to lose."

It took Gustavo less than an hour to organize the climb. Each of the climbers would carry a pair of the seat-cushion snowshoes that Fito had invented, and a pair of the sunglasses Fito's cousin Eduardo had made by cutting lenses from tinted plastic sun visors in the cockpit and stringing them together with copper wire. The snowshoes would keep the climbers from sinking into the soft snow, and the sunglasses would shield their eyes from the fierce glare of the sun on the snow-covered slopes. Otherwise they were poorly protected. They wore only sweaters pulled over light cotton shirts and thin summer trousers. They all wore lightweight moccasins on their feet. The others would be climbing in canvas sneakers. None of them wore gloves, and they had no blankets with them, but it was a clear day, winds were light, and the bright sun warmed us enough to make the mountain air bearable. If the climbers stuck to their plan and returned to the Fairchild before sundown, the cold should not be a danger.

"Pray for us," Gustavo said, as the climbers set off. Then we watched the three of them stride across the glacier toward the high summits in the distance, following the path the Fairchild had plowed through the snow. As they made their way slowly up the slope and into the distance, their bodies grew smaller and smaller until they were just three tiny specks inching their way up the white face of the mountain. They seemed as small and fragile as a trio of gnats as they climbed, and my respect for their courage had no end.

All morning we watched them climb, until they disappeared from view, then we kept vigil until late afternoon, scouring the slopes for any signs of movement. As the light faded there was still no sign of them. Then darkness fell and the bitter cold forced us back into the shelter of the fuselage. That night, stiff winds battered the Fairchild's hull and forced jets of snow in through every chink and crevice. As we huddled and shivered in our cramped quarters, our thoughts were with our friends on the open slopes. We prayed earnestly for their safe return, but it was hard to be hopeful. I tried to imagine their suffering, trapped in the open in their flimsy clothes, with nothing to shield them from the killing wind. All of us knew very well what death looked like now, and it was easy for me to imagine my friends lying stiff in the snow. I pictured them like the bodies I'd seen at the burial site outside the fuselage—the same waxy, blue-tinged pallor on the skin, the senseless, rigid faces, the crust of frost clinging to the eyebrows and the lips, thickening the jaw, whitening the hair.

I saw them that way, lying motionless in the dark, three more friends who were now mere frozen *things*. But where, exactly, had they fallen? This question began to fascinate me. Each had found the exact moment and place of his death. When was my moment? Where was my place? Was there a spot in these mountains where I would finally fall and lie like the rest, frozen forever? Was there a place like this for each of us? Was this our fate, to lie scattered in this nameless place? My mother and sister here at the crash site; Zerbino and the others on the slopes; the rest of us wherever we lay when death decided to take us? What if we learned that escape was impossible? Would we simply sit here and wait to die? And if we did, what would life be like for the last few survivors, or, worse, for the very last one? What if that last one was me? How long could I stay sane, sitting alone in the fuselage at night, with only ghosts for company, and the only sound the constant growl of the wind? I tried to silence these thoughts by joining the others in another prayer for the climbers, but in my heart I wasn't sure whether I was praying for their safe return or simply for the grace of their souls, for the grace of all our souls, because I knew that even as we lay in the relative safety of the fuselage, death was closing in. *It is only a matter of time,* I told myself, *and perhaps the ones on the mountain tonight are the lucky ones, because for them the wait is over.*

"Maybe they have found some shelter," someone said.

"There is no shelter on that mountain," Roberto replied.

"But you climbed, and you survived," someone pointed out.

"We climbed in daylight and still we suffered," Roberto answered. "It must be forty degrees colder up there at night."

"They are strong," someone offered. Others nodded and, out of respect, held their tongues. Then Marcelo, who had not spoken for hours, broke the silence.

"It's my fault," he said softly. "I have killed you all."

We all understood his despondency and had seen this coming.

"Don't think that way, Marcelo," said Fito. "We all share the same fate here. No one blames you."

"I chartered the plane!" Marcelo snapped. "I hired the pilots! I scheduled the matches and persuaded you all to come."

"You did not persuade my mother and my sister," I said. "I did that, and now they're dead. But I cannot take the blame for this. It's not our fault that a plane falls from the sky."

"Each of us made his own choice," someone said.

"You are a good captain, Marcelo, don't lose heart."

But Marcelo was losing heart, very rapidly, and it troubled me to see him in such misery. He had always been a hero to me. When I was in grade school, he was already a rugby standout for Stella Maris, and I loved watching him play. He had a commanding, enthusiastic presence on the field and I always admired the joy and confidence with which he played the game. Years later, when I found myself playing beside him for the Old Christians, my respect for his athletic gifts only deepened. But it was more than his rugby prowess that won my respect. Like Arturo, Marcelo was different from the rest of us, more principled, more mature. He was a devout Catholic who followed all the teachings of the Church and tried his best to live a virtuous life. He was not a self-righteous person; in fact, he was one of the humblest guys on the team. But he knew what he believed, and often, using the same authority and quiet charisma with which he pushed us to be better teammates, he would coax us to be better men. He was constantly chiding Panchito and me, for example, about our restless obsession with the opposite sex. "There is more to life than chasing girls," he would tell us with a wry smile. "You two need to grow up a little, and get serious about your lives."

Marcelo himself had vowed to be a virgin until he married, and a lot of the guys teased him about this. Panchito especially thought it was laughable—no women until you are married? For Panchito, this was like asking a fish not to swim. But Marcelo took the jokes in stride, and I was always impressed by the seriousness and self-respect with which he carried himself. In many ways, he was very different from Arturo, the ardent *socialista* with the heretical notions of God, but like Arturo, he seemed to know his own mind well. He had thought carefully about all the important issues of his life, and he knew with clarity where he stood. For Marcelo, the world was an orderly place, watched over by a wise and loving God who had promised to protect us. It was our job to follow His commandments, to take the sacraments, to love God and to love others as Jesus had taught us. This was the wisdom that formed the foundation of his life and shaped his character. It was also the source of his great confidence on the field, his sure-footedness as our captain, and the charisma that made him such a strong leader. It is easy to follow a man who has no doubts. We had always trusted in Marcelo completely. How could he allow himself to falter now, when we needed him the most?

Perhaps, I thought, *he was never as strong as he seemed.* But then I understood: Marcelo had been broken not because his mind was weak, but because it was too strong. His faith in the rescue was absolute and unyielding: *God would not abandon us. The authorities would never leave us here to die.*

When we heard the news that the search had been canceled, it must have felt to Marcelo like the earth beneath his feet had begun to crumble. God had turned His back, the world had been turned upside down, and all the things that had made Marcelo such a great leader—his confidence, his decisiveness, his unshakable faith in his own beliefs and decisions—now prevented him from adjusting to the blow and finding a new balance. His certainty, which had served him so well in the ordinary world, now robbed him of the balance and flexibility he needed to adjust to the strange new rules by which we were battling for our lives. When the ground rules changed, Marcelo shattered like glass. Watching as he quietly sobbed in the shadows, I suddenly understood that in this awful place, too much certainty could kill us; ordinary civilized thinking could cost us our lives. I vowed to myself that I would never pretend to understand these mountains. I would never get trapped by my own expectations. I would never pretend to know what might happen next. The rules here were too savage and strange, and I knew I could never imagine the hardships, setbacks, and horrors that might lie ahead. So I would teach myself to live in constant uncertainty, moment by moment, step by step. I would live as if I were dead already. With nothing to lose, nothing could surprise me, nothing could stop me from fighting; my fears would not block me from following my instincts, and no risk would be too great.

THE WINDS BLEW all that night, and few of us slept, but at last morning came. One by one we brushed the frost from our faces, slipped our feet into our frozen shoes, and forced ourselves to our feet. Then we gathered outside the plane and began to scan the mountains for signs of our lost friends. The skies were clear, the sun had already warmed the air, and the winds had weakened into a light breeze. Visibility was quite good, but after hours of watching we had spotted no movement on the slopes. Then, in late morning, someone shouted.

"Something is moving!" he said. "There, above that ridge!"

"I see it, too!" said someone else.

I stared at the mountain and finally saw what the others were seeing: three black dots on the snow.

"Those are rocks," someone muttered.

"They weren't there before."

"Your mind is playing tricks," sighed someone else.

"Just watch. They are moving."

A little lower on the slope was a dark outcrop of rock. Using this rock as a reference point, I kept my gaze on the dots. At first I was sure they were stationary, but after a minute or two it was clear that the dots had moved closer to the outcrop. It was true!

"It's them! They're moving!"

"Puta carajo! They are alive!"

Our spirits soared and we slapped and shoved each other in our happiness.

"Vamos, Gustavo!"

"Come on, Numa! Come on, Daniel!"

"Come on, you bastards! You can make it!"

It took the three of them two hours to work their way down the slope and across the glacier, and all that time we shouted encouragement to them and celebrated as if our friends had returned from the dead. But the celebration ended abruptly when they got close enough for us to see their condition. They were stooped and battered, too weak to lift their feet from the snow as they shuffled toward us, leaning on each other for support. Gustavo was squinting and groping as if he'd gone blind, and all three seemed so weary and unstable that I thought the lightest breeze might blow them down. But the worst thing was the look on their faces. They seemed to have aged twenty years overnight, as if the mountain had blasted the youth and vigor from their bodies, and in their eyes I saw something that had not been there before—the unsettling combination of dread and resignation you sometimes see on the faces of very old men. We rushed to meet them, then helped them into the fuselage and gave them cushions to lie on. Roberto examined them immediately. He saw that their feet were nearly frozen. Then he noticed the tears streaming from Gustavo's bleary eyes.

"It was the glare on the snow," said Gustavo. "The sun was so strong . . ."

"Didn't you use your sunglasses?" Roberto asked.

"They broke," said Gustavo. "It feels like sand in my eyes. I think I am blind."

Roberto put some drops in Gustavo's eyes—something he'd found in a suitcase that he thought might soothe the irritation—and wrapped a T-shirt around Gustavo's head to shade his damaged eyes from the light. Then he told the rest of us to take turns rubbing the climbers' frozen feet. Someone brought them large portions of meat, and the climbers ate ravenously. After they had rested, they began to talk about the climb.

"The mountain is so steep," said Gustavo. "In places it is like climbing a wall. You have to clutch the snow in front of you to pull yourself up."

"And the air is thin," said Maspons. "You gasp, your heart pounds. You take five steps and it feels like you have run a mile."

"Why didn't you come back before night?" I asked them.

"We climbed all day and were only halfway up the slope," said Gustavo. "We didn't want to come back and tell you we had failed. We wanted to see beyond the mountains, we wanted to come back with good news. So we decided to find shelter for the night, then climb again in the morning."

The climbers told us how they had found a level place near a rocky outcrop. They made a short wall out of large stones they found lying about, and huddled behind this wall, hoping it would shield them from the wind at night. After so many nights freezing in the fuselage, the climbers didn't think it was possible to suffer much more from the cold. They quickly discovered they were wrong.

"The cold up on those slopes is indescribable," said Gustavo. "It rips the life from you. It's as painful as fire. I never thought we would live until morning."

They told us how they had suffered horribly in their light clothing, punching each other in the arms and legs to keep the blood moving in their veins, and lying close together to share the warmth of their bodies. As the hours crawled by, they were certain their decision to stay on the mountain had cost them their lives, but somehow they lasted until dawn, and finally they felt the first rays of sun warming the slopes. Amazed to be alive, they let the sunshine thaw their frozen bodies, then they turned to the slope and resumed the climb.

"Did you find the tail?" Fito asked.

"We only found pieces of wreckage and some luggage," Gustavo answered. "And some bodies." Then he explained how they had found the remains of people who had fallen from the plane, many of them still strapped to their seats. "We took these things from the bodies," he said, pulling out some watches, wallets, religious medallions, and other personal effects he had taken from the corpses.

"The bodies were very high up the slope," said Gustavo, "but we were still far from the summit. We didn't have the strength to keep climbing, and we didn't want to get trapped for another night."

Later that night, when things were quiet in the fuselage, I went to Gustavo.

"What did you see up there?" I asked. "Did you see beyond the peaks? Did you see any green?"

He shook his head wearily. "The peaks are too high. You can't see far."

"But you must have seen something."

He shrugged. "I saw between two peaks, into the distance . . ."

"What did you see?"

"I don't know, Nando, something yellowish, brownish, I couldn't really tell, it was a very narrow angle. But one thing you should know: When we were high on the mountain I looked down at the crash site. The Fairchild is a tiny speck in the snow. You can't tell it from a rock or a shadow. There is no hope that a pilot could see it from a plane. There was never any chance we would be rescued."

THE NEWS THAT the search had been canceled convinced even the most hopeful among us that we were on our own, and that our only chance of survival now was to save ourselves. But the failure of Gustavo's mission disheartened us, and as days passed, our spirits were battered further by the realization that Marcelo, in his self-doubt and despair, had quietly abdicated his role as our leader. There seemed to be no one to take his place. Gustavo, who had led by his courage and resourcefulness from the very first moments of our ordeal, had been devastated by the mountain, and could not regain his strength. Roberto was still a strong presence, and we had come to rely on his cleverness and keen imagination, but he was an extremely headstrong young man, far too irritable and belligerent to inspire the kind of trust we'd had in Marcelo. Rapidly, in the absence of a single strong leader, a looser, less formal style of leadership emerged. Alliances formed, based on previous friendships, similar temperaments, and common interests. The strongest of these alliances was the one made up of Fito and his cousins Eduardo Strauch and Daniel Fernandez. Of the three, Fito was the youngest and the most prominent. He was a quiet boy, and at first I thought he was almost painfully shy, but he soon proved himself to be bright and level-headed, and while he had an unflinching grasp of how steeply the odds were stacked against us, I knew he intended to fight with all his strength to help us all survive. The three cousins were extremely close, and with Daniel and Eduardo consistently following Fito's lead, they presented a unifying force that gave them a great deal of influence over all the decisions we made. This was a good thing for all of us. "The cousins," as we called them, gave us a strong, stable center that prevented the group from disintegrating into factions, and saved us from all the conflict and confusion that might have caused. They also were able to convince most of the survivors that our lives were in our own hands now, and that each of us had to do everything he could to survive. Yielding to that advice, and to Javier's pleading, Liliana finally began to eat. One by one, the rest of the holdouts—Numa, Coche, and the others—did the same, telling themselves that drawing life from the bodies of their dead friends was like drawing spiritual strength from the body of Christ when they took Communion. Relieved that they were nourishing themselves, I didn't dispute their rationale, but for me, eating the flesh of the dead was nothing more than a hard, pragmatic choice I had made to survive. I was moved by the knowledge that even in death, my friends were giving me what I needed to live, but I felt no uplifting sense of spiritual connection with the dead. My friends were gone. These bodies were objects now. We would be fools if we didn't use them.

As the days passed, we became more efficient at processing the meat. Fito and the cousins took responsibility for cutting the flesh and rationing it to us, and soon they had devised an efficient system. After cutting the meat into small pieces, they would arrange it on pieces of aluminum and let it dry in the sun, which made it much easier to stomach. On the rare occasion when we had a fire they even cooked it, which improved its taste dramatically. For me, eating the meat became easier over time. Some could not overcome their revulsion, but all of us were eating enough now to hold starvation at bay. Out of respect for me, the others had promised not to touch the bodies of my mother and sister, but even so, there were enough bodies to last us for weeks if we rationed the meat carefully. To make the food last even longer, we eventually began to eat the kidneys, the livers, and even the hearts. These internal organs were highly nutritious, and as grisly as it may sound, by this point in the ordeal, most of us had grown numb to the horror of friends being butchered like cattle.

Still, eating human flesh never satisfied my hunger, and it never gave me back my strength. I was still wasting away, like the others, and the small amount of food we allowed ourselves each day only slowed the process of starvation. Time was running out, and I knew that soon I would be too weak to climb. This became my greatest fear, that we would grow so weak that escape would become impossible, that we would use up all the bodies, and then we'd have no choice but to languish at the crash site as we wasted, staring into each other's eyes, waiting to see which of our friends would become our food. That horrible scenario preoccupied me, and sometimes it took all my discipline to keep myself from ignoring the wishes of the others and setting off on my own. But the near disaster of Gustavo's expedition had given me a new understanding of how difficult the climb would be. Like all the others, I was stunned by what the mountains had done to Gustavo, who was famous for his toughness and stamina on the field. Why should I believe I could conquer the mountain when he could not? In moments of weakness I would surrender to despair. *Look at these mountains,* I would tell myself. *It's impossible, we are trapped here. We are finished. All of our suffering has been in vain.*

But each time I gave in like this to defeat and self-pity, the face of my father would drift up from memory, reminding me of his suffering, and of the promise I had made to return to him. At times, when I thought I couldn't stand the cold or the thirst or the gnawing terror for one more second, I'd feel a powerful urge to surrender. "You can end this whenever you want," I would tell myself. "Lie down in the snow. Let the cold take you. Just rest. Be still. Stop fighting."

These were comforting, seductive thoughts, but if I savored them too long the voice in my mind would interrupt me. *When you climb, make sure every fingerhold is a good one. Don't trust a rock to hold you, test every step. Probe the snow for hidden crevasses. Find good shelter for the nights . . .*

I would think about climbing, and that would remind me of my promise to my father. I would think of him and let my heart fill with love for him, and this love would be stronger than my suffering, or my fear. After two weeks on the mountain, my love for my father had taken on the irresistible power of a biological drive. I knew that someday I would have to climb, even though I'd be climbing to my doom. But what did it matter? I was a dead man already. Why not die in the mountains, fighting for each step, so that when I died, I would die one step closer to home? I was ready to face such a death, but as inevitable as that death seemed, I still felt a flicker of hope that I might somehow stumble through the wilderness and make it home. The thought of leaving the fuselage terrified me, even though I couldn't wait to leave. I knew that somehow I would find the courage to face the mountains; I also knew I would never be brave enough to face them alone. I needed a companion for the journey, someone who would make me stronger and better, and so I began to study the others, weighing their strengths, their temperaments, their performance under pressure, trying to imagine which of these ragged, starving, frightened boys I would most want by my side.

Twenty-four hours earlier the question would have had a simple answer: I would want Marcelo, our captain, and Gustavo, whose strength of character I had always admired. But now Marcelo was in despair, and Gustavo had been battered and blinded by the mountain, and I feared that neither one of them would recover in time to go with me. So I turned my eye to the other healthy survivors, and as I watched them, a few quickly caught my attention. Fito Strauch had proven his bravery in the first attempt to climb the mountain, and had earned all our respect for his calmness and clear thinking throughout the ordeal. Fito's cousins, Eduardo and

Daniel Fernandez, were a great source of strength for him, and I wondered at times how he would perform on his own in the mountains, but Fito was definitely high on my list. So was Numa Turcatti. Numa had impressed me from the start, and as the days passed my respect for him had deepened. Although he had been a stranger to most of us before the crash, he had quickly won the friendship and admiration of all the survivors. Numa made his presence felt through quiet heroics: no one fought harder for our survival, no one inspired more hope, and no one showed more compassion for the ones who suffered most. Even though he was a new friend for most of us, I believe Numa was the best loved man on the mountain.

Daniel Maspons, who had climbed bravely with Gustavo, was another candidate. So was Coco Nicholich, whose selflessness and composure had impressed me. Antonio Vizintin, Roy Harley, and Carlitos Paez were all healthy and strong. And then there was Roberto, the brightest, most difficult, most complicated character on the mountain.

Roberto had always been hard to handle. The son of a renowned cardiologist in Montevideo, he was brilliant, self-confident, egotistical, and interested in following no one's rules but his own. Because of his contrary nature, he was constantly in trouble at school, and it seemed his mother was always being called into the headmaster's office to endure another conference about Roberto's transgressions. He simply refused to be told what to do. For example, Roberto had a horse that he would ride to school each morning, even though the Christian Brothers repeatedly forbade him to bring the animal onto school grounds. Roberto simply ignored them. He would tie the horse to the bicycle rack, it would work its tether free, and an hour or so later the Brothers would find it wandering in the garden, munching their prized shrubs and flowers. He also spurred the big animal through the crowded streets of Carrasco, galloping along sidewalks and through busy intersections so fast that the horse's shoes struck sparks on the pavement. Drivers swerved and pedestrians lurched out of his way. Our neighbors constantly complained, and once or twice the police spoke to Roberto's father, but Roberto continued to ride.

Hoping to find a constructive outlet for Roberto's unruliness, the Christian Brothers encouraged him to play rugby, where his forceful nature made him a formidable presence on the field. He played left wing, the same position as Panchito played on the right, but where Panchito would gracefully dodge and weave his way past tacklers toward the try-line, Roberto preferred to batter a more direct path through the opposition, one head-on collision after another. He was not one of our bigger players, but his thick legs were so impressively developed that, along with his famous muscle-headedness, they earned him the nickname *Músculo*—"Muscles." Powered by such sturdy limbs and such natural belligerence, Roberto was more than a match for much larger opponents, and he loved nothing more than to lower his shoulder and send some oversized, would-be tackler flying.

Roberto loved rugby, but it didn't cure his stubbornness as the Christian Brothers had hoped. Roberto was Roberto, on the field or off, and even in the middle of a hard-fought match, he refused to be told what to do. Our coaches prepared us well for each match, with scripted plays and strategies, and the rest of us tried as hard as we could to follow the game plan. But Roberto always reserved the right to improvise at will. Usually this meant he would keep the ball when he should have passed it, or would hurl himself headlong into an opponent when the coaches wanted him to dance into the open. As he grudgingly endured the coaches' reprimands, the dark glare in his piercing eyes showed defiance and impatience. He chafed at being told what to do. He simply felt his own way was better. And he lived this way in every facet of his life. Roberto's strong-mindedness made him a challenging friend, and even in the comfortable circumstances of our lives in Carasco, he could be arrogant and overbearing. In the pressure-packed atmosphere of the fuselage, his conduct was often insufferable. He routinely ignored decisions made by the group and turned on anyone who challenged him, raining down rants and insults in the belligerent falsetto he used when his blood was hot. He could be brutally inconsiderate: If he had to leave the plane at night to urinate, for example, he simply stepped on the arms and legs of whoever happened to be sleeping in his path. He slept where he wanted, even if it meant shoving others aside from the places they had chosen. Dealing with Roberto's quick temper and confrontational manner created stress we did not need and cost us energy we could not afford to squander, and more than once his hardheaded abrasiveness almost led to fights.

But, despite his difficult nature, I respected Roberto. He was the most intelligent and ingenious of us all. Without his quick-witted medical care in the wake of the crash, many of the boys who were now recovering from their injuries might well be dead, and his creative thinking had solved many problems in ways that made us safer or more comfortable on the mountain. It was Roberto who realized that the Fairchild's seat covers could be removed and used as blankets, an innovation that may have saved us all from freezing. Most of the simple tools we used, and our crude selection of medical supplies, had been improvised by him from articles he'd scavenged from the wreckage. And for all his egotistical bluster, I knew he felt a strong sense of responsibility toward the rest of us. After seeing how Arturo and Rafael suffered at night as they lay on the floor of the plane (and bellowing at them fiercely to stop their pathetic moaning), Roberto spent hours the next morning fashioning the swinging hammocks that gave those two injured boys some relief from their pain. It was not compassion, exactly, that spurred him to do these things, it was more a sense of duty. He knew his gifts and abilities, and it simply made sense to him to do what he knew no one else could do.

I knew Roberto's resourcefulness would be a great advantage in any attempt to escape. I also trusted his realistic view of our situation—he understood how desperate things were, and that our only hope was to save ourselves. But more than anything I wanted him with me simply because he was Roberto, the most determined and strong-willed person I had ever known. If there was anyone in our group who could stand up to the Andes through sheer stubbornness alone, Roberto was the one. He would not be the easiest traveling companion, and I worried that his difficult nature might plunge us into conflict on our way, sabotaging whatever slim chance we had to reach civilization. But, intuitively, I understood that Roberto's willfulness and strong sense of self would be the perfect complement to the wild impulses that drove me to flee blindly into the wild. With my manic urge to escape, I would be the engine that pulled us through the mountains; Roberto's cantankerous spirit would be the clutch that prevented me from revving out of control. I had no way of knowing what kind of hardships lay ahead in the wilderness, but I knew Roberto would make me stronger and better on the journey. He was the one I needed by my side, and when the time seemed right and we were alone together, I asked him to come with me on the trek.

"We must do it, Roberto, you and I," I said. "We have the best chance of anyone here."

"You're crazy, Nando," he snapped, his voice rising in pitch. "Look at these fucking mountains. Do you have any idea how high they are?"

I gazed at the highest peak. "It seems maybe two or three times the Pan de Azúcar," I said, referring to the tallest "mountain" in Uruguay.

Roberto snorted. "Don't be an idiot!" he screeched. "There's no snow on the Pan de Azúcar! It is only fifteen hundred feet high! This mountain is ten times higher, at least!"

"What choice do we have?" I answered. "We have to try. For me, the decision is made. I am going to climb, Roberto, but I am afraid. I cannot do it alone. I need you to come with me."

Roberto shook his head ruefully. "You saw what happened to Gustavo," he said. "And they only made it halfway up the slope."

"We can't stay here," I said. "You know that as well as I do. We need to leave as soon as possible."

"No way!" shouted Roberto. "It would have to be planned. We must do it the smartest way. We need to think through every detail. How would we climb? Which slope? Which direction?"

"I think of these things constantly," I said. "We will need food, water, warm clothing . . ."

"How would we keep ourselves from freezing at night?" he asked.

"We will find shelter beneath rocks," I said, "or maybe dig caves in the snow."

"Timing is very important," he said. "We would have to wait for the weather to improve."

"But we can't wait so long that we are too weak to make the climb," I told him.

Roberto was silent for a moment. "It will kill us, you know," he said.

"It probably will," I replied, "but if we stay here we are dead already. I cannot do this alone, Roberto. Please, come with me."

For a moment Roberto seemed to study me with his penetrating gaze, as if he'd never seen me before. Then he nodded toward the fuselage. "Let's go inside," he said. "The wind is picking up and I am fucking cold."

IN THE DAYS that followed, we were all preoccupied with discussions of our plan to climb out of the cordillera, and I soon realized that the others were beginning to trust in this plan as desperately as they had once trusted in the certainty of rescue. Because I'd been the first to speak openly about our need to escape, and because they knew I would certainly be one of the ones who tried, many of the survivors began to see me as a leader. Never in my life had I assumed such a role—I was the one who always drifted along, riding the current, letting others show the way. I certainly didn't feel like a leader now. Couldn't they see how confused and frightened I was? Did they really want a leader who felt in his heart that all of us were already doomed? For my part, I had no desire to lead anyone; I needed all my strength just to keep myself from falling apart. I worried I was giving them false hope, but in the end I decided that false hope was better than no hope at all. So I kept my thoughts to myself. They were dark thoughts, mostly, but one night something remarkable happened. It was after midnight, the fuselage was dark and cold as always, and I was lying restlessly in the shallow, groggy stupor that was as close as I ever got to genuine sleep, when, out of nowhere, I was jolted by a surge of joy so deep and sublime that it nearly lifted me bodily from the floor. For a moment the cold vanished, as if I'd been bathed in a warm, golden light, and for the first time since the plane had crashed, I was certain I would survive. In excitement, I woke the others.

"Guys, listen!" I cried. "We will be okay. I will have you home by Christmas!"

My outburst seemed to puzzle the others, who only muttered softly and went back to sleep. In moments my euphoria passed. I tried all night to recapture the feeling, but it had slipped away. By morning my heart was filled once more with nothing but doubts and dread.

Chapter Six

Tomb

By the last week in October, we had chosen the group that would leave the crash site and try to reach help. There was no question in anyone's mind that I was going—they would have had to tie me to a rock to keep me from leaving. Roberto had finally agreed to go with me. Fito and Numa would round out the team. The other survivors approved of the choices, and began to refer to us as "the expeditionaries." It was decided that we would receive larger rations of food to build our strength. We would also be given the warmest clothing and the best places to sleep, and would be excused from our routine chores so that we could conserve our energy for the trek.

Having a designated team of expeditionaries made our plans for escape seem real at last, and, in response, the spirits of the group began to rise. And after two weeks on the mountain, we found other reasons to hope: despite so much suffering and so many horrors, none of us had died since our eighth day on the mountain, when I'd lost Susy. With all the frozen bodies lying in the snow, we had enough food to keep us alive, and though we still suffered through the freezing nights, we knew that as long as we huddled in the shelter of the Fairchild, the cold would not kill us. Our situation was still critical, but we began to feel that we had passed the point of crisis. Things seemed more stable. We had resolved the immediate threats that faced us, and now we would play a waiting game, resting and strengthening ourselves while we waited for the weather to improve, then we would climb. Perhaps we had seen the last of the horrors. Perhaps all twenty-seven of us were destined to survive. Why else would God have saved us? Many of us were comforted by these thoughts as we filed into the fuselage on the evening of October 29 and prepared ourselves for sleep.

It was a windy night. I settled on the floor, and Liliana lay down next to me. For a while she talked quietly with Javier, who lay facing her. As always, they talked about their children. Liliana worried about them every moment, and Javier would comfort her, telling her that surely their grandparents were taking good care of them. I was touched by the tenderness between them. They shared such an intimacy, such a sense of partnership. It was as if they were a single person. Before the crash, they had been living the life I'd dreamed of—a strong marriage, the joys of a loving home and family. I wondered if they would ever return to that life. And what about me? Would my own chance for such happiness die with me in this frozen hell? I let my thoughts wander: Where, at this very moment, was the woman I would marry? Was she wondering about her future, too—who she would marry and where he might be?

Here I am, I thought, *freezing my ass at the top of the world, and thinking of you . . .*

After a while, Javier tried to sleep and Liliana turned to me.

"How is your head, Nando?" she asked. "Does it still hurt?"

"Only a little," I said.

"You should rest more."

"I am glad you decided to eat," I told her.

"I want to see my children," she said. "And if I do not eat, I will die. I do it for them."

"How is Javier?"

"He is still so sick," she sighed. "I pray with him often. He feels certain God will give us a chance."

"Do you think so?" I asked. "Do you think God will help us? I'm so confused. I am so filled with doubt."

"God has saved us so far," she said. "We must trust Him."

"But why would God save us and let the others die? My mother, my sister, Panchito, Guido? Didn't they want God to save them?"

"There is no way to understand God or his logic," she replied.

"Then why should we trust Him?" I asked. "What about all the Jews who died in concentration camps?" I said. "What about all the innocents killed in plagues and purges and natural disasters? Why would He turn His back on them, but still find time for us?"

Liliana sighed, and I felt the warmth of her breath on my face. "You are getting too complicated," she said, with softness in her voice. "All we can do is love God and love others and trust in God's will."

Liliana's words did not convince me, but her warmth and kindness comforted me. I tried to imagine how much she must long for her children, and said a prayer that they should be together again, then I closed my eyes and drifted off into my usual bleary halfslumber. I dozed for a while, perhaps half an hour, and then I woke, frightened and disoriented, as a huge and heavy force thumped against my chest. Something was terribly wrong. I felt an icy wetness pressing against my face, and a crushing weight bore down on me so hard that it forced the air from my chest. After a moment of confusion, I realized what had happened—an avalanche had rolled down the mountain and filled the fuselage with snow. There was a moment of complete silence, then I heard a slow, wet creak as the loose snow settled under its own weight and packed around me like rock. I tried to move, but it felt as if my body were encased in concrete, and I couldn't even wiggle a finger. I managed a few shallow breaths, but soon snow packed into my mouth and nostrils and I began to suffocate. At first the pressure in my chest was unbearable, but as my awareness dimmed, I stopped noticing the discomfort. My thoughts grew calm and lucid. "This is my death," I told myself. "Now I will see what lies on the other side." I felt no strong emotion. I didn't try to shout or struggle. I simply waited, and as I accepted my helplessness, a sense of peace overtook me. I waited patiently for my life to end. There were no angels, no revelations, there was no long tunnel leading to a golden loving light. Instead, I sensed only the same black silence I had fallen into when the Fairchild hit the mountain. I drifted back into that silence. I let my resistance fade. It was over. No more fear. No more struggle. Just bottomless silence, and rest.

Then a hand clawed the snow from my face and I was yanked back into the world of the living. Someone had dug a narrow shaft down through several feet of snow to reach me. I spat the snow from my mouth and gulped cold air into my lungs, although the weight of the snow on my chest made it difficult to draw a full breath.

I heard Carlitos's voice above me. "Who is it?" he shouted.

"Me," I sputtered. "It's Nando."

Then he left me. I heard chaos above me, voices shouting and sobbing.

"Dig for the faces!" someone shouted. "Give them air!"

"Coco! Where is Coco?"

"Help me here!"

"Has anyone seen Marcelo?"

"How many do we have? Who is missing?"

"Someone count!"

Then I heard Javier's voice shouting hysterically, "Liliana? Liliana? Help her! Hold on, Liliana! Oh, please, hurry, find her!"

The chaos lasted just a few minutes, then the fuselage fell silent. A few moments later they dug me out, and I was able to lift myself up from the snow. The dark fuselage was lit eerily by the flames of the cigarette lighter Pancho Delgado was holding. I saw some of my friends lying motionless. Other boys were rising from the snow like zombies from the grave. Javier was kneeling beside me, with Liliana in his arms. I knew from the way her arms and head hung limply that she was dead. I shook my head in disbelief as Javier began to sob. "No," I said flatly. "No." As if I could argue with what had just happened. As if I could refuse to allow it to be real. I glanced at the others standing around me. Some were weeping, some were com-

ABOVE: The 1964 team picture of the Stella Maris High School rugby squad. Guido Magri is seated fourth from the left. I am standing in the top row, far right. (*Unknown*)

During the Old Christians' 1971 rugby trip to Chile, I pose with Roberto Canessa and teammate Eduardo Deal, with the Andes rising in the background. (*Unknown*)

The Old Christians on a Chilean practice field in 1971. Guido Magri kneels at far left and Panchito Abal kneels two men to his left. I am standing second from the right, with Marcelo Perez in front of me. *(Unknown)*

At a rugby match in Uruguay, 1971. Guido Magri, standing, far right, is about to toss the ball into the scrum. *(Unknown)*

Antonio "Tintin" Vizintin backs me up as we keep our eyes on the ball during a 1971 match in Uruguay. *(Unknown)*

Rugby action, Uruguay, 1971. I am leaping to fight for the ball in a line out. Marcelo Perez is at the far right. *(Unknown)*

I glare at the camera
after a tough game in
Uruguay, 1971.
(Unknown)

With my sisters at a party
in 1970. Graciela is on the
left, Susy is on the right.
(Unknown)

My sister Susy, 1970. *(Unknown)*

My parents, Xenia and Seler Parrado, 1970. *(Unknown)*

In mid-November, at the wrecked tail section with Roy Harley (*top*), Roberto Canessa (*left*), and Antonio Vizintin (*front*), during our failed efforts to fix the Fairchild's radio. Hanging from the ragged roof of the tail, just to

Harley's left are the little red shoes my mother purchased in Mendoza.
(*Group of Survivors/Corbis*)

On clear days we sat outside to warm ourselves in the sun and escape the dark, damp interior of the fuselage. On a bright day in early December, from left to right: Alvaro Mangino, Carlitos Paez, Daniel Fernandez (*in white cap*), Coche Inciarte (*with his hand on Daniel's shoulder*), and Pancho Delgado. (*Gamma*)

A picture of me drinking a cup of melted snow inside the tail section of the plane. *(Group of Survivors/Corbis)*

In December, the nights were still frigid, but the days were mild and the unfiltered sun was strong enough to burn us. Here, from left to right, are Eduardo Strauch, Pancho Delgado, and Gustavo Zerbino posing against the backdrop of the cordillera. *(Group of Survivors/Corbis)*

In the days before our final attempt to climb the peaks to the west, Pancho Delgado (*sitting on fuselage roof*) and Roberto Canessa (*standing to Pancho's right*) are stitching together squares of insulation to make the sleeping bag we will carry with us on the journey. Resting in the foreground are Fito Strauch (*left*) and Carlitos Paez (*right*). In the row behind them, from left to right, are Gustavo Zerbino, Eduardo Strauch, me, and Javier Methol. (*Group of Survivors/Corbis*)

The frantic note I scribbled for the peasant. Before wrapping it around a rock and throwing it across the river to him, I turned it over and scrawled on the back, with a lipstick I'd found in my mother's luggage, "CUANDO VIENE?" ("When will you come?") For complete translation of the note, see page 222. (© Bettmann/Corbis)

Sergio Catalan (*center*), the peasant who found us in the mountains and led rescuers to us at Los Maitenes, sits with Roberto and me as we wait for rescue helicopters to arrive. (*EL PAIS de Uruguay, Colección Caruso*)

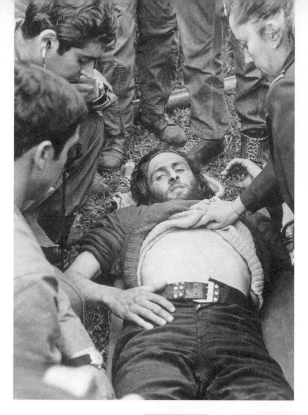

The first medics to arrive at Los Maitenes huddle around Roberto, who is wearing the belt he had taken from the body of Panchito Abal. *(EFE)*

As Roberto receives treatment, I am reluctantly preparing myself to lead the helicopter rescue team on a risky flight to the Fairchild's crash site. *(Associated Press)*

As Chilean helicopters thunder in the overcast skies above our heads, the mounted police take Roberto and me across the shallow river to the spot where the helicopters will land. In the background are reporters and photographers, who had found us before the Chilean Air Force did. *(Courtesy of Copesa)*

I am on horseback behind an officer of the mounted police as we watch the helicopters break through the cloud cover. *(Empresa Periodística La Nación)*

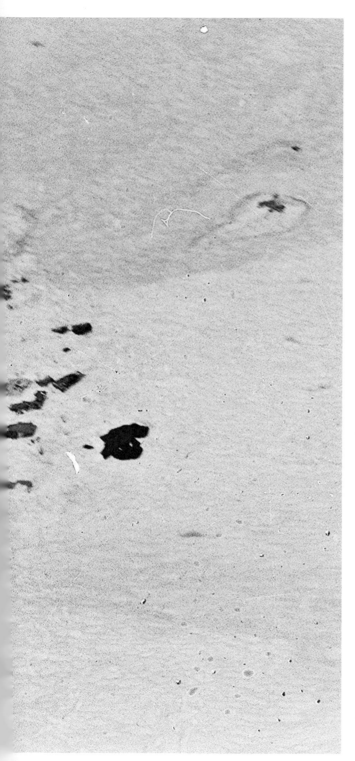

After a terrifying flight through the cordillera, we found ourselves hovering above the crash site, and I watched from the helicopter as my friends rejoiced at our arrival.
(EL PAIS de Uruguay, Colección Caruso)

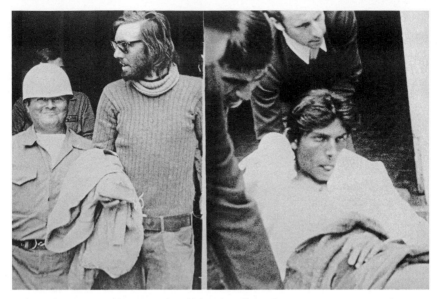

When the rescue helicopters landed at a military base near San Fernando, I refused to be carried to the waiting ambulances on a stretcher. "I have walked across the Andes," I told myself. "I can walk a few more steps." Others, like Alvaro Mangino, right, had spent all their strength in the mountains and needed assistance. *(© Bettmann/CORBIS)*

On the day of the rescue, darkness fell before all the survivors could be taken from the mountain, so six of them had to spend another night at the crash site. From left to right: Fito Strauch, Gustavo Zerbino, Coche Inciarte, Roy Harley, Pancho Delgado, and Moncho Sabella. Two members of the Chilean rescue team are seated at the far left and far right. *(Group of Survivors/CORBIS)*

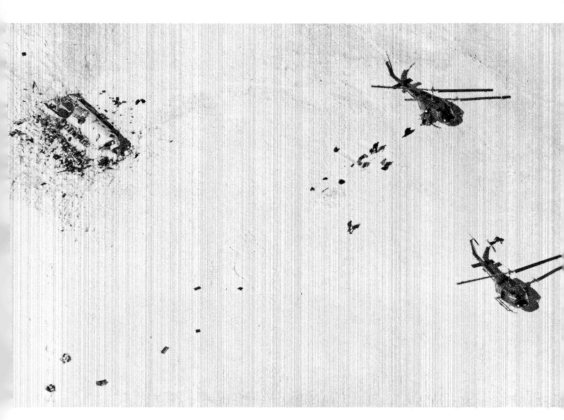

On December 23, while the rest of us were already being cared for at the hospital in San Fernando, rescue teams returned to the crash site to retrieve the last of the survivors. This aerial shot shows them leaving the fuselage behind them as they walk toward the waiting helicopters. *(Associated Press)*

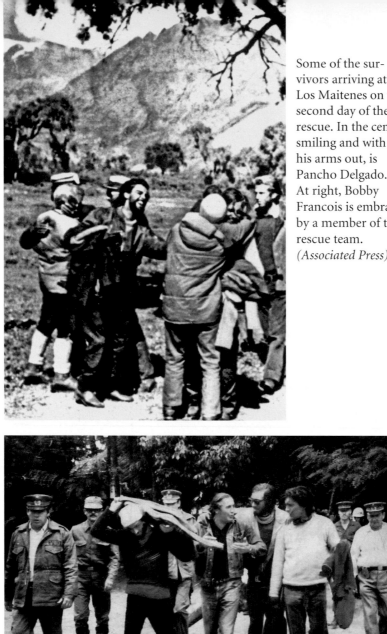

Some of the survivors arriving at Los Maitenes on the second day of the rescue. In the center, smiling and with his arms out, is Pancho Delgado. At right, Bobby Francois is embraced by a member of the rescue team. *(Associated Press)*

Just moments after the helicopters landed at the military base in San Fernando, I walk toward the ambulances with my arm around Carlos Paez-Villaro, the father of Carlitos Paez, who is in the white sweater to my left. Roberto Canessa is in the white cap, to my right. *(Unknown)*

News of our rescue touched off a media frenzy. Shortly after their arrival at the hospital in Santiago, Pancho Delgado (left, smiling, with his face raised) and Antonio Vizintin (center front, in a hospital gown with his back to camera) find themselves mobbed by reporters and photographers.
(*Empresa Periodística La Nación*)

Some of the survivors relaxing at the hospital in Santiago. From left to right: Moncho Sabella, Fito Strauch, Antonio Vizintin, Bobby Francois, Pancho Delgado, and Gustavo Zerbino. *(Associated Press)*

Carlitos Paez is embraced by his father, Carlos Paez-Villaro, who had stalked the Andes for weeks in his own desperate search for his son *(EFE)*

Roy Harley in the arms of his mother as he arrives at the military base near San Fernando. *(Clarin Contenidos)*

Christmas 1972 with the survivors and their families at the Sheraton San Cristobol Hotel in Santiago. I raise my glass high in celebration, but with my mother and sister gone, it is a bittersweet moment for me. *(Associated Press)*

December 30, 1972, my first day back in Carrasco after the Andes ordeal. My beloved motorcycle, which my father had sold to a friend, was returned to me, and I wasted no time getting it on the road. *(Unknown)*

With my friend and Autodelta teammate Chippy Breard (*center*), I am speaking with racing legend Jackie Stewart (*right*) at the 1974 Argentinian F1 Gran Prix in Buenos Aires. *(Armando Rivas)*

During a 1975 race at El Pinar race track, near Montevideo, I watch the action with fellow Uruguayan driver Josè P. Passadore. *(Unknown)*

A driver change during the Silverstone Tourist Trophy competition at Silverstone, England, in 1977. I am standing, wearing a helmet and waiting to take the wheel as my teammate Mario Marquez exits the car. We took second place in this long-distance event. *(Jorge Mayol)*

Summer 2003, somewhere in the Great Plains. I am posing with my 1400cc Titan 2000, on my way to a motorcycle rally in Sturgis, South Dakota, to celebrate the one hundredth anniversary of the Harley-Davidson company. *(Gonzalo Mateu)*

With Veronique and my father, Christmastime, 2003.
(*Courtesy of the Parrado family*)

With my wife, Veronique, in Punta del Este, 2004. *(Jean Pierre Banowicz)*

The ladies of my life. My wife, Veronique (*center*), with my daughters, Cecilia (*left*) and and Veronica (*right*). *(Jean Pierre Banowicz)*

The Parrados, 2004. From left: Cecilia, Veronique, Veronica, and me. *(Jean Pierre Banowicz)*

OPPOSITE: A survivor reunion, December 22, 2004. Fifteen survivors gathered, plus Rafael Ponce de Leon, who during the disaster used the ham radio in his Montevideo basement to keep our parents informed of rescue efforts and to spread news of our rescue. Top row, left to right: Antonio "Tintin"Vizintin, Gustavo Zerbino, Roy Harley, Javier Methol, Roberto "Bobby" Francois, Alfredo "Pancho" Delgado, Eduardo Strauch, Adolfo "Fito"Strauch, me, and Roberto Canessa. Bottom row: Josè Luis "Coche" Inciarte, Alvaro Mangino, Carlos Pàez, Ramòn "Moncho" Sabella, Ponce de Leòn, and Daniel Fernandez. Pedro Algorta is missing from the picture. *(Veronique van Wassenhove)*

March 2003. On one of many trips to the grave near the crash site in the Andes, I hang some flowers on the simple steel cross. *(Carlos Cardoso)*

In the Andes, March 2005. On our way to surprise Sergio Catalan at his fiftieth wedding anniversary, Roberto Canessa and I run into him on a deserted mountain trail near his village. "Good man," I tell him, "we are lost again!" (*Veronique van Wassenhove*)

The wreckage of the Fairchild after all the survivors have been rescued. The row of chairs to the left was our "lounge" area, where we sunned ourselves on clear days. To the right, near the base of the fuselage, you can see the body of one of the victims of the disaster. *(Keystone/Gamma)*

forting Javier, others were simply gazing into the shadows with dazed looks on their faces. For a moment no one spoke, but when the shock eased, the others told me what they'd seen.

It began with a distant roar on the mountain. Roy Harley heard the noise and jumped to his feet. Seconds later the avalanche swept through the makeshift wall at the rear of the fuselage, burying him to the hips. In horror, Roy saw that all of us sleeping on the floor had been buried in snow. Terrified that all of us were dead and he was alone on the mountain, Roy began to dig. He quickly uncovered Carlitos, Fito, and Roberto. As each boy was uncovered, he also began to dig. They scrambled back and forth on the surface of the snow, searching frantically for our buried friends, but despite their efforts they were not fast enough to save us all. Our losses were heavy. Marcelo was dead. So were Enrique Platero, Coco Nicholich, and Daniel Maspons. Carlos Roque, the Fairchild's mechanic, and Juan Carlos Menendez had died beneath the falling wall. Diego Storm, who, on the third day of the ordeal, had saved my life by dragging me into the warmth of the fuselage while I still lay in a coma, had suffocated under the snow. And Liliana, who, just moments earlier, had spoken such kind words of comfort to me, was also gone. Gustavo had helped Javier dig for her, but too much time had passed, and when they found her she had died.

It is hard to describe the depths of the despair that fell upon us in the wake of the avalanche. The deaths of our friends staggered us. We had allowed ourselves to believe that we had passed the point of danger, but now we saw that we would never be safe in this place. The mountain could kill us in so many ways. What tortured me most was the capriciousness of death. How could I make sense of this? Daniel Maspons had been sleeping only inches to my right. Liliana had been just as close on my left. Both were dead. Why them and not me? Was I stronger? Smarter? Better prepared? The answer was clear: Daniel and Liliana wanted to live as much as I did, they were just as strong and they fought just as hard to survive, but their fate was decided by a simple stroke of bad luck—they chose their spots to sleep that night, and that decision killed them. I thought of my mother and Susy choosing their seats on the plane. I thought of Panchito switching seats with me just moments before the crash. The arbitrariness of all these deaths outraged me, but it frightened me, too, because if death here was so senseless and random, nothing, no amount of courage or planning or determination, could protect me from it.

Sometime later that night, as if to mock me for my fears, the mountain sent a second avalanche roaring down the slopes. We heard it coming and braced for the worst, but the snow simply rolled over us this time. The Fairchild had already been buried by snow.

THE WRECKAGE OF the Fairchild had always been a drafty and crowded shelter, but in the aftermath of the avalanche it became a truly hellish place. The snow that invaded the fuselage was so deep that we couldn't stand; we had barely enough headroom now to crawl about the plane on hands and knees. As soon as we had the stomach for it, we stacked the dead at the rear of the plane where the snow was deepest, which left only a small clearing near the cockpit for the living to sleep. We packed into that space—nineteen of us now, jammed into an area that might have comfortably accommodated four—with no choice but to squeeze together, our knees, feet, and elbows tangled in a nightmare version of a scrum. The air in the fuselage was thick with dampness from the snow, which gave the cold an even meaner edge. All of us had been covered with snow, which quickly melted from the heat of our bodies, and soon our clothing was soaked through. To make matters worse, all our possessions now lay buried beneath several feet of snow on the fuselage floor. We had no makeshift blankets to warm us, no shoes to protect our feet from the cold, and no cushions to insulate us from the frozen surface of the snow, which was now the only surface for us to rest on. There was so little clearance above our heads that we were forced to rest with our shoulders slumped forward and our chins pressed to our chests, but still, the backs of our heads bumped the ceiling. As I struggled in the jostling heap of bodies to find a comfortable position, I felt panic rising in my throat and I had to fight the urge to scream. How much snow lay above us? I wondered. Two feet? Ten feet? Twenty feet? Were we buried alive? Had the Fairchild become our coffin? I could *feel* the oppression of the snow all around us. It insulated us from the noise of the wind outside and altered sounds inside the plane, creating a thick, muffled silence, and giving our voices a subtle echo, as if we were speaking at the bottom of a well. I thought, *Now I know how it feels to be trapped in a submarine on the ocean floor.* Despite the cold, there was clammy sweat beneath my collar. I felt the walls of the fuselage close in on me. All my claustrophobic fears—of being trapped by the mountains around us, of being shut off from escape and cut off from my father—were being realized in an absurdly literal way. I was trapped inside an aluminum tube under tons of hardened snow. Teetering on the verge of panic, I remembered the peaceful acceptance I'd felt under the avalanche, and for a moment I wished they had found Liliana instead of me.

The following hours were some of the darkest of the entire ordeal. Javier wept miserably for Liliana, and almost all the other survivors mourned the loss of at least one especially close friend. Roberto had lost his closest amigo, Daniel Maspons. Carlitos had lost Coco Nicholich and Diego Storm. We all mourned for Marcelo and Enrique Platero. The deaths of our friends left us feeling more helpless and vulnerable than ever. The mountain had given us another show of force, and there was nothing we could do in response except to sit shivering in a miserable tangle on our hard bed of snow. Minutes passed like hours. Soon some of the survivors began to cough and wheeze, and I realized that the air in the fuselage was growing stale. The snow had sealed us in so tightly that we'd been cut off from fresh air. If we didn't find an air supply soon, we would suffocate. I spotted the tip of an aluminum cargo pole jutting up from the snow. Without thinking, I drew it from the snow, grasped it like a lance, and, resting on my knees, began to drive the pole's pointed tip into the ceiling. Using all my strength, I stabbed the ceiling again and again until somehow I managed to punch through the Fairchild's roof. I pushed the pole upward, feeling the resistance of the snow above the plane. Then the resistance ended and the pole broke free. We were not hopelessly buried. The Fairchild was covered by no more than a few feet of snow.

When I removed the pipe, fresh air flowed in through the hole I'd made, and we all breathed easier as we settled back into our pack and tried to sleep. That night was endless. When dawn finally arrived, the windows of the fuselage brightened slightly as the dim light filtered down through the snow. We wasted no time trying to dig our way out of our aluminum tomb. We knew that because of the way the plane was tilted on the glacier, the windows on the right side of the cockpit faced skyward. With tons of snow blocking our usual exit at the rear of the aircraft, we decided these windows would be our best route of escape. But the way to the cockpit was also clogged with snow. We began to dig toward it, using shards of metal and broken pieces of plastic as shovels. There was only room for one man to work at a time, so we took turns digging in fifteen-minute shifts, one man chipping away at the rock-hard snow and the rest of us shoveling the loosened snow to the rear of the plane. In the dim light, I couldn't help thinking that my bearded, emaciated, disheveled friends looked like desperate prisoners tunneling their way out of a cell in the Siberian Gulag.

It took hours to burrow a passage through the cockpit, but finally Gustavo dug his way to the pilot's seat, and, standing on the dead body of the pilot, was able to reach the window. He pushed against the window, hoping to force it out of its frame, but the snow pressing down on the glass was too heavy, and he couldn't muster the strength. Roberto tried next, but he did no better. Finally, Roy Harley climbed onto the pilot's seat and, with a furious shove, pushed the window free. Climbing through the opening he'd created, Roy dug up through a few feet of snow until he broke the surface and was able to look around. A storm was pounding the mountain with high winds and pelting snow that stung his face. Squinting into the wind, Roy saw that the avalanche had buried the fuselage completely. Before climbing back down to us, he glanced at the sky. He saw no break in the clouds.

"There's a blizzard," he said, when he climbed back down into the fuselage. "And the snow all around the plane is too deep to walk on. I think we would sink into it and be lost. We are trapped inside until the storm ends, and it doesn't look like it will end soon."

Trapped by the weather, we had no choice but to hunker down in our wretched prison and endure our misery one long moment at a time. To brighten our mood, we discussed the only thing that gave us comfort—our plans to escape—and as these discussions progressed, a new idea emerged. Two failed efforts to climb to the mountains above us had convinced many in the group that escape to the west was impossible. Now they were turning their attention to the broad valley that sloped away from the crash sight down the mountainside to the east. Their theory was that if we were as close to Chile as we believed, then all water in this region must drain through the Chilean foothills and into the Pacific Ocean to the west. That would include all the snow melting in this region of the cordillera. That water must find a way to flow west, they reasoned, and if we could find the path of that flow down through the cordillera, we would find our route of escape.

I did not have much faith in this plan. For one thing, I couldn't believe the mountains would let us off so easily. It also seemed insane to ignore the one fact we knew to be true—*to the west is*

Chile—and follow a path that would almost certainly take us deeper into the heart of the Andes. But as the others decided to place their faith in this new plan, I did not argue. I don't know why. Maybe my thinking was muddled because of altitude or dehydration or lack of sleep. Maybe I was relieved to be spared the terror of facing the mountain. For some reason I accepted their decision without question, even though I felt it was a waste of time. All I knew was that we must leave this place, and that we must start soon.

"As soon as the blizzard ends, we must go," I told them.

Fito disagreed. "We must wait for the weather to get better," he said.

"I am tired of waiting," I replied. "How do we know the weather will ever get better in this damned place?"

Then Pedro Algorta remembered a conversation he'd had with a taxi driver in Santiago. "He said that summertime in the Andes comes like clockwork on November fifteenth," Pedro said.

"That's only a little more than two weeks, Nando," said Fito. "You can wait that long."

"I will wait," I answered. "But only until November fifteenth. If no one else is ready to go by then, I will go alone."

THE DAYS WE spent trapped beneath the avalanche were the grimmest of the ordeal. We could not sleep, or warm ourselves, or dry our soaking clothes. Trapped inside as we were, Fito's water-making machines were useless to us, and the only way to ease our thirst was to gnaw chunks of the filthy snow on which we were crawling and sleeping. Hunger presented a more complicated problem. With no access to the bodies outside, we had no food and we rapidly began to weaken. We were all well aware that the bodies of the avalanche victims lay within easy reach, but we were slow to face the prospects of cutting them. Until now, when meat had been cut, it had been done outside the fuselage, and no one but the ones doing the cutting had had to see it. We never knew whose body the flesh had been taken from. Also, after lying for so many days under the snow, the bodies outside had frozen so solidly it was easier to think of them as lifeless objects. There was no way to objectify the bodies inside the fuselage. Just a day earlier they had been warm and animated. How could we eat flesh that would have to be cut from these newly dead bodies right before our eyes? Silently, we all agreed that we would rather starve as we waited out the storm. But by October 31, our third day under the avalanche, we knew we couldn't hold out any longer. I can't recall who it was, Roberto or Gustavo, perhaps, but someone found a piece of glass, swept the snow from one of the bodies, and began to cut. It was a horror, watching him slice into a friend, listening to the soft sounds of the glass ripping at the skin and sawing at the muscle below. When a piece of flesh was handed to me, I was revolted. As before, the meat had been dried in the sun before we ate it, which weakened its taste and gave it a more palatable texture, but the chunk of flesh Fito gave me now was soft and greasy, and streaked with blood and bits of wet gristle. I gagged hard when I placed it in my mouth, and had to use all my willpower to force myself to swallow. Fito had to urge many of the others to eat—he even forced some into the mouth of his cousin Eduardo. But some, including Numa and Coche, who, even under the best of circumstances, could barely stomach human flesh, could not be persuaded to eat. I was especially troubled by Numa's obstinacy. He was an expeditionary, a great source of strength for me, and I did not like the idea of challenging the mountains without him.

"Numa," I said to him, "you have to eat. We need you with us when we hike out of here. You must stay strong."

Numa grimaced and shook his head. "I could barely swallow the meat before," he said. "I could never stand it like this."

"Think of your family," I told him. "If you want to see them again, you must eat."

"I'm sorry, Nando," he said, turning away from me. "I simply can't."

I knew there was more to Numa's refusal than simple disgust. On some level, he had had enough, and his refusal to eat was his rebellion against the inescapable nightmare our lives had become. I felt the same. Who could survive such a litany of horrors as we had been forced to endure? What had we done to deserve such misery? What was the meaning of our suffering? Did our lives have any value? What kind of God could be so cruel? These questions plagued me every moment, but somehow I understood that thoughts like these were dangerous. They led to nothing but an impotent rage that quickly soured into apathy. In this place, apathy meant death, so I fought off the questions by conjuring thoughts of my family at home. I pictured my sister Graciela with her new baby boy. I wanted so badly to be an uncle to him. I still had the red baby shoes my mother had bought for him in Mendoza, and I imagined myself slipping them on his little feet, kissing his head, whispering to him, *Soy tu tío, Nando.* I thought of my grandmother Lina, who had my mother's bright blue eyes and loving smile. What would I give to feel her arms around me in this terrible place? I even thought of my dog, Jimmy, a playful boxer, who went with me everywhere. It broke my heart to think of him lying sadly on my empty bed, or waiting by the front door for me to come home. I thought about friends in Montevideo. I dreamed of visiting my old haunts. I remembered all the small comforts—swimming at the beach, soccer games and car races, the pleasure of sleeping in my own bed, and the kitchen full of food. Was there really a time when I'd been surrounded by such treasures, when so much happiness had been within my reach? It all seemed so distant now, so unreal.

As I shivered in the clammy snow, racked with despair and forced to chew the raw, wet gobs of flesh that had been hacked from my friends before my eyes, it was hard to believe in anything before the crash. In those moments I forced myself to think of my father, and I promised once more that I would never stop fighting to make it home. Sometimes this would give me a sense of hope and peace, but often, as I glanced at our sorry condition and the horrors that surrounded us, it was hard to connect myself to the happy life I'd had before, and for the first time, my promise to my father began to ring hollow. Death was drawing closer; its stink was growing stronger all around me. There was something sordid and rank in our suffering now, a sense of darkness and corruption that soured my heart.

I dreamed very little in the mountains—I rarely slept soundly enough to dream—but one night, as I slept under the avalanche, I saw myself lying on my back with my arms extended to the side. My eyes were closed. "Am I dead?" I asked myself. "No, I can think, I am alert." Now a dark figure stood over me. "Roberto? Gustavo? Who are you? Who is there?"

No answer. I saw something glitter in his hand, and I realized he was holding a shard of glass. I tried to rise to my feet but I couldn't force myself to move.

"Get away from me! Who the hell are you? What are you doing?"

The figure knelt beside me and started to cut me with the glass. He took small pieces of my flesh from my forearm and passed them back to other figures standing behind him."

"Stop!" I screamed. "Stop cutting, I am alive!"

The others put my flesh in their mouths. They started to chew. "No! Not yet!" I cried. "Don't cut me!"

The stranger kept working, slicing at my arm. I realized he could not hear me. Then I realized that I felt no pain.

"Oh God! Am I dead? Have I died? Oh no, please, God, please . . ."

The next moment I woke with a jolt.

"Are you okay, Nando?" It was Gustavo, lying beside me.

My heart was pounding. "I had a nightmare," I said.

"It's okay," he said, "you are awake now."

Yes, I said to myself, *I am awake now, everything is fine.*

OCTOBER 31, our third day under the avalanche, was Carlitos's nineteenth birthday. Lying beside him in the fuselage that night, I promised him we would celebrate his birthday when we were home. "My birthday is December ninth," I told him. "We'll all go to my parents' place in Punta del Este and celebrate all the birthdays we missed."

"Speaking of birthdays," he said, "tomorrow is my father's birthday, and my sister's birthday, too. I have been thinking about them, and now I am certain I will see them again. God has saved me from the crash and from the avalanche. He must want me to survive and return to my family."

"I don't know what to think about God anymore," I said.

"But can't you feel how near He is to us?" he said. "I feel His presence so strongly here. Look how peaceful the mountains are, how beautiful. God is in this place, and when I feel His presence I know we will be all right." Like Carlitos, I had seen beauty in the mountains, but for me it was a lethal beauty, and we were the blemish on that beauty that the mountain wanted to erase. I wondered if Carlitos truly understood what trouble we were in, but still I admired him for the courage of his optimism.

"You are strong, Nando," he said. "You will make it. You will find help."

I said nothing. Carlitos began to pray.

"Happy birthday, Carlitos," I whispered, then I tried to sleep.

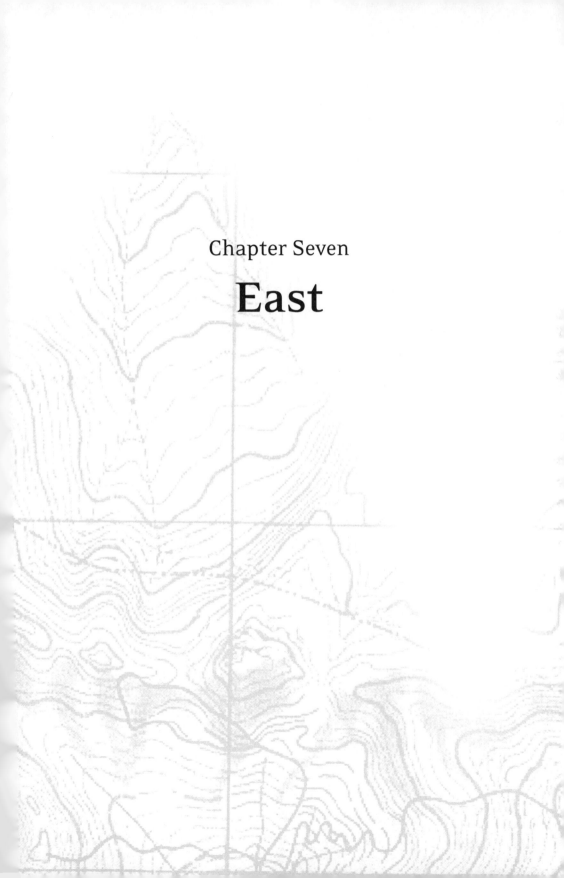

Chapter Seven

East

THE BLIZZARD FINALLY ended on the morning of November 1. The skies were clear and the sun was strong, so a few of the guys climbed out onto the roof of the fuselage to melt snow for drinking water. The rest of us began the slow process of removing the tons of snow that packed the Fairchild's interior. It took eight days to clear the fuselage, chipping at the rock-hard snow with our flimsy plastic shovels and passing each scoopful back through the cabin, man to man, until we could toss it outside. As an expeditionary, I was officially excused from such grueling labor, but I insisted on working anyway. Now that the date of our escape had been chosen, I could not rest. I had to keep busy, fearing that idle moments might weaken my resolve, or drive me insane.

While we worked to make the fuselage livable again, my fellow expeditionaries Numa, Fito, and Roberto prepared for the trek. They made a sled by tying a nylon strap to one half of a hard-shell plastic suitcase, and loaded it with whatever gear they thought we could use: the nylon seat covers we would use as blankets, Fitos's seat-cushion snowshoes, a bottle in which we would melt water, and other supplies. Roberto had fashioned knapsacks for us by tying off the legs of trousers and threading nylon straps through the pantlegs in such a way that we could sling them over our backs. We packed the knapsacks with more gear, but left room for the meat that Fito and his cousins were cutting for us and cooling in the snow. We all watched the weather closely, waiting for signs that spring was on its way, and by the second week in November it seemed that winter was easing its grip. When there was sun, temperatures were mild, as high as the mid-forties. But overcast days were cold, and even the slightest wind gave the air an icy edge. Nights were still frigid and storms still swept the mountains, often with little warning, and the thought of being trapped on the open slopes in a blizzard was one of my greatest concerns.

In the first week of November we decided to add Antonio Vizintin to the ranks of the expeditionaries. Antonio, or "Tintin" as we called him, was one of the strongest of all the survivors. Broad-shouldered and with legs like tree trunks, he was a prop for the Old Christians, a position he played with the strength of a bull. He also had a bull's temperament. Tintin could be just as hot-tempered and overbearing as Roberto, and I worried that facing the mountains with these two great hardheads at my side might be a recipe for disaster. But Tintin was not as complicated as Roberto; he lacked Roberto's raging ego and the need to tell others what to do. In terms of physical strength, Tintin had endured our weeks on the mountain as well as any of us, and despite my concerns, I was happy he would join us, thinking that with five expeditionaries rather than four, we would improve the odds of at least one of us getting through alive. But as soon as we added this new member to our team, we lost another, as Fito was stricken by a case of hemorrhoids so severe that they bled down his legs and made walking even short distances an agony. There was no way he could cross the mountains in such pain, so it was agreed that we would travel with four, and Fito would stay behind.

As the day of our departure grew nearer, I felt the spirits of the group rise as their confidence in the prospects of our mission increased. I didn't share their confidence. I still knew in my heart that the only way to escape these mountains was to follow the path that led up the slopes of the terrifying peaks to the west, but I didn't resist the decision of the others to try the eastern route. I told myself that, if nothing else, the easier trek to the east would be a good training mission for this more difficult journey to come. In truth, I think it was simpler than that. I had suppressed my anxieties and my maddening urge to escape too long. I couldn't stay at the crash site one moment longer. The idea of leaving this place, no matter what direction we headed, was too attractive to resist. If the others insisted on going east, I would go with them. I would do anything to be *anyplace* but here. But, deep down, I knew this trek was nothing more than a prelude, and I worried it would cost us precious time. All of us were growing weaker by the hour, and a few seemed to be sinking at an alarming rate. Coche Inciarte was one of the weakest. Coche, a longtime fan of the Old Christians, was one of the ones who dwelt in the background. He was famous for bumming cigarettes and wheedling his way into the warmest sleeping positions, but always with great charm, and it was impossible not to like him. Coche had an open and amiable spirit, a sharp wit, and an irresistible smile. His jovial spirit brightened our mood even in the darkest moments, and his gentle humor was a good buffer for the more aggressive personalities in the group. By diffusing tensions and making us smile, Coche was helping, in his way, to keep us all alive.

Like Numa, Coche was one of those who had refused to eat when we first cut meat from the bodies of the dead. He had changed his mind a few days later, but he was still so repulsed by the idea of eating human flesh that he had never been able to force down enough food to keep himself strong. He had grown shockingly thin, and his immune system had been so severely compromised that his body could no longer fight off infection. As a result, minor wounds on his legs had gone septic, and now large, fierce boils bulged from his reed-thin legs.

"What do you think?" he asked me, as he drew his pantleg to his knee and swiveled a calf flirtatiously from side to side. "Pretty skinny, huh? Would you go for a girl with legs as skinny as these?" He had to be in great pain from those angry sores on his legs, and I knew he was as frightened and weak as any of us, but still, he was Coche, and he still found a way to make me laugh.

As bad as Coche might have been, Roy Harley seemed worse. Roy also found it hard to eat human flesh, and so his tall, broad-shouldered frame had been rapidly stripped of fat and muscle. Now he walked with a hunched and uncertain stride, as if his bones were a flimsy collection of sticks held together by pale, sagging skin. Roy's mental state was also deteriorating. He had always been a rugged and courageous player for the Old Christians, but the mountain had depleted all his emotional reserves, and now he seemed to live constantly at the brink of hysterics, jumping at noises, weeping at the slightest provocation, and always with his face drawn tight in a grimace of apprehension and extreme despair.

Many of the younger boys were weakening, especially Moncho Sabella, but Arturo and Rafael were the worst off, by far. Although he had suffered terribly from the first minute of the crash, Rafael had lost none of his fighting spirit. He remained courageous and defiant, and he still began every day with a loud proclamation of his intention to survive, a brave gesture from which we all drew strength. Arturo, on the other hand, had grown even quieter and more introspective than usual, and when I sat with him now, I sensed he was nearing the end of his fight.

"How are you feeling, Arturo?"

"I'm so cold, Nando," he said. "There's not much pain. I can't feel my legs anymore. It's hard to breathe."

His voice was growing soft and thin, but his eyes brightened as he motioned me closer and spoke with gentle urgency. "I know I am getting closer to God," he said. "Sometimes I feel His presence so close to me. I can feel His love, Nando. There's so much love, I want to cry."

"Try to hold on, Arturo."

"I don't think it will be long for me," he said. "I feel myself being pulled to Him. Soon I will know God, and then I will have the answers to all your questions."

"Can I get you some water, Arturo?"

"Nando, I want you to remember, even in this place, our lives have meaning. Our suffering is not for nothing. Even if we are trapped here forever, we can love our families, and God, and each other as long as we live. Even in this place, our lives are worth living."

Arturo's face was lit with a serene intensity when he said this. I kept my silence, for fear that my voice would crack if I tried to speak.

"You will tell my family that I love them, won't you? That's all that matters to me now."

"You will tell them yourself," I said.

Arturo smiled at the lie. "I am ready, Nando," he continued. "I made my confession to God. My soul is clean. I will die with no sins."

"What's this?" I laughed. "I thought you didn't believe in the kind of God who forgives your sins."

Arturo looked at me and managed a thin, self-deprecating grin. "At a time like this," he said, "it seems wise to cover all the angles."

All through the first week of November, Arturo grew weaker and more distant. His best friend, Pedro Algorta, stayed close to him through it all, bringing him water, keeping him warm, and praying with him. One night, Arturo started to cry softly. When Pedro asked Arturo why he was sobbing, Arturo replied, with a faraway gaze in his eyes, "Because I am so close to God." The following day Arturo developed a high fever. For forty-eight hours he was delirious, slipping in and out of consciousness. On his last night, we helped him down off the hammock so he could sleep beside Pedro, and sometime before morning, Arturo Nogueira, one of the bravest men I've ever known, quietly died in the arms of his best friend.

ON THE MORNING of November 15, Numa, Roberto, Tintin, and I stood outside the fuselage, looking down the valley that sloped off to the east ready to begin our escape. Numa was beside me, and though he was trying to hide it, I could see he was in pain. Since the avalanche, he had forced himself to eat, despite his revulsion, knowing he'd need all his strength for the expedition. Still, like Coche, he could not stomach more than a few scraps at a time—sometimes he could not make himself swallow at all—and while his will remained strong, it was clear that his body had weakened. A few nights earlier, someone trying to make his way across the dark fuselage had stepped on Numa's calf as he lay on the floor. An ugly bruise quickly appeared, and when Roberto saw how badly the leg had swollen, he advised Numa to drop out of the expedition. Numa assured Roberto that the bruise was nothing to be concerned about, and he firmly refused to let us leave without him.

"How are you feeling?" I asked him, after we had gathered our things and said good-bye to the others. "Are you sure you can make it on that leg?"

Numa shrugged. "It's nothing," he said. "I'll be fine."

As we set off down the slope, the weather was overcast and the air was chilly but the winds were light, and despite all my misgivings about the eastern trip, it felt good to be leaving the crash site at last. At first we made good progress moving down the slope, but after an hour or so of hiking, the skies darkened, temperatures dropped, and snow began to squall in violent spirals all around us. In the blink of an eye, a heavy storm rolled over us. Knowing that every second counted, we fought our way back up the slope and stumbled into the fuselage, frightened and half-frozen, just as the storm matured into a full-blown blizzard. As stiff winds rocked the plane, Roberto and I exchanged a sober glance. We understood, without speaking, that if the storm had hit just an hour or two later, trapping us farther from shelter on the open slopes, we would now be dead or dying.

The blizzard, one of the worst we'd had in all our weeks in the Andes, kept us penned in the fuselage for two long days. While we waited out the storm, Roberto grew more concerned with Numa's leg. There were two large sores now, each almost as large as a billiard ball. As Roberto lanced and drained the sores, he realized Numa was in no shape to hike through the mountains.

"Your legs are getting bad," said Roberto. "You'll have to stay behind."

For the first time on the mountain, Numa's temper flared. "My leg is fine!" he shouted. "I can bear the pain!"

"Your leg is septic," said Roberto. "If you would eat more, your body would be strong enough to fight off the infection."

"I am not staying behind!"

Roberto glared at Numa and, with his characteristic bluntness, said, "You are too weak. You will only slow us down. We can't afford to take you."

Numa turned to me. "Nando, please, I can make it. Don't make me stay."

I shook my head. "I'm sorry, Numa," I said, "I agree with Roberto. Your leg is bad. You should stay here." As others gave the same advice, Numa fumed and drew into himself. I knew how badly he wanted to be with us, and how hard it would be for him to watch us leave. I knew I would not be able to stand such a disappointment, and I hoped this setback would not crush Numa's spirit.

THE BLIZZARD FINALLY spent itself, and on the morning of November 17 we woke to find a clear, calm day. Without much fanfare, Roberto, Tintin, and I gathered our things and set off once more down the slopes, this time in bright sunshine and light breezes. There was little talking. I quickly fell into the rhythm of my strides, and as the miles passed the only sound in the world was the crunching of my rugby shoes in the snow. Roberto, who was dragging the sled, had pulled ahead of us, and after about an hour and a half of hiking I heard him shout. He was standing on a tall snowdrift, and when we joined him there and looked beyond the drift we saw what he was pointing at—the remains of the Fairchild's tail section were lying a few hundred yards ahead. In minutes we had reached the tail. Suitcases were scattered everywhere, and we tore through them to get at the treasures inside: socks, sweaters, warm trousers. Happily we tore off the tattered, filthy rags on our backs and dressed in clean clothes.

Inside the tail we found more luggage, filled with more clothing. We also found some rum, a box of chocolates, some cigarettes, and a small camera loaded with film. The plane's small galley area was in the tail, and there we found three small meat pastries that we immediately devoured, and a moldy sandwich wrapped in plastic, which we saved for later.

We were so excited by all this unexpected booty that we almost forgot about the radio batteries, which Carlos Roque had told us were somewhere in the tail. After a short search, we found the batteries in a recessed space behind a hatch in the tail's exterior hull. They looked larger than I expected. We also found some empty Coca-Cola crates in the luggage hold behind the galley, which we took outside and used as fuel for a fire. Roberto roasted some of the meat we'd brought with us, and we ate with great appetite. We peeled the mold off the sandwiches we'd found, and ate them, too. As night fell, we spread clothes from the suitcases on the floor of the luggage hold and laid down to rest. Working with wires he'd stripped from the walls of the tail section, Roberto connected the airplane's batteries to a light fixture bolted to the ceiling, and for the first time we had light after sunset. We read some magazines and comic books we had salvaged from the luggage, and I took some pictures of Roberto and Tintin with the camera we had found. I thought that if we didn't make it out alive, someone might find the camera and develop the film, and they would know that we had lived, at least for a while. For some reason, this was important to me.

It was luxuriously warm and spacious in the luggage hold—what a pleasure to stretch my legs, and to roll into any position I chose—and soon we grew drowsy. Roberto extinguished the light, we closed our eyes, and all of us enjoyed the best night of sleep we'd had since the plane fell into the mountains. In the morning we were tempted to stay for a while in these cozy quarters, but we reminded ourselves of the others and their hopes for our expedition, and soon after waking, we were once again trekking east.

It snowed that morning, but by late morning the skies cleared, the sun was hot on our shoulders, and we perspired heavily in our warm clothing as we hiked. After so many weeks of frigid temperatures, the sudden heat exhausted us quickly, and at noon we were forced to rest in the shade of a rocky outcrop. We ate some of our meat and melted some snow for water, but even after we'd refreshed ourselves, none of us had the energy to continue, so we decided to camp at the rock for the night.

The sun grew stronger as the afternoon passed, but at sunset, temperatures began to plummet. We dug into the snow for shelter and wrapped up in our blankets, but as the hard chill of night fell upon us, these things seemed to offer us no protection at all. This was my first night outside the fuselage, and it only took a few moments to understand how terribly Gustavo, Numa, and Maspons must have suffered when they spent their long night on the open slopes. Our night was no better. The cold bore down on us so aggressively that I feared my blood had frozen solid in my veins. Huddling together for warmth, we shuddered in each other's arms. We discovered that by making a sandwich of our bodies—one of us lying between the others—we could keep the guy in the middle of the sandwich warm. We lay this way for hours, taking turns at the middle position, and though we didn't sleep at all, we survived until daylight. When morning finally came, we climbed out of our poor shelter and warmed ourselves in the first rays of the sun, staggered by what we'd lived through, and stunned to be alive.

"We won't last another night like that," said Roberto. He was gazing to the east, at the mountains that seemed to have grown larger and more distant as we trekked.

"What are you thinking?" I asked.

"I don't think this valley ever turns west," he said. "We are only walking deeper into the cordillera."

"You may be right," I said. "But the others are counting on us. Maybe we should go a little farther."

Roberto scowled. "It's hopeless!" he snapped, and I heard that angry falsetto creeping into his voice. "Are we any good to them if we're dead?"

"Then what should we do?"

"Let's get the batteries from the tail and take them to the Fairchild," he said. "We can drag them on the sled. If we can make the radio work, we can save ourselves without risking our lives."

I had no more faith in the radio than I had had in the prospects of trekking east, but I told myself we had to explore every hope, no matter how slim. So we gathered our things and returned to the tail section. It took only moments to remove the batteries from the plane and set them side by side on our Samsonite sled. But when Roberto tried to drag the sled forward, it dug deep into the snow and wouldn't budge.

"Damn, these are too heavy," he said. "There is no way we can drag them up to the plane."

"We can't carry them," I said.

Roberto shook his head. "No," he said, "but we can get the radio from the Fairchild and bring it here. We'll bring Roy with us. Maybe he can figure out how to connect it to the batteries."

I didn't like the sound of this. I was certain the radio was damaged beyond repair, and I feared that Roberto's attempts to fix it would only distract him from what we now knew more clearly than ever was our only chance to survive: climb the mountains to the west.

"Do you really think we can make it work?" I asked.

"How do I know?" snapped Roberto. "But it's worth a try."

"I'm worried we will waste too much time."

"Do you have to argue about everything?" he cried. "This radio could save our lives."

"Okay," I said, "I will help you. But if it doesn't work, then we climb. Do we have a deal?"

Roberto nodded, and after allowing ourselves two more luxurious nights in the tail's luggage hold, we set off in the afternoon of November 21 to climb our way back to the fuselage. The walk down the valley from the crash site had been easy—so easy, in fact, that I hadn't appreciated the steepness of the slopes. Now, just minutes into our uphill trek, we found ourselves pushed to the limits of our stamina. In places we faced inclines as sharp as forty-five degrees, and the snow was often as deep as my hips. Battling up the mountain quickly sapped my strength. I was gasping for air, my muscles were burning with fatigue, and I found myself forced to rest for thirty seconds or more after every few steps. Our progress was excruciatingly slow; it had taken us less than two hours to descend from the Fairchild to the tail; it would take us twice as long to make the same trip in reverse.

We reached the crash site in midafternoon, and the survivors at the fuselage gave us a somber greeting. It was six days since we had left them, and they had hoped we'd be close to civilization by now. Our return had dashed those hopes, but that was not the only reason for their low spirits; while we were gone, Rafael Echavarren had died.

"At the end he was delirious," Carlitos told me, "He kept calling to his father to come get him. On his last night, I made him pray with me and that calmed him a little. A few hours later he began to gasp for air, then he was gone. Gustavo and I tried to revive him, but it was too late."

Rafael's death was a serious blow. He had become such a symbol of courage and defiance for us that to see him struck down after all his brave resistance was one more reason to believe that the mountain would sooner or later claim us all. Was there no rhyme or reason to our suffering? This one struggles bravely and is taken away, that one doesn't fight at all and still survives? Since the avalanche, some of the others had clung to the belief that God had seen nineteen of us through that disaster because we were the ones he'd chosen to survive. Rafael's passing made it harder to believe that God was paying any attention at all.

As we settled into the fuselage that night, Roberto explained the reason for our return. "The route to the east is no good," he said. "It only leads deeper into the mountains. But we found the tail section, and most of the luggage. We brought warm clothes for everyone. And lots of cigarettes. But the good news is we found the batteries."

The others listened quietly as Roberto explained his plan to fix the Fairchild's radio. It was worth a try, they all agreed, but there was little enthusiasm in their reaction. There was a new look in their eyes now, of weary acceptance. Some of them had the dim, vacant stare I'd seen in pictures of concentration camp survivors. Just weeks ago, these were all vigorous young men. Now they stooped and wobbled when they walked, like feeble old men, and their clothing hung loose on the hard angles of their bony hips and shoulders. They were looking more and more like animated corpses, and I knew that I looked no better. I felt their hopes were flickering, and I couldn't blame them. We had suffered so much, and the signs were so bad: despite his brave resistance, Rafael was dead. Our escape to the east had failed. Two attempts to climb the mountains to the west had ended in near disaster. It seemed that every door we tried to walk through was slammed in our faces. Yes, they agreed, we should try the radio. But none of them seemed to see any reason to expect that it would work.

The next morning, Roberto and I started working to remove the Fairchild's radio. The cockpit was packed with dials, toggles, and complex instrumentation, and in our ignorance it took some guesswork to decide what was part of the radio and what was not. Finally we figured out that the radio was made up of two components, one anchored in the cockpit's control panel and the other hidden behind a plastic panel in the wall of the luggage compartment. The component in the control panel, to which the earphones and microphone were attached, came out easily after we'd removed a few screws. The second component, tucked into a dark, cramped, and shallow cavity in the wall, was anchored more firmly and was much more difficult to get at. Working clumsily with our fingers and the bits of metal and plastic we used for tools, we struggled to loosen the bolts and clips holding the transmitter in place, but it was two frustrating days before we were able to remove it from the wall. When we finally pulled it free and set it beside the component from the cockpit, I saw the futility of our efforts.

"Carajo!" I cried. "Look at this mess!"

Bristling from the back of each component was a crazy tangle of tiny electrical wires. "This is impossible, Roberto! How will we ever match these wires?"

Roberto ignored me, and carefully counted the wires on each component.

"There are sixty-seven wires coming out of the back of this piece," he said, "and sixty-seven coming out of the transmitter."

"But which wire connects to which?" I said. "It's impossible! There are too many combinations."

"Do you see these markings?" he replied. "Each wire has a different mark. The marks will tell us which wires match."

"I don't know, Roberto," I said. "All this time we are spending, and we don't even know if the radio still works."

Roberto's eyes flashed with anger. "This radio can save our lives!" he snapped. "We owe it to ourselves to try this before we go off blundering into the mountains and throw our lives away."

"Okay! Okay!" I said, to calm him. "*Está bien.* But let's ask Roy to take a look."

I called Roy over and showed him the radio. He frowned and shook his head.

"I don't think this can be fixed," he said.

"We *are* going to fix it," Roberto replied. "*You* are going to fix it."

"I can't fix this!" Roy cried, his voice growing thin and shrill in protest. "It's much too complicated. I don't know the first thing about a radio like this!"

"Get hold of yourself, Roy," said Roberto. "We're going to take this radio to the tail. You are coming with us. We are going to make this radio work and we are going to use it to call for help."

Roy's eyes went wide with terror at the news. "I can't go there!" he shrieked, "I'm too weak! Look at me! I can barely walk. Please, I won't make it to the tail and back!"

"You'll make it because you have to," Roberto replied.

"But this radio is ruined!" he wailed. "It's impossible!"

"Maybe it is," said Roberto, "but we have to try, and you're the only one who has a chance of making it work."

Roy's face crumpled and he began to sob. The thought of leaving the fuselage terrified him, and in the following days he pleaded with anyone who would listen that he should be excused from the mission. Fito and the cousins were firm with him, insisting that he go. They pressured him to think of the good of the others. They even forced him to train for the mission by walking back and forth outside the fuselage. Roy reluctantly obeyed, but often he would weep as he paced in the snow.

Roy was no coward. I knew that about him long before the crash, from the way he played rugby and from how he lived his life. In the early days of our ordeal, while he was still strong, he had been a productive member of our group. Roy had been at Marcelo's side as they organized the plane in the immediate aftermath of the crash, and had helped Marcelo with the difficult work of building the wall that kept us all from freezing. And I couldn't forget that if not for Roy's quick action in the wake of the avalanche, we all would have suffocated beneath the snow. But he was very young. I knew his suffering had shattered his nerves, and it was clear to see how the ordeal had ravaged his body. He was a skeleton covered in skin now, one of the thinnest and weakest among us, and I should have felt as much compassion for him as I felt for the others. In all our time on the mountain, I had rarely grown angry with any of my fellow survivors. I understood their fears, and the pressures they were under, especially the younger guys, so it was easy to be patient with them when their suffering made them selfish or lazy or afraid. Roy had suffered as much as any of the others, and he deserved the same consideration from me, but as he weakened and his emotional state continued to crumble, I found myself infuriated by his frequent displays of distress, and for some reason it became more and more difficult for me to show him kindness. So, when he begged me, in desperation, not to make him go with us to the tail, I didn't even look him in the eyes.

"We are leaving soon," I snapped. "You'd better be ready."

Roberto spent several days studying the radio, and as I waited for him to finish, I grew more and more concerned about Numa. Since we had dropped him from the expeditionary team, his spirits had tumbled. Withdrawn into a brooding silence, he had grown furious with himself and the way his body had betrayed him. He was irritable and morose, and, worst of all, he refused to eat anything at all. As a result, he lost weight more rapidly, and the sores on his legs got worse. There were two large boils on his leg now, each larger than a golf ball, and each of them clearly infected. But what worried me most was the look of resignation in his eyes. Numa was one of the strongest and most selfless of all the survivors, and he had battled as bravely as anyone to keep us all alive. But now that he could battle for us no longer, and had only himself to care for, he seemed to be losing heart. One night I sat beside him and tried to raise his spirits.

"Are you going to eat something for me, Numa?" I asked. "We are going to the tail soon. It would be nice to see you eat before I leave."

He shook his head feebly. "I can't. It is too painful for me."

"It's painful for all of us," I said, "but you must do it. You must remember it is only meat now."

"I only ate before to strengthen myself for the trip," he said. "What reason do I have to force myself now?"

"Don't give up," I told him. "Hold on. We are going to get out of here."

Numa shook his head. "I am so weak, Nando. I can't even stand anymore. I don't think I'm going to last much longer."

"Don't talk that way, Numa. You will not die."

Numa sighed. "It's okay, Nando," he said. "I have examined my life, and I know that if I die tomorrow, I have still had wonderful years."

I laughed. "That's exactly what Panchito used to say," I said. "And he lived his life according to those words. He was reckless, daring; he always thought that things would go his way. And usually they did."

"He was famous for that," said Numa. "How old was he?"

"He was only eighteen. But he lived so many lifetimes, had so many adventures, and, *macho,* he made love to so many beautiful girls."

"Maybe that's why God took him," said Numa. "So that there would be a few girls for the rest of us."

"There will be plenty of girls for you, Numa," I said. "But first you must eat, and live. I want you to live."

Numa smiled and nodded. "I will try," he said. But later, when they brought him some meat, I saw him wave it away.

We left the next morning at 8:00 a.m., and made fast progress down the slope. As we approached the tail, I spotted a red leather bag lying in the snow, and immediately recognized it as my mother's cosmetics case. Inside I found some lipstick that I could use to protect my lips from the sun, some candy, and a little sewing kit. I stashed these items in our knapsacks and kept hiking. Less than two hours after leaving the Fairchild, we were once again at the tail.

We rested that first day. The next morning, Roy and Roberto started working on the radio. They worked hard, trying to make the proper connections to the battery, but they were feeling their way by trial and error, and just when it seemed they were making progress, the wires would flash and sizzle and we'd hear a loud electrical pop. Roberto would swear and badger Roy to be more careful, and they'd start over.

Daytime temperatures were milder now, and the snow around the tail was melting fast. Suitcases that had been buried only days ago, when we first found the fuselage, were now lying in plain view. While Roy and Roberto tinkered with the radio, Tintin and I rummaged through the suitcases scattered around the tail. In one of the bags we found two bottles of rum. We opened one of the bottles and took a few swigs.

"We'll save the other," I said. "We can use it when we climb."

Tintin nodded. We both knew the radio would never work, but Roy and Roberto were still working furiously. They tinkered with it all afternoon and into the next morning. I was getting anxious to finish this experiment, and get back to the fuselage, where we could prepare for the climb.

"How much longer do you think, Roberto?" I asked.

He glanced at me with irritation in his eyes. "It will take as long as it takes," he grumbled.

"We're running low on food," I said. "I think Tintin and I should go back and get more."

"That's a good idea," he said. "We'll keep working."

Tintin and I gathered our things, and in minutes we were climbing up the valley toward the Fairchild. Once again I was struck by how much more difficult it was to climb these slopes than it was to descend them. We trudged for hours, stopping frequently to gasp for air, and finally reached the plane in late afternoon. Once again we received a sullen welcome, and I couldn't help noticing that the others seemed to have grown even weaker and more listless than when we'd left them.

"We came for more meat," I said. "The radio is taking longer than expected."

Fito frowned. "We are running low on food. We've been looking everywhere for the bodies that were lost in the avalanche, but the snow is so deep and we are so tired. We even climbed up the slopes several times to fetch the bodies that Gustavo found when he climbed."

"Don't worry," I said, "Tintin and I will dig."

"How is it going with the radio?"

"Not well," I said. "I don't think it is going to work."

"We are running out of time," said Fito. "Every one of us is weak. The food won't last much longer."

"We need to go west," I said. "It may be impossible, but it is our only chance. We have to go as soon as possible."

"Does Roberto think the same?"

"I don't know what he is thinking," I said. "You know Roberto. He will do what he wants to do."

"If he refuses," said Fito, "I will go with you."

I smiled warmly at Fito. "That's brave of you," I said, "but with those sores in your ass, you can barely walk fifteen feet. No, we must persuade Roberto to go west, and to go very soon."

Tintin and I stayed at the fuselage for two days, digging through the snow in search of fresh bodies. When we found what we were looking for, Fito and his cousins cut the meat for us, and after resting a while, we hiked down the glacier once more. We reached the tail section at midmorning and found Roy and Roberto hard at work on the radio. They thought they had the connections right, but when they powered up the radio, they heard nothing but static. Roy thought the radio's antenna, which had been damaged in the crash, might be defective, so he made a new one from copper wire he stripped from the electrical circuits in the tail. Roy and Roberto attached the new antenna to the Fairchild's radio, and stretched the long copper wires on the snow. The radio worked no better. Roy disconnected the antenna and attached it to the small transistor radio, which he'd brought along. The long antenna gave the transistor a strong signal. Roy tuned in a station with some music that we liked, and went back to work. Moments later the music was interrupted by a bulletin, and we heard the surprising news that the Uruguayan air force was sending a specially equipped Douglas C-47 to search for us.

Roy whooped in joy at the news. Roberto turned to me, smiling broadly.

"Did you hear that, Nando!? They're looking for us!"

"Don't get your hopes up," I said. "Remember what Gustavo said—from the slopes the Fairchild is just another speck on the glacier."

"But this is a specially equipped plane," said Roberto.

"And the Andes are huge," I said. "They don't know where we are. Even if they do find us, it could take months."

"We need to make a sign for them," Roberto said, ignoring my skeptical glare. In minutes he had us gathering suitcases and arranging them on the snow in the shape of a large cross.

When we'd finished, I asked Roberto about the radio.

"I don't think we can fix it," he said. "We should go back to the plane."

"And get ready to go west," I said, "as we agreed."

Roberto nodded absently and went to gather his things. As I rounded up my own gear, Tintin came to me with a small rectangular piece of cloth insulation he had taken from the tail. "This stuff is wrapped around all the pipes in there," he said. "There must be some way we can use it."

I felt the material between my fingers. It was light and strong, fluffy inside, with a tough, smooth fabric cover. "Maybe we can use it to line our clothes," I said. "It seems like it would keep us warm."

Tintin nodded, and we went into the tail. In moments we had stripped all the insulation from the pipes and stuffed it into our knapsacks. As we worked, we heard a racket outside, and when we looked, we saw Roy angrily stomping the radio to pieces.

"He should save his energy," I said to Tintin. "This climb is going to be tough."

We set off up the slope in midmorning. The skies were overcast as we departed, and the ceiling was very low, but temperatures were mild and the weather was calm. Roberto and Tintin were in the lead, Roy was straggling behind me. As before, fighting up the slope through the knee-deep snow was exhausting, and we stopped often to rest. I knew Roy was suffering from the effort, so I kept my eye on him, and slowed my pace to keep him from slipping too far behind. About an hour into our trek, I glanced at the sky as I rested, and was startled by what I saw. The clouds had swollen and turned an ominous dark gray. They hung so low I felt I could touch them. Then, as I watched, the clouds rushed at us, like the crest of a killer wave. Before I could react, the sky seemed to fall, and we were swept up in one of the blitzkrieg blizzards that those who know the Andes call a "white wind." In a matter of seconds, everything was chaos. The temperature plummeted. The wind shoved and tugged at me so fiercely I had to stagger back and forth to keep from falling down. Snow swirled in thick whirlpools around me, stinging my face and robbing me of my bearings. I squinted into the blizzard, but visibility was close to zero now, and I saw no sign of the others. For a moment I panicked. "Which way is up?" I asked myself. "Which way do I go?"

Then I heard Roberto's voice, sounding faint and distant in the huge roar of the storm.

"Nando! Can you hear me?"

"Roberto! I am here!"

I looked behind me. Roy had vanished.

"Roy? Where are you?"

There was no response. About thirty feet behind me, I saw a blurred gray heap in the snow, and I realized Roy had fallen.

"Roy!" I bellowed. "Come on!"

He didn't move, so I stumbled down the slope to the spot where he lay. He was curled up in the snow, his knees drawn up to his chest and his arms wrapped around his body.

"Move your ass!" I shouted. "This storm will kill us if we don't keep moving!"

"I can't," Roy whimpered. "I can't go another step."

"Get up, you bastard!" I shouted. "We'll die here!"

Roy looked up at me, his face twisted into a grimace of fear. "No, please," he sobbed, "I can't. Just leave me."

The storm was gathering power by the second, and as I stood over Roy, the winds gusted so ferociously I thought they would lift me off my feet. We were trapped in a total white-out now. I had completely lost my sense of direction, and my only hope of making it back to the fuselage was to follow the tracks Roberto and Tintin were leaving. But the heavy snow was rapidly burying their footprints. I knew they would not wait for us—they were fighting for their lives, too—and I knew that each second I stayed with Roy brought us both closer to disaster. I looked down at Roy. His shoulders were quaking as he wept, and he was already half-covered in snow.

I have to leave him or I will die, I thought. *Can I do it? Do I have it in me to leave him here to die?* I did not answer these questions in words, but with action. Without another thought, I turned away from Roy and followed the tracks of the others up the slope. As I staggered against the force of the winds, I pictured Roy lying in the snow. I thought of him watching my shadow disappear into the storm. It would be the last thing he ever saw. *How long will it take for him to lose consciousness?* I wondered. *How long will he suffer?* I was perhaps fifteen yards away now, and I couldn't erase the picture of him from my mind: slumped on the snow, so helpless, so pathetic, so *defeated*. I felt a wild surge of contempt for his weakness and lack of courage, or at least that was what it felt like then. In retrospect, things look quite different. Roy was no weakling. He had suffered more than most of us and had found the strength to endure, but he was so young and his body had been ravaged so badly that all his resources, physical and mental, had simply been overwhelmed. We were all being forced toward our limits, but Roy had been pushed too hard and too fast. It bothers me now that I did not show him more patience and encouragement in the mountains, and I have realized, after years of reflection, that the reason I treated him as I did was that I saw too much of myself in him. I know now that the grating whine in Roy's trembling voice was unbearable to me because it was such a vivid expression of the terror I felt in my own heart, and that the twisted grimace he wore on his face maddened me only because it was a mirror of my own despair. When Roy surrendered and lay down in the snow I knew he had reached the end of his struggle. He had found the place where death would take him at last. Thinking of Roy lying still on the slope, slowly disappearing beneath the snow, I was forced to wonder how close my own moment of surrender might be. Where was the place where my own will and strength would fail? Where, and when, would I give up the struggle and lie down, frightened and defeated like Roy, in the soft comfort of the snow?

This was the true source of my anger: Roy was showing me my future, and in that moment I hated him for it.

Of course, there was no time for such introspective thought on that storm-swept mountain. I was acting on instinct alone, and as I pictured Roy sobbing in the snow, all the scorn and derision I had felt toward him in the last few weeks exploded into a murderous fury. Impulsively, I swore like a madman into the gusting winds. *"Mierda! Carajo! La reconcha de la reputisima madre! La reputa madre que lo recontra mil y una parió!"* I was out of my mind with anger, and before I knew it, I was crashing down the slope to where Roy had fallen. When I reached him, I kicked him savagely in the ribcage. I fell on him, slamming my knees into his side. Kneeling on him, I balled my fist and battered him with hard punches. As he rolled and screamed in the snow, I abused him verbally just as viciously as I attacked him with my fists.

"You son of a whore!" I shouted, "You filthy bastard! Get on your fucking feet, you miserable motherfucker. Stand up or I'll kill you! You bastard, I swear it." I had struggled, since my first moment on the mountain, to maintain my composure and avoid wasting energy venting my angers and fears. But now, as I hovered over Roy, I felt my soul emptying itself of all the fear and venom that my time on the mountain had given me. I stomped Roy's hips and shoulders with my rugby boots. I shoved him into the snow. I called him every foul name I could think of, and insulted his mother in ways I do not like to remember. Roy wept and screamed as I abused him, but finally he rose to his feet. I shoved him forward, so hard that he almost fell again. And I kept shoving him roughly, forcing him to stumble up the slope a few feet at a time.

We battled through the blizzard. Roy suffered terribly from the exertion, and my own strength was rapidly fading. The aggressiveness of the storm was frightening. As I struggled to breathe the thin air, the swirling winds would snatch my breath away, then force it down my throat again, forcing me to sputter and choke as if I were drowning. The cold hammered me, and wading through the deep, heavy snow pushed me beyond exhaustion. Soon my muscles were utterly spent, and each step required a monumental act of will. I kept Roy in front of me, where I could keep shoving him forward, and we climbed foot by foot. But after a few hundred yards he slumped forward and fell, and I knew he had spent the last of his strength. This time I didn't try to rouse him. Instead I reached around him and lifted him from the snow. Even through all the layers of his clothing, I could feel how thin and weak he had become, and my heart softened. "Think of your mother, Roy," I told him, with my lips pressed to his ear so he could hear me in the storm. "If you want to see her again, you must suffer for her now." His jaw was slack, and his eyes were rolling up under their eyelids. He was on the verge of passing out, but still he managed a feeble nod: he would fight. For me, this moment of bravery was as remarkable as any of the other acts of courage and strength that we saw in the mountains, and now, when I think of Roy, I always think of him in this moment, as a hero.

Roy leaned against me, and together we climbed. He struggled with all he had, but soon we reached a point where the slope swept upward in a sharp incline. Roy looked at me calmly, in resignation, knowing the climb was simply beyond his strength. I squinted into the stinging snow, trying to gauge the steepness of the rise, then I tightened my grip around Roy's waist, and with what little strength I still had, I lifted him off the ground, so that I bore his weight on my shoulder. Then, taking one slow, labored step at a time, I carried him up the rise. Light was fading now, and the tracks of the others were difficult to see. I climbed by intuition, and as I felt my way toward the crash site, I was constantly tormented by the thought that I had drifted off course and was walking into the wild. But finally, as the last lights of afternoon were fading, I saw the faint silhouette of the Fairchild through the heavy snow. I was dragging Roy more than carrying him now, but with the plane in sight I felt a boost of energy, and at last we reached the plane. The others took Roy from my shoulders as we stumbled into the fuselage. Roberto and Tintin had collapsed on the floor, and I fell heavily beside them. I couldn't stop shivering, and my muscles burned and quivered with the most profound exhaustion I'd ever felt. *I've burned myself out,* I thought. *I will never recover. I will never have the strength to climb out of here.* But I was too tired to care. I burrowed into the heap of bodies pressing around me, drawing warmth from the others, and for the first time I fell asleep quickly and slept soundly for hours.

In the morning, I rested. The days I'd spent away from the Fairchild had given me perspective, and now I saw with fresh eyes the gruesomeness that had become a normal part of our daily lives. There were piles of bones scattered outside the fuselage. Large body parts—someone's forearm, a human leg from hip to toes—were stored near the opening of the fuselage for easy access. Strips of fat were spread on the roof of the fuselage to dry in the sun. And for the first time I saw human skulls in the bone pile. When we first started eating human flesh, we consumed mostly small pieces of meat cut from the large muscles. But as time passed and the food supply diminished, we had no choice but to broaden our diet. For some time, we had been eating livers, kidneys, and hearts, but meat was in such short supply now that we would have to split skulls to get at the brains inside. While we'd been away, some of the survivors had been driven by their hunger to eat things we couldn't stomach before: the lungs, parts of the hands and feet, and even the blood clots that form in the large blood vessels of the hearts. To the ordinary mind, these actions may seem incomprehensibly repulsive, but the instinct to survive runs very deep, and when death is so near, a human being gets used to anything. Still, despite the extreme depths of their hunger, and their desperate efforts to scour the slopes for bodies that had been lost, they had not broken their promise to Javier and me: the bodies of my mother, my sister, and Liliana, all in easy reach, had not been touched; they still lay whole under the snow. It moved me to think that even at the brink of starvation, a promise still meant something to my friends. The mountains had caused us such loss and anguish. They had stolen away our best friends and loved ones, forced us to face intolerable horrors, and changed us in ways that would take years to understand. But despite all the suffering my friends had endured, the principles of friendship, loyalty, compassion, and honor still mattered to them. The Andes had done so much to crush us, and each of us knew he was clinging to life by a thread. But we hadn't surrendered to primitive instincts of self-survival. We were still fighting together, as a team. Our bodies were weakening, but our humanity survived. We hadn't let the mountains steal away our souls.

IN THE FIRST WEEK of December, we began to prepare in earnest for the westward climb. Fito and the cousins cut meat for us and stored it in the snow, while Antonio, Roberto, and I gathered the clothing and equipment we would need for the journey. An odd mixture of excitement and gloom hung over us as we readied ourselves for the final expedition. The earlier attempts to climb, and our failed expedition to the east, had shown us the daunting power of the Andes, but they had also schooled us in the fundamentals of mountain survival. We were still spectacularly ill equipped to challenge the wilderness around us, but at least we understood a little more clearly just how dangerous the mountains could be. We knew, for example, that we would face two great challenges on our journey. The first would be the severe demands that high-altitude climbing exerts upon the body. We had learned, from hard experience, that the thin mountain air turns even the slightest effort into a grueling test of stamina and will. There was nothing we could do about that, except to leave before we grew too weak, and to pace ourselves on the climb.

The second challenge would be to protect ourselves from exposure, especially after sundown. At this time of year we could expect daytime temperatures well above freezing, but the nights were still cold enough to kill us, and we knew now that we couldn't expect to find shelter on the open slopes. We needed a way to survive the long nights without freezing, and the quilted batts of insulation we'd taken from the tail section gave us our solution. The insulation was in small, rectangular patches, each about the size of a magazine. Since returning from the tail, we'd been stuffing the insulation between layers of our clothing, and we found that, despite their lightness and thinness, they were very effective in shielding us from the cold at night. As we brainstormed about the trip, we realized we could sew the patches together to create a large warm quilt. Then we realized that by folding the quilt in half and stitching the seams together, we could create an insulated sleeping bag large enough for all three expeditionaries to sleep in. With the warmth of three bodies trapped by the insulating cloth, we might be able to weather the coldest nights.

Carlitos took on the challenge. His mother had taught him to sew when he was a boy, and with the needles and thread from the sewing kit I'd found in my mother's cosmetics case, he began to work. It was meticulous labor, and he had to make sure all his stitching was strong enough to withstand hard use. To speed the progress, Carlitos taught others to sew, and we all took our turns, but many of us were too thick-fingered for the job; Carlitos, Coche, Gustavo, and Fito turned out to be our best and fastest tailors.

While the work progressed, Tintin and I prepared for the trek, but Roberto was slow in gathering his gear. Worried that he was having second thoughts about the climb, I approached him one afternoon while he was resting outside the fuselage.

"The sleeping bag will be finished soon," I said. "Everything else is ready. We should leave as soon as possible."

Roberto shook his head. "It would be foolish to leave just as they are looking for us again," he said.

"We had a deal," I said. "The radio didn't work, now it's time to go west."

"Yes, we will go west," he replied. "Let's just give them some time."

"How much time?"

"Let's give them ten days," said Roberto. "It only makes sense to give them a chance."

"Look, Roberto," I said, "no one knows better than you that we don't have that much time. In ten days, half of us could be dead."

Roberto shot me a belligerent glare. "So what is your brilliant idea, Nando?" he snapped. "To stomp off into the mountains just when we know a rescue team is trying to find us?"

"They're not a rescue team," I answered. "They're looking for bodies. They're in no hurry to find us."

Roberto scowled and turned away. "It's not time," he muttered. "It's too soon."

BY THE MIDDLE of the first week in December, the sleeping bag was finished. Our gear was all gathered, the meat for the trip was cut and packed into socks, and everyone knew the time had come for our departure—everyone but Roberto, who found one maddening reason after another to delay the trip. First he complained that the sleeping bag wasn't strong enough, and insisted it be reinforced. Then he said he couldn't leave while Coche and Roy and the others needed his medical attention so badly. Finally he declared that he hadn't rested up sufficiently for the climb, and would need several more days to gather his strength. Fito and the cousins tried to pressure him into action, but Roberto angrily rejected their authority. He lashed out at anyone, in fact, who suggested he was dragging his feet, and he loudly made it clear that he would not leave one moment before he was ready.

As the rest of us grew more annoyed with his stubbornness, Roberto became increasingly tense and confrontational. He bullied the weaker boys. He picked fights without provocation. Once, after some trivial squabble, he grabbed his close friend Alvaro Mangino by the hair and slammed him against the wall. Moments later, full of remorse, he apologized to Mangino and they embraced, but I had seen enough. I followed Roberto and waited until we were alone.

"This can't continue," I told him. "You know it's time to go."

"Yes," said Roberto, "we will go soon, but we must wait for the weather to improve."

"I'm tired of waiting," I said softly.

"I told you," he snapped, "we'll leave when the weather is better!"

I was trying to stay calm, but Roberto's aggressive tone set me off. "Look around!" I shouted. "We are running out of food! Our friends are dying. Coche has started to rave at night. He doesn't have much time left. Roy is even worse, skin and bone. Javier is fading, and the younger guys, Sabella, Mangino, Bobby, they are all so weak. And look at *us!* You and I are wasting away by the hour. We have to climb before we're too weak to stand!"

"You listen to me, Nando," Roberto shot back, "we had a bad storm two days ago. Do you remember that? If it had caught us on the slopes, it would have killed us."

"And an avalanche would kill us," I said, "or we could fall into a crevasse. We could loose our footing and fall a thousand feet onto the rocks! We can't eliminate these risks, Roberto, and we can't wait any longer!"

Roberto glanced away, dismissing my comments. I rose to my feet.

"I picked a date, Roberto. I am leaving the morning of December twelfth. If you aren't ready, I'll go without you."

"You can't go without me, you stupid bastard."

"You heard me," I said, as I walked away. "I'm leaving on the twelfth. With you or without you."

DECEMBER 9 WAS my twenty-third birthday. That night in the fuselage, the guys gave me one of the cigars we'd found in the luggage at the tail.

"It's not Punta del Este, as we planned," joked Carlitos, "but that *is* a Havana cigar."

"The quality is lost on me," I said, choking as I inhaled. "All I know is that the smoke is warm."

"We missed our birthdays," said Carlitos, "but I know in my heart we will be with our families for Christmas. You will make it, Nando. I am certain of it."

I didn't answer Carlitos, and I was glad the shadows of the fuselage hid the doubt in my eyes. "Get some sleep," I told him, then I blew a cloud of expensive Cuban smoke in his face.

On December 10, Gustavo and I spoke with concern about Numa. "He asked me to check a sore on his backside," Gustavo said, "and I got a look under his clothes. There is no flesh at all on his bones. He can't last more than a couple of days."

I left Gustavo and knelt at Numa's side.

"How are you feeling, Numa?"

Numa smiled weakly. "I don't think it will be much longer for me."

I saw a look of acceptance in his eyes. He was facing his death with courage, and I did not want to dishonor this by telling him lies.

"Try to hold on," I said. "We'll be climbing soon. We are going west, at last."

" 'To the west is Chile,' " he said, with a weary smile.

"I will get there or die trying."

"You will make it, you are strong."

"*You* must be strong, Numa, for your family. You will see them again."

Numa just smiled. "It's funny," he said. "I think most men die regretting errors they have made in their lives, but I have no regrets. I have tried to live a good life. I have tried to treat people well. I hope God will take that into account."

"Don't talk like that, Numa."

"But I'm at peace," he said. "I'm ready for whatever lies ahead."

ON THE MORNING of December 11, Numa slipped into a coma. He was dead that afternoon. Numa was one of the best of us, a young man who seemed to have no bad side, a person whose compassion and generosity never wavered, no matter how much he suffered. It maddened me that such a man should die from a simple bump to the leg, a minor bruise, the kind of injury that in the ordinary world would not have deserved a second thought.

As I looked at my friends, I wondered if their families, who had sent them off as hearty young men, would even know them now, with their faces drawn, their brows and sunken cheeks ridged with bone, like the withered faces of gargoyles and goblins, and most of them barely strong enough to stand without wobbling. Whatever hope they had managed to keep alive was fading now, I could see it in their eyes. Their bodies were dry and empty husks. Life was fading from them the way the color fades from a fallen leaf. I thought of all the others who had died, and imagined their ghosts gathering around us, twenty-nine gray figures huddled in silence on the snow, and Numa taking his place among them. So much death, so many lives cut short. I felt a heavy sense of weariness overtake me.

Enough of this, I muttered. *Enough.* It was time to bring the story to a close. I found Roberto outside the fuselage, slumped against the hull of the Fairchild. "Everything is ready," I told him. "Tintin and I are set to go. Tomorrow morning we leave. Are you coming with us?"

Roberto glanced at the mountains to the west. I saw in his eyes that he was as shaken by Numa's death as the rest of us. "Yes," he said. "I'll be ready. It's time to go."

∧ ∧ ∧

ON THE EVENING of December 11, our sixtieth evening in the Andes, I sat outside the fuselage, on one of the seats we'd dragged out from inside the plane, and stared west at the mountains that blocked me from my home. As night fell, the largest of the mountains, the one I'd have to climb, grew darker and more forbidding. I saw no hostility in it, just hugeness and power and cruel indifference. It was hard to convince myself that the moment I had longed for and feared had finally arrived. My mind was a blizzard of questions. *What is it like to freeze to death?* I wondered. *Is it a painful death or an easy one? Is it fast or slow? It seems like a lonely way to die. How does one die of exhaustion? Do you simply drop in your tracks? It would be horrible to starve to death, but I would rather starve than fall. Please, God, don't let me fall. That is my greatest fear—to slide down some steep slope for hundreds of feet, clutching at the snow, knowing I am heading for a cliff and a long, hopeless drop to the rocks a thousand feet below. What would it feel like to fall that far? Would my mind shut itself down to spare me the horror, or would I be lucid until I hit the ground? Please, God, protect me from that kind of death.*

Suddenly an image flashed in my mind. I saw myself from above, as a motionless figure curled in the snow. The life was ebbing from my body. I had found my limits, the place and the moment of my death. What would that moment be like? What would be the last thing that I saw? The snow? The sky? The shadow of a rock? The face of a friend? Would I be alone? Would my eyes be open or shut when my spirit left my body? Would I accept my death peacefully, as I did under the avalanche, or would I wail and claw for one more moment of life?

Death felt so real, so close, and, feeling its presence, I began to tremble, knowing I didn't have the courage to face what lay ahead.

I cannot do this. I don't want to die. I resolved that I would tell the others I had changed my mind. I was staying. Perhaps Roberto was right, and the rescuers would find us after all . . .

But I knew better. We were almost out of food. How long would it be until we ran out completely, and began the horrific wait for someone to die? Who would go first? How long would we wait to cut him? And what would it be like for the last one left alive? I looked again at the mountain, and knew that nothing it could do to me would be worse than the future that waited for me here. I spoke to the mountain, hoping there was mercy in its slopes. "Tell me your secrets," I whispered. "Show me how to climb." The mountain, of course, was silent. I gazed at the soaring ridges, trying, with an amateur's eye, to trace the best path to the summit. But soon night was falling. The slopes disappeared into darkness. I went inside the Fairchild, lay down with my friends one last time, and tried to sleep.

Chapter Eight

The Opposite
of Death

IF I SLEPT AT ALL that night, it was never for more than a few restless moments at a time, and when the first light of morning glowed weakly in the Fairchild's windows, I had been lying awake for hours. Some of the others were up, but none of them spoke to me as I rose from the floor and readied myself to go. I had dressed for the mountain the night before. Next to my skin were a cotton polo shirt and a pair of woolen slacks. They were women's slacks I'd found in someone's luggage—Liliana's, probably—but after two months in the mountains I had no trouble slipping them over my bony hips. I had three pairs of jeans over the slacks, and three sweaters over the polo. I wore four pairs of socks, and now I covered the socks with plastic supermarket bags to keep them dry in the snow. I stuffed my feet into my battered rugby boots and carefully tied the laces, then I pulled a wool cap over my head and topped it with the hood and shoulders I'd cut from Susy's antelope coat. Everything I did that morning had the feel of ceremony, of consequence. My thoughts were razor sharp, but reality seemed muffled and dreamlike, and I had the feeling I was watching myself from a distance. The others stood by quietly, not sure what to say. I had left them before, when we'd set off on the eastern trek, but I'd known from the start that that trip was merely an exercise. This morning I felt a heavy sense of finality about my departure, and the others felt it, too. After so many weeks of intense camaraderie and common struggle, there was suddenly a distance between us. I had already begun to leave them.

I grabbed the aluminum pole I would use as a walking stick, and took my backpack down from the luggage compartment above me. It was packed with my rations of meat and whatever odds and ends I thought might be useful—some bands of cloth I could wrap around my hands to keep them warm, a lipstick to protect my blistered lips from the wind and sun. I had readied the pack before going to bed. I wanted my departure to be as swift and simple as possible; delays would only give me time to lose my nerve.

Roberto had finished dressing. We exchanged a silent nod, then I slipped Panchito's watch onto my wrist and followed him outside. There was a sharp chill in the air, but the temperature was well above freezing. It was a perfect day for climbing; the wind was light and the sky was brilliant blue.

"Let's hurry," I said. "I don't want to waste this weather."

Fito and the cousins brought us some meat for breakfast. We ate quickly. There was very little talk. When it was time to leave, we stood to say our good-byes. Carlitos stepped forward and we embraced. He was smiling happily, and his voice was full of strong encouragement. "You will make it!" he said. "God will protect you!" I saw the wild hope in his eyes. He was so thin, so weak, his dark eyes had sunk deep into his skull and the skin was drawn tightly across the bones of his face. It broke my heart to think that I was his hope, that this hopeless trek we were about to begin was his only chance of survival. I wanted to shake him, to let my tears flow, to scream at him, *What the fuck am I doing, Carlitos? I am so afraid! I don't want to die!* But I knew that if I allowed those feelings to rise in me, what was left of my courage would crumble. So, instead, I handed him one of the tiny red shoes my mother had purchased in Mendoza for my nephew. The shoes were magical for me because my mother had chosen them with such love for her grandson, and had handled them so tenderly on the plane. "Keep this," I told him. "I'll keep the other one. When I come back for you, we'll have a pair again."

The others said good-bye with embraces and glances of quiet

encouragement. Their faces showed so much hope and so much fear, it was hard for me to look them in the eyes. After all, I was the one who had planned the expedition. I was the one who had insisted most forcefully that it was possible to reach Chile on foot. I know the others saw my behavior as confident and optimistic, and perhaps it gave them hope. But what looked to them like optimism was really nothing of the sort. It was panic. It was terror. The urge that drove me to trek west was the same urge that drives a man to jump from the top of a burning building. I had always wondered how a person thinks in such a moment, perched on the ledge, cringing from the flames, waiting for the split second when one death makes more sense than another. How does the mind make such a choice? What is the logic that tells you the time has come to step into thin air? This morning I had my answer. I smiled at Carlitos, then turned away before he saw the anguish in my eyes. My gaze fell on the soft mound of snow marking the place where my mother and sister were buried. In all the time since their deaths, I had not allowed myself a single sentimental thought about them. But now I relived the moment when I laid Susy in her shallow grave and covered her with the sparkling snow. Two months had passed since that day, but I could still see her face very clearly as the white crystals fell softy across her cheeks and brow. *If I die,* I thought, *my father will never know how I comforted her and kept her warm, and how peaceful she looked in her white grave.*

"Nando, are you ready?"

Roberto was waiting. The mountain was behind him, its white slopes blazing in the early sunlight. I reminded myself that those brutal peaks were all that blocked my path to my father, and that the time had finally come to begin the long walk home, but these thoughts inspired no courage. I was very close to panic. All the fears that had tormented me since the moment I woke from my coma were converging, and I trembled like a doomed man about to climb the steps to the gallows. If I were alone, I might have whimpered like a baby, and the only thought in my mind was the plea of a frightened child: *I do not want to go.* For months I had sustained myself with thoughts of my escape, but now, on the verge of that escape, I wanted desperately to stay with my friends. I wanted to huddle with them in the fuselage tonight, to talk with them about our homes and our families, to be comforted by their prayers and the warmth of their bodies. The crash site was an awful place, soaked in urine, smelling of death, littered with ragged bits of human bone and gristle, but to me it suddenly felt safe and warm and familiar. I wanted to stay there. How badly I wanted to stay.

"Nando," said Roberto, "it's time to go."

I glanced at the graves once again, then turned to Carlitos.

"If you run out food," I said, "I want you to use my mother and Susy."

Carlitos was speechless for a moment, then he nodded. "Only as a last resort," he said softly.

Roberto called again. "Nando?"

"I'm ready," I said. We waved one last time and then began to climb.

None of us had much to say as we followed the gentle incline of the glacier up to the mountain's lower slopes. We thought we knew what lay ahead, and how dangerous the mountain could be. We had learned that even the mildest storm could kill us if it trapped us in the open. We understood that the heavily corniced snow on the high ridges was unstable, and that the smallest avalanche would whisk us down the mountain like a broom sweeping crumbs. We knew that deep crevasses lay hidden beneath the thin crust of frozen snow, and that rocks the size of television sets often came crashing down from crumbling outcrops high on the mountain. But we knew nothing about the techniques and strategies of mountaineering, and what we didn't know was enough to kill us.

We didn't know, for example, that the Fairchild's altimeter was wrong; the crash site wasn't at seven thousand feet, as we thought, but close to twelve thousand. Nor did we know that the mountain we were about to challenge was one of the highest in the Andes, soaring to the height of nearly seventeen thousand feet, with slopes so steep and difficult they would test a team of expert climbers. Experienced mountaineers, in fact, would not have gone anywhere near this mountain without an arsenal of specialized gear, including steel pitons, ice screws, safety lines, and other critical gadgets designed to keep them safely anchored to the slopes. They would carry ice axes, weatherproof tents, and sturdy thermal boots fitted with crampons—metal spikes that provide traction on the steepest, iciest inclines. They would be in peak physical condition, of course, and they would climb at a time of their own choosing, and carefully plot the safest route to the top. The three of us were climbing in street clothes, with only the crude tools we could fashion out of materials salvaged from the plane. Our bodies were already ravaged from months of exhaustion, starvation, and exposure, and our backgrounds had done little to prepare us for the task. Uruguay was a warm and low-lying country. None of us had ever seen real mountains before. Prior to the crash, Roberto and Tintin had never even seen snow. If we had known anything about climbing, we'd have seen we were already doomed. Luckily, we knew nothing, and our ignorance provided our only chance.

Our first task was to choose a path up the slopes. Experienced climbers would have quickly spotted a ridge winding down from the summit to meet the glacier at a point less than a mile south of the crash site. If we had known enough to hike to that ridge and climb its long, narrow spine, we would have found better footing, gentler slopes, and a safer and swifter path to the top. We never even noticed the ridge. For days I had marked with my eye the spot where the sun set behind the ridges, and, thinking that the best path was the shortest path, we used that point to chart a beeline path due west. It was an amateurish mistake that would force us to weave our way up the mountain's steepest and most dangerous slopes.

Our beginning, though, was promising. The snow on the mountain's lower flank was firm and fairly level, and the cleats of my rugby boots bit well into the frozen crust. Driven by an intense adrenaline surge, I moved quickly up the slope, and in no time I had pulled fifty yards ahead of the others. But soon I was forced to slow my pace. The slope had grown much steeper, and it seemed to grow steeper yet with every step, like a treadmill that constantly increases its incline. The effort left me gasping in the thin air, and I had to rest, with my hands on my knees, after every few yards of progress.

Soon the sun was strong enough to warm us as we climbed, but it warmed the snow as well, and the firm surface beneath my feet began to weaken. Now, with every step, my foot was breaking through the thinning crust and I would sink up to my knees in the soft, deep drifts below. Each step required extreme effort. I would lift my knee almost to my chest to clear my boot from the snow. Then I would swing that foot forward, shift my weight onto it, and break through the ice again. In the thin air I had to rest, exhausted, after every step. When I looked behind me I saw the others struggling, too. I glanced at the sun above us, and realized that we had waited too long that morning to start the climb. Logic told us it would be wiser to climb in daylight, so we'd waited for the sun to rise. Experts, on the other hand, know that the best time for climbing is in the predawn hours, before the sun can turn the slopes to mush. The mountain was making us pay for another amateur mistake. I wondered what other blunders lay ahead, and how many of them we'd be able to survive.

Eventually all the crust melted away, and we were forced to wade uphill through heavy drifts that sometimes were as deep as my hips. "Let's try the snowshoes!" I shouted. The others nodded, and in moments we had slipped Fito's makeshift snowshoes off our backs and strapped them to our feet. They worked well at first, allowing us to climb without sinking into the snow. But the size and bulk of the cushions forced us to bow our legs as we walked, and to swing our feet in unnaturally wide circles to keep the fat cushions from colliding. To make things worse, the stuffing and upholstery quickly became soaked with melted snow. In my exhausted state, I felt as if I were climbing the mountain with manhole covers bolted to my shoes. My spirits were rapidly sinking. We were already on the verge of exhaustion, and the real climbing hadn't even begun.

THE INCLINE OF the mountain grew steadily sharper, and soon we reached slopes that were too steep and windblown to hold deep drifts of snow. With relief, we removed the snowshoes, strapped them to our backs, and kept climbing. By midmorning we had worked our way to a dizzying altitude. The world around us now was more blue air and sunlight than rock and snow. We had literally climbed into the sky. The sheer altitude and the yawning openness of the vast slopes left me reeling with a sense of dreamlike disbelief. The mountain fell away so steeply behind me now that when I looked down on Tintin and Roberto, I saw only their heads and shoulders outlined against two thousand feet of empty sky. The angle of the slope was as steep as a roofer's ladder, but imagine a ladder you could climb to the moon! The height made my head swim and sent tingling spasms along my hamstrings and spine. Turning to look behind me was like pirouetting on the ledge of a skyscraper.

On steep, open slopes like these, where the incline seems intent on tipping you off the mountain and good handholds are hard to find, experts would use safety lines tethered to steel anchors driven into rock or ice, and they'd count on their crampons to give their footing a secure grip on the mountainside. We had none of those things, but only the fading strength of our arms, legs, fingertips,

and freezing toes, to keep us from sailing off into the blue void behind us. I was terrified, of course, but still I could not deny the wild
beauty all around me—the flawless sky, the frosted mountains, the
glowing landscape of deep virgin snow. It was all so vast, so perfect,
so silent and still. But something troubling was hiding behind all
that beauty, something ancient and hostile and profound. I looked
down the mountain to the crash site. From this altitude it was just a
ragged smudge on the pristine snow. I saw how crass and out of
place it seemed, how fundamentally *wrong*. Everything about us
was wrong here—the violence and racket of our arrival, our garish
suffering, the noise and mess of our lurid struggle to survive. None
of it fit here. *Life* did not fit here. It was all a violation of the perfect
serenity that had reigned here for millions of years. I had sensed it
the first time I gazed at this place: we had upset an ancient balance,
and balance would have to be restored. It was all around me, in the
silence, in the cold. Something wanted all that perfect silence back
again; something in the mountain wanted us to be still.

BY LATE MORNING we had climbed some two thousand feet from
the crash site and were probably fourteen thousand feet or more
above sea level. I was moving inch by inch now as a vicious
headache tightened like an iron ring around my skull. My fingers
felt thick and clumsy, and my limbs were heavy with fatigue. The
slightest effort—lifting my head, turning to speak to Roberto—left
me sucking for air as if I'd just run a mile, but no matter how forcefully I inhaled, I couldn't fill my lungs. I felt as if I were drawing
breath through a piece of felt.

I would not have guessed it at the time, but I was suffering from
the effects of high altitude. The physiological stress of climbing in
oxygen-depleted air is one of the great dangers mountain climbers
face. Altitude sickness, which generally strikes in the zone above
eight thousand feet, can cause a range of debilitating symptoms,

including headache, intense fatigue, and dizziness. Above twelve thousand feet, the condition can lead to cerebral and pulmonary edemas, both of which can cause permanent brain damage and rapid death. At high altitude, it's hard to escape the effects of mild and moderate altitude disease, but the condition is worsened by rapid climbing. Experts recommend that climbers ascend no more than one thousand feet per day, a rate that gives the body a chance to acclimate itself to the thinning air. We had climbed twice that far in a single morning, and were making matters worse by continuing to climb when our bodies desperately needed time to rest.

In response, my oxygen-starved body was struggling to cope with the thinning air. My heart rate soared and my blood thickened in my veins—the body's way of conserving oxygen in the bloodstream and sending it more rapidly to vital organs and tissues. My respiration rate rose to the brink of hyperventilation, and with all the moisture I lost as I exhaled, I was becoming more severely dehydrated with every breath. To supply themselves with the huge amounts of water needed to stay safely hydrated at high altitude, expert climbers use portable gas stoves to melt pots of snow, and they guzzle gallons of fluids each day. Our only source of fluids was the snow we gulped in handfuls, or melted in the glass bottle we had in one of the packs. It did little good. Dehydration was rapidly sapping our strength, and we climbed with a constant, searing thirst.

AFTER FIVE OR SIX hours of hard climbing, we had probably ascended some 2,500 feet, but for all our striving, the summit seemed no closer. My spirits sagged as I gauged the vast distance to the top, and realized that each of my tortured steps brought me no more than fifteen inches closer. I saw with brutal clarity that we had taken on an inhuman task. Overwhelmed with fear and a sense of futility, I felt the urge to sink to my knees and stay there. Then I heard the calm voice in my head, the voice that had steadied me in so many moments of crisis. "You are drowning in distances," it said. "Cut the mountain down to size." I knew what I had to do. Ahead of me on the slope was a large rock. I decided I would forget about the summit and make that rock my only goal. I trudged for it, but like the summit it seemed to recede from me as I climbed. I knew then that I was being tricked by the mountain's huge scale of reference. With nothing on those vast empty slopes to give me perspective—no houses, no people, no trees—a rock that seemed ten feet wide and a hundred yards away might really be ten times larger and more than a mile distant. Still, I climbed toward the rock without resting, and when I finally got there I picked another land-mark and started all over again.

I climbed that way for hours, focusing my attention completely on some target—a rock, a shadow, an unusual ruffle in the snow—until the distance to that target became all that mattered in the world. The only sounds were my own heavy breathing and the rhythmic crunch of my shoes in the snow. My pace soon became automatic, and I slipped into a trance. Somewhere in my mind I still longed for my father, I still suffered from fatigue, I still worried that our mission was doomed, but now those thoughts seemed muted and secondary, like a voice on a radio playing in another room. *Step-push, step-push.* Nothing else mattered. Sometimes I promised myself I'd rest when the next goal was reached, but I never kept my promise. Time melted away, distances dwindled, the snow seemed to glide beneath my feet. I was a locomotive lumber-ing up the slope. I was lunacy in slow motion. I kept up that pace until I had pulled far ahead of Roberto and Tintin, who had to shout to make me stop. I waited for them at an outcrop that offered a level place to rest. We ate some meat and melted some snow to drink. None of us had much to say. We all knew the kind of trouble we were in.

"Do you still think we can make it by nightfall?" asked Roberto. He was looking at the summit.

I shrugged. "We should look for a place to camp."

I looked down to the crash site. I could still make out the tiny shapes of our friends watching us from seats they'd dragged outside the fuselage. I wondered how things looked from their perspective. Could they tell how desperately we were struggling? Were their hopes beginning to fade? If at some point we stopped moving, how long would they wait for us to start moving again? And what would they do if we didn't? These thoughts occurred to me only as passing observations. I was no longer in the same world as the boys down below. My world had narrowed, and the feelings of compassion or responsibility I had felt for the other survivors were now crowded out by my own terror and my own furious struggle to survive. I knew it was the same for Tintin and Roberto, and while I was certain we would fight side by side as long as possible, I understood that each of us, in his desperation and fear, was already alone. The mountain was teaching me a hard lesson: camaraderie is a noble thing, but in the end death is an opponent each of us would face in solitude.

I looked at Roberto and Tintin, resting sullenly on the ledge of rock. "What did we do to deserve this?" muttered Roberto. I looked up the mountain, searching for a cliff or a boulder that might give us shelter for the night. I saw nothing but a steep endless blanket of snow.

As we worked our way up the mountain, that snow-cover gave way to an even more difficult landscape. Now rocks were jutting from the snow, some of them huge and impossible to climb. Massive ridges and outcrops above us blocked my view of the slope ahead, and I was forced to choose my path by instinct. Often I chose wrong, and found myself trapped under an impassable ledge, or at the base of a vertical rock wall. Usually I could backtrack, or inch my way diagonally across the slope to find a new path. Sometimes I had no choice but to press on.

At one point in the early afternoon, I found my way blocked by an extremely steep, snow-covered incline. I could see a level rock shelf at the far upper edge. Unless we could climb the incline diagonally and scramble up onto that narrow shelf, we'd have to backtrack. That could cost us hours, and with sunset growing closer by the minute, I knew that was not an option. I looked back at Tintin and Roberto. They were watching to see what I would do. I studied the incline. The slope was sheer and smooth, there was nothing to grip with my hands. But the snow looked stable enough to support me. I'd have to dig my feet into the snow and keep my weight tilted forward as I climbed. It would all be a matter of balance.

I began to climb the frozen wall, carving the snow with the edges of my shoes and pressing my chest against the slope to keep from toppling backwards. The footing was stable, and with great caution I inched my way to the rock ledge and scrambled up onto level ground. I waved to Tintin and Roberto. "Follow my steps," I shouted. "Be careful, it is very steep."

I turned away from them and began to climb the slopes above me. Moments later I glanced back to see that Roberto had made it across the incline. Now it was Tintin's turn. I began climbing again, and had ascended thirty yards or so when a terrified shout echoed up the mountain.

"I'm stuck! I can't make it!"

I turned to see Tintin frozen in the middle of the incline.

"Come on, Tintin!" I shouted. "You can do it!"

He shook his head. "I can't move."

"It's the backpack!" said Roberto. "It's too heavy."

Roberto was right. The weight of Tintin's backpack, which he carried very high on his back, was pulling him off the face of the mountain. He was struggling to shift his balance forward, but there was nothing to offer him a handhold, and the look on his face told me he could not hold out for long. From my vantage point I could see the dizzying drop behind him, and I knew what would happen if Tintin fell. First he would swim away from us for a long time in thin air, then he would hit the slope, or an outcrop, and tumble down the mountain like a rag doll until some drift or crag eventually brought his broken body to a stop.

"Tintin, hold on!" I shouted. Roberto was at the lip of the rock shelf above the incline, stretching his arm down to Tintin. His reach was short by inches. "Take off your backpack!" he shouted. "Give it to me!" Tintin removed the backpack carefully, struggling to keep his balance as he slowly worked the straps off his arms and handed it up to Roberto. Without the weight of the backpack, Tintin was able to find his balance and climb safely up the incline. When he reached the ledge, he slumped to the snow. "I can't go any farther," he said. "I'm too tired. I can't lift my legs."

Tintin's voice betrayed his exhaustion and fear, but I knew we had to climb until we found a sheltered place to rest for the night, so I kept going, leaving the others no choice but to follow. As I climbed, I scanned the slopes in every direction, but the mountain was so rocky and steep there was no safe place to spread our sleeping bag. It was late afternoon now. The sun had drifted behind the western ridges, and shadows were already stretching down the slopes. The temperature began to fall. At the crash site below, I saw that our friends had retreated into the fuselage to escape the cold. A clot of panic was rising in my throat as I frantically searched the slopes for a safe, level place to spend the night.

At twilight I scaled a tall rock outcropping to get a better view. As I climbed, I wedged my right foot in a small crevice in the rock, then, with my left hand, reached up to grab a horn of boulder jutting from the snow. The boulder seemed solid, but when I pulled myself up, a rock the size of a cannon ball broke free and plummeted past me.

"Watch out! Watch out below!" I shouted. I looked down to see Roberto beneath me. There was no time to react. His eyes widened as he waited for the impact of the rock, which missed his head by inches. After a moment of stunned silence, Roberto glared at me. "You son of a bitch! You son of a bitch!" he shouted. "Are you trying to kill me? Be careful! Watch what the fuck you are doing!" Then he fell silent and leaned forward, and his shoulders started to heave. I realized he was crying. Hearing his sobs, I felt a pang of hopelessness so sharp I could taste it on my tongue. Then I was overtaken by a sudden, inarticulate rage. "*Fuck* this! *Fuck* this!" I muttered. "I have had *enough!* I have had *enough!*" I just wanted it to be over. I wanted to rest. To sink into the snow. To lie still and quiet. I can't remember any other thoughts, so I don't know what led me to keep going, but once Roberto had gathered himself, we started climbing again in the fading light. Finally I found a shallow depression in the snow beneath a large boulder. The sun had warmed the boulder all day, then the heat radiating from the rock had melted out this compact hollow. It was cramped, and its floor tilted sharply down the slope, but it would shelter us from the nighttime cold and wind. We laid the seat cushions on the floor of the hollow to insulate us from the cold, then spread the sleeping bag over the cushions. Our lives depended upon the bag, and the body warmth it would conserve, but it was a fragile thing, sewn together crudely with strands of copper wire, so we handled it with great care. To keep from tearing the seams, we removed our shoes before sliding in.

"Did you pee?" asked Roberto, as I eased myself into the bag. "We can't be getting in and out of this bag all night."

It reassured me that Roberto was becoming his grumbling self again.

"I peed," I answered. "Did you pee? I don't want you peeing in this bag."

Roberto huffed at me. "If anyone pees in the bag it will be you. And be careful with those big feet."

When the three of us were all inside the sleeping bag, we tried to get comfortable, but the ground beneath us was very hard, and the floor of the hollow was so steep we were almost standing up, with our backs pressed to the mountain and our feet braced against the downhill rim of the hollow. That small rim of snow was all that kept us from sliding down the slope. We were all exhausted, but I was far too frightened and cold to relax.

"Roberto," I said, "you are the medical student. How does one die of exhaustion? Is it painful? Or do you just drift off?"

The question seemed to irk him. "What does it matter how you die?" he said. "You'll be dead and that's all that matters."

We were quiet for a long time. The sky was as black as ink now, and studded with a billion brilliant stars, each of them impossibly clear and blazing like a point of fire. At this altitude I felt I could reach out and touch them. In another time and place I would have been awestruck by all this beauty. But here, and now, it seemed a brutal show of force. The world was showing me how tiny I was, how weak and insignificant. And temporary. I listened to my own breathing, reminding myself that as long as I drew breath I was still alive. I promised myself I would not think of the future. I would live from moment to moment and from breath to breath, until I had used up all the life I had.

THE TEMPERATURE DROPPED so low that night that the water bottle we carried shattered from the cold. Huddled together in the sleeping bag, we kept ourselves from freezing, but still we suffered terribly. In the morning we placed our frozen shoes in the sun and rested in the bag until they thawed. Then, after eating and packing our things, we began to climb. The sun was bright. It was another perfect day.

We were climbing above fifteen thousand feet now, and with every hundred yards or so the incline of the mountain tilted closer to the vertical. The open slopes were becoming unclimbable, so we began to work our way up the rocky edges of the winding couloirs—the steep plunging ravines that gashed the side of the mountain. Experienced climbers know couloirs can be killing zones—their shape makes them efficient chutes for all the rocks that tumble down the mountain—but the packed snow inside them gave us good footing, and the tall rock walls at their rims gave us something firm to grip.

At times, one edge of a couloir would lead us to an impassable point. Then I would work my way across the snow-covered center of the couloir to the opposite edge. As we climbed the couloirs, I found myself worrying more and more about the lethal void behind me. Perhaps it was the dizzying altitude, perhaps it was fatigue or a trick of my oxygen-starved brain, but I felt that the emptiness at my back was no longer a passive danger. Now it had presence and intention, very bad intention, and I knew that if I didn't resist it with all my strength, it would lure me off the mountain and toss me down the slope. Death was tapping me on the shoulder, and the thought of it made me slow and tentative. I second-guessed every movement, and lost faith in my balance. I realized with searing clarity that there were no second chances here, there was no margin for error. One slip, one moment of inattention, one bit of bad judgment, would send me headlong down the slope. The tug of the void was constant. It wanted me, and the only thing that could keep me from it was the level of my own performance. My life had collapsed to a simple game—climb well and live, or falter and die—and my consciousness had narrowed until there was no room in my thoughts for anything but a close and careful study of the rock I was reaching for, or the ledge on which I was about to brace my foot. Never had I felt such a sense of concentrated presence. Never had my mind experienced such a pure, uncomplicated sense of purpose.

Put the left foot there. Yes, that edge will hold. Now, with the left hand, reach up for the crack in that boulder. Is it sturdy? Good. Lift yourself. Now, put the right foot on that ledge. Is it safe? Trust your balance. Watch the ice!

I forgot myself in the intensity of my concentration, forgot my fears and fatigue, and for a while I felt as if everything I had ever been had disappeared, and that I was now nothing more than the pure will to climb. It was a moment of pure animal exhilaration.

I had never felt so focused, so driven, so fiercely alive. For those astonishing moments, my suffering was over, my life had become pure flow. But those moments did not last. The fear and exhaustion soon returned, and climbing once again became an ordeal. We were very high on the mountain now, and altitude was making my motions heavy and my thinking slow. The slopes had become almost vertical and were harder than ever to climb, but I told myself that inclines this steep could only mean we were nearing the summit. To steady myself, I imagined the scene I'd see from the summit just as I'd imagined it so many times before—the rolling hills partitioned into green and brown parcels of farmland, the roads leading off to safety, and somewhere a hut or a farmhouse . . .

How we continued to climb, I cannot say. I was shivering uncontrollably from cold and fatigue. My body was on the verge of complete collapse. Only the simplest thoughts could take shape in my mind. Then, in the distance above me, I saw the outline of a sloping ridge in sharp relief against a background of clear blue sky, and no more mountain above it. The summit! "We made it!" I shouted, and with renewed energy I clawed my way to the ridge. But as I pulled myself over its edge, the ridge gave way to a level shelf several yards wide, and above the shelf the mountain rose again. It was the steep angle of the slope that had fooled me. This was only another trick of the mountain, a false summit. And it wasn't the last. We spent the afternoon struggling toward one false summit after another until, well before sunset, we found a sheltered spot and decided to pitch our camp.

Roberto was sullen that night as we lay in the sleeping bag. "We will die if we keep climbing," he said. "The mountain is too high."

"What can we do but climb?" I asked.

"Go back," he said. For a moment I was speechless.

"Go back and wait to die?" I asked.

He shook his head. "Do you see across there, that dark line on the mountain? I think it's a road." Roberto pointed across a wide valley to a mountain ridge miles away.

"I don't know," I said. "It looks like some sort of fault line in the rock."

"Nando, you can barely see," he snapped. "I tell you it's a road!"

"What are you thinking?" I asked.

"I think we should go back and follow that road. It must lead somewhere."

That was the last thing I wanted to hear. Since the moment we'd left the fuselage, I had secretly been tormented by doubts and misgivings. *Are we doing the right thing? What if rescuers come while we're in the mountains? What if the farmlands of Chile are not just over the ridge?* Roberto's plan seemed like lunacy, but it forced me to consider other options, and I did not have the heart for that now.

"That mountain must be twenty-five miles away," I said. "If we hike there and climb to that black line, and find that it is just a layer of shale, we won't have the strength to return."

"It's a road, Nando, I'm sure of it!"

"Perhaps it's a road, perhaps it's not," I replied. "The only thing we know for sure is that to the west is Chile."

Roberto scowled. "You've been saying that for months, but we'll break our necks before we get there."

Roberto and I argued about the road for hours, but as we settled down to sleep, I knew the matter had not been resolved. I woke the next morning to yet another clear sky.

"We've been lucky with the weather," said Roberto. He was still inside the sleeping bag.

"What have you decided?" I asked him. "Are you going back?"

"I'm not sure," he said. "I need to think."

"I'm going to climb," I said, "maybe we'll reach the summit soon."

Roberto nodded. "Leave your packs here," he said. "I'll wait until you return."

I nodded. The thought of going on without Roberto terrified me, but I had no intention of turning back now. I waited for Tintin to gather his pack, then we turned to the slope and began to climb. After hours of slow progress, we found ourselves trapped at the base of a cliff towering hundreds of feet above us. Its face was almost dead vertical and covered with hard-packed snow.

"How can we climb this?" asked Tintin.

I studied the wall. My mind was sluggish, but soon I remembered the aluminum walking stick strapped to my back.

"We need a stairway," I said. I drew the stick off my back, and with its sharp tip, I began to carve crude steps into the snow. Using the steps like the rungs of a ladder, we continued to climb. It was excruciating work, but I kept at it with the dull persistence of a farm animal, and we ascended one slow step at a time. Tintin followed behind me. He was frightened, I know, but he never complained. In any case, I was just dimly aware of his presence. My attention was focused on the task at hand: *Dig, climb, dig, climb.* I felt, at times, that we were climbing the sheer sides of a frozen skyscraper, and it was very difficult to keep my balance as I dug, but I no longer worried about the void at my back. I respected it, but I had learned to tolerate its presence. A human being, as I've said before, gets used to anything.

It was an agonizing process, inching up the mountain that way, and the hours passed slowly. Sometime in late morning I spotted blue sky above a ridgeline and worked my way toward it. After so many false summits, I had learned to keep my hopes in check, but this time, as I climbed over the ridge's edge, the slope fell away flat and I found myself standing on a gloomy hump of rock and wind-scoured snow. It dawned on me slowly that there was no more mountain above me. I had reached the top.

I don't remember if I felt any joy or sense of achievement in that moment. If I did, it vanished as soon as I glanced around. The summit gave me an unobstructed 360-degree view of creation. From here I could see the horizon circling the world like the rim of a colossal bowl, and in every direction off into the fading blue distance, the bowl was crowded with legions of snow-covered mountains, each as steep and forbidding as the one I had just climbed. I understood immediately that the Fairchild's copilot had been badly mistaken. We had not passed Curicó. We were nowhere near the western limits of the Andes. Our plane had fallen somewhere in the middle of the vast cordillera.

I don't know how long I stood there, staring. A minute. Maybe two. I stood motionless until I felt a burning pressure in my lungs, and realized I had forgotten to breathe. I sucked air. My legs went rubbery and I fell to the ground. I cursed God and raged at the mountains. The truth was before me: for all my striving, all my hopes, all my promises to myself and my father, it would end like this. We would all die in these mountains. We would sink beneath the snow, the ancient silence would fall over us, and our loved ones would never know how hard we had struggled to return to them.

In that moment all my dreams, assumptions, and expectations of life evaporated into the thin Andean air. I had always thought that *life* was the actual thing, the natural thing, and that death was simply the end of living. Now, in this lifeless place, I saw with a terrible clarity that *death* was the constant, death was the base, and life was only a short, fragile dream. I was dead already. I had been born dead, and what I thought was my life was just a game death let me play as it waited to take me. In my despair, I felt a sharp and sudden longing for the softness of my mother and my sister, and the warm, strong embrace of my father. My love for my father swelled in my heart, and I realized that, despite the hopelessness of my situation, the memory of him filled me with joy. It staggered me: The mountains, for all their power, were not stronger than my attachment to my father. They could not crush my ability to love. I felt a moment of calmness and clarity, and in that clarity of mind I discovered a simple, astounding secret: Death has an opposite, but the opposite is not mere living. It is not courage or faith or human will. The opposite of death is *love*. How had I missed that? How does anyone miss that? Love is our only weapon. Only love can turn mere life into a miracle, and draw precious meaning from suffering and fear. For a brief, magical moment, all my fears lifted, and I knew that I would not let death control me. I would walk through the godforsaken country that separated me from my home with love and hope in my heart. I would walk until I had walked all the life out of me, and when I fell I would die that much closer to my father. These thoughts strengthened me, and with renewed hope I began to search for pathways through the mountains. Soon I heard Tintin's voice calling to me from the slope below.

"Do you see any green, Nando?" he cried. "Do you see any green?"

"Everything will be fine," I called down to him. "Tell Roberto to come up and see for himself." While I waited for Roberto to climb, I pulled a plastic bag and the lipstick from my backpack. Using the lipstick as a crayon, I wrote the words MT. SELER on the bag and stuffed it under a rock. *This mountain was my enemy,* I thought, *and now I give it to my father. Whatever happens, at least I have this as my revenge.*

It took three hours for Roberto to climb the steps. He looked around for a few moments, shaking his head. "Well, we are finished," he said flatly.

"There must be a way through the mountains," I said. "Do you see there, in the distance, two smaller peaks with no snow on them? Maybe the mountains end there. I think we should head that way."

Roberto shook his head. "It must be fifty miles," he said. "And who knows how much farther after we reach them? In our condition, how can we make such a trek?"

"Look down," I said. "There is a valley at the base of this mountain. Do you see it?"

Roberto nodded. The valley wound through the mountains for miles, in the general direction of the two smaller peaks. As it neared the small mountains, it split into two forks. We lost sight of the forks as they wound behind larger mountains, but I was confident the valley would take us where we needed to go.

"One of those forks must lead toward the small mountains," I said. "Chile is there, it's just farther than we thought."

Roberto frowned. "It's too far," he said. "We'll never make it. We don't have enough food."

"We could send Tintin back," I said. "With his food and what's left of ours, we could easily last twenty days."

Roberto turned away and looked off to the east. I knew he was thinking about the road. I looked west again, and my heart sank at the thought of trekking through that wilderness alone.

We were back at camp by late that afternoon. As we ate together, Roberto spoke to Tintin. "Tomorrow morning we are going to send you back," he said. "The trip will be longer than we thought, and we're going to need your food. Anyway, two can move faster than three." Tintin nodded in acceptance.

In the morning Roberto told me he had decided to stay with me. We embraced Tintin and sent him down the mountain.

"Remember," I said as he left us, "we will always be heading west. If rescuers come, send them to find us!"

We rested all that day in preparation for the trek that lay ahead. In the late afternoon we ate some meat and crawled into the sleeping bag. That evening, as the sun slipped behind the ridge above us, the Andes blazed with the most spectacular sunset I had ever seen. The sun turned the mountains to gleaming gold, and the sky above them was lit with swirls of scarlet and lavender. It occurred to me that Roberto and I were probably the first human beings to have such a vantage point on this majestic display. I felt an involuntary sense of privilege and gratitude, as humans often do when treated to one of nature's wonders, but it lasted only a moment. After my education on the mountain, I understood that all this beauty was not for me. The Andes had staged this spectacle for millions of years, long before humans even walked the earth, and it would continue to do so after all of us were gone. My life or death would not make a bit of difference. The sun would set, the snow would fall . . .

"Roberto," I said, "can you imagine how beautiful this would be if we were not dead men?" I felt his hand wrap around mine. He was the only person who understood the magnitude of what we had done and of what we still had to do. I knew he was as frightened as I was, but I drew strength from our closeness. We were bonded now like brothers. We made each other better men.

In the morning we climbed the steps to the summit. Roberto stood beside me. I saw the fear in his eyes, but I also saw the courage, and I instantly forgave him all the weeks of arrogance and bullheadedness. "We may be walking to our deaths," I said, "but I would rather walk to meet my death than wait for it to come to me."

Roberto nodded. "You and I are friends, Nando," he said. "We have been through so much. Now let's go die together."

We walked to the western lip of the summit, eased ourselves over the edge, and began to make our way down.

Chapter Nine

"I See a Man . . ."

THE HIGHEST REACHES of the mountain's western face were snow covered and extremely steep, and the view down the mountain, a view no other human had ever seen, was a bone-chilling sight. The steepness of the slopes and the sheer dizzying altitude—we'd be climbing *down* toward the clouds—stole my courage, and I had to force myself to move. As we slipped off the summit, I realized immediately that descending the mountain would be even more terrifying than the ascent. Climbing a mountain is a struggle, an attack, and every step up is a small victory over the force of gravity. But descending is more like surrender. You are no longer fighting gravity, but trying to strike a bargain with it, and as you lower yourself carefully from one treacherous foothold to another, you know that, given the slightest chance, it will pull you off the mountain and into the blue void of the sky.

"Carajo! I am a dead man," I muttered to myself. "What are we doing in this place?" It took great effort to find my courage, but I did, and I began to work my way carefully down the sheer inclines at the very top of the mountain. The slopes here were too steep to hold snow, and the wind had scoured the mountain down to bare rock, so we lowered ourselves inch by inch, grasping the edges of boulders jutting from the soil, and jamming our boots into spaces between small rocks. Sometimes we crab-walked down the slope, with our backs to the mountain, and other times we descended with our backs to the sky. Each step was treacherous—rocks that looked firmly fixed to the mountain would break away under our feet, and we would have to scramble for something solid to hold on

to. With no expertise to guide our descent, we lacked the ability to look ahead and plan the safest route down the mountain. We thought only about surviving the next step, and at times our haphazard path would lead us to an impassable wall, or to the lip of an outcrop jutting out from the slope like a balcony, with a heart-stopping view to the base of the mountain, thousands of feet below. Neither of us knew the first thing about technical rock-climbing, but we managed to work our way over or around these obstacles, or we would climb down through narrow clefts between them. Sometimes we had no choice but to hop from one rock to another, with nothing but a few thousand feet of thin air below us.

We descended this way for more than three hours, covering no more than fifty yards, but finally the rocks gave way to open slopes under a heavy snow cover. Slogging through the hip-deep snow was not as frightening as the more technical climb above, but it was exhausting, and we were constantly fooled by the rolling, softly sculpted slopes. Again and again, what began as a gentle slope would lead to an ice wall or a hidden cliff or an impossibly steep drop. Each dead end forced us to retrace our steps and find another route. When we had made our way a few hundred yards down the mountain, the footing changed dramatically. Because this portion of the western-facing mountain was exposed each day to afternoon sun, much of the snow had melted off, and more of the mountain's rocky surface was exposed. The dry ground gave us easier passage than the knee-deep snow above, but in places it was covered by a layer of loose stones and shale several inches deep. This rubble made for dangerously unstable footing, and more than once I lost my grip and had to clutch desperately at rocks and clumps of ice to keep myself from sliding down the mountain. When we could, we slid down on our backsides, or we lowered ourselves down in huge, rubble-strewn couloirs and followed them down the mountain. At midday, after some five hours on the mountain, we reached a point where the slopes lay in the shadow of a mountain to the west. The snow cover here was deep again, and as I gazed down the smooth, white surface, an idea came to me. Without thinking things through, I tossed one of the seat cushions onto the snow and sat on it. Grasping my aluminum walking stick in both hands, I drew up my legs, nudged myself forward, and began to ride the cushion down the slope. In seconds I knew I had done something very stupid. The surface of the snow was hard and slick, and in just a few yards I had reached an alarming velocity. Riding my motorcycle on the open roads in Uruguay had given me a feel for speed, and I'm sure I must have been flying down that slope as fast as sixty miles an hour. In an effort to slow my fall, I drove my aluminum walking stick into the snow, and dug in my heels, but this had no effect at all, except to throw my body weight forward. I knew that if I tumbled off the cushion and cartwheeled down the mountain, I could break every bone in my body, so I stopped trying to slow myself and simply held on, flying past rocks and hurtling over bumps, with no way of stopping or steering. Finally a wall of snow appeared before me, and I realized I was sailing toward it on a collision course. *If there's rock beneath that snow,* I thought, *I'm a dead man.* Seconds later I slammed into the snowbank at full speed, and though the impact stunned me, the deep snow softened the blow and I survived. As I dug myself out of the berm and brushed myself off, I heard Roberto's shrill falsetto shouting from above. I couldn't make out the words, but I knew he was beside himself at my recklessness.

I waved my arms to show him I was okay, and rested while he picked his way carefully down to meet me. We continued down the slope together, and by late afternoon we had made it about two-thirds of the way down the mountain. At the crash site, the shadow cast by the mountains to the west cut the days short. But here on the western side daylight lasted into the evening, and I wanted to use every moment of our time.

"Let's keep going until the sun sets," I said.

Roberto shook his head. "I need to rest."

I saw that he was exhausted. I was, too, but the anxiety and desperation that drove me was stronger than my fatigue. For long months, my compulsive urge to escape had been bottled up inside me. It was free now, and raging out of control. We had conquered the mountain that kept us trapped at the crash site, and now an open valley lay ahead, pointing the way toward home. How could we stop to rest?

"Another hour," I said.

"We need to stop," Roberto snapped. "We must be smart about this, or we will burn ourselves out." Roberto's eyes were bleary with weariness, but there was determination in them, too, and I knew there was no use arguing. We spread the sleeping bag on a flat, dry rock, climbed in, and rested for the night.

Because of the lower altitude, and perhaps because of the solar energy stored in the rock we slept on, the night was not uncomfortably cold. The next morning was December 15, the fourth day of our journey. I roused Roberto as the sun rose and we set off down the slope. When we reached the bottom of the mountain, sometime near noon, we found ourselves standing at the entrance to the valley that we hoped would be our pathway to civilization. Glacial ice streamed along the gently sloping valley floor, winding like a river through the great mountains that rose on either side. From a distance, the snow-covered glacier looked as smooth as glass, but this was an illusion. Up close, we saw that the snow on the surface of the glacier had fractured into millions of small, icy boulders and jagged plates. It was difficult ground, and we stumbled with each step as if we were trekking on piles of concrete rubble. The big chunks of snow rolled and shifted beneath our feet. Our ankles wobbled, and our feet slipped and jammed into the narrow spaces between the chunks. It was difficult and painful progress, and we had to be careful about every single step—we both knew that in this wilderness a broken ankle would be a death sentence. I wondered what I'd do if one of us was injured. Would I leave Roberto? Would he leave me?

We stumbled over the glacier all that day, until the hours bled together. Both of us were struggling on the rough terrain, but I kept up my lunatic pace and was always drawing farther and farther ahead of Roberto. "Slow down, Nando!" he would shout. "You are going to kill us!" I would badger him, in return, to move faster, and I resented the time we wasted every time I waited for him to catch up. Still, I knew he was right. Roberto was nearing the end of his strength. My strength was fading, too. Painful cramps had seized my legs, making every step an agony, and my breathing was too rapid and shallow. I knew we were walking ourselves to death, but I couldn't make myself stop. Time was running out for us, and the weaker I grew, the more frantic I became to keep moving. My pain, my body, didn't matter anymore; it was just a vehicle now. I would burn myself to ashes if that was what it took to get home.

Temperatures were mild enough that we could walk after sunset, and sometimes I was able to persuade Roberto to trek late into the night. Even in our battered state, we were awed by the wild beauty of the Andes after dark. The skies were the deepest indigo blue, and clustered with blazing stars. Moonlight softened the rugged peaks surrounding us, and gave the snowfields an eerie glow. Once, as we descended a slope in the valley, I saw dozens of shadowy figures ahead, like hooded monks gathered to pray in the moonlight. When we reached these figures, we found that they were tall pillars of snow—*penitentes,* as geologists call them— carved at the bases of snowy slopes by swirling wind. There were dozens of them, standing silently side by side, and we had to find a path through them as if we were weaving our way through a forest of frozen trees. Sometimes I watched my shadow gliding beside me on the snow, and used it as proof that I was real, I was here. But often I felt like a ghost on those moonlit snowfields, a spirit trapped between the worlds of the living and the dead, guided by nothing more than will and memory, and an indestructible longing for home.

ON THE MORNING of December 18, the seventh day of our trek, the punishing snow cover began to give way to scattered patches of gray ice and fields of sharp loose rubble. I was weakening rapidly. Each step now required supreme effort, and a total concentration of my will. My mind had narrowed until there was no room in my consciousness for anything but my next stride, the careful place-ment of a foot, the critical issue of moving forward. Nothing else mattered—my weariness, my pain, the plight of my friends on the mountain, not even the hopelessness of our efforts. All that was forgotten. I'd forget Roberto, too, until I'd hear him calling and turn to see that once again he had fallen far behind. It was a kind of self-hypnosis, probably, brought on by the mesmerizing effects of my rhythmic breathing, the repetitive crunch of my boots on the rocks and snow, and the litany of Hail Marys I constantly chanted. In this trancelike state, distances vanished and hours flowed. Few conscious thoughts broke this spell, and when they did, they were simple ones.

Watch that loose rock . . .

Did we bring enough food?

What are we doing here? Look at these mountains! We are fucked!

At one point during this phase of the trek, I noticed that the sole of my right rugby boot was tearing loose from the upper. I realized that if my shoe failed in this rugged terrain, I was done for, but my reaction to this problem was oddly detached. My mind showed me a picture of myself hobbling shoeless on ridges of rock and ice until my bare foot was too bloody to continue. Then I saw myself crawl-ing, until my hands and knees were shredded. Finally, I fell to my belly and dragged myself with my elbows until my strength was gone. At that point, I assumed, I would die. In my altered state of mind, these images did not distress me. In fact, I found them reassuring. If the shoe fell apart, I had a plan. There were things I could do. There would still be space between my death and me.

I hiked for miles in this dreamlike state. Distant. Removed. There were times, however, when the power and beauty of the mountains yanked me out of my dull self-absorption. It would happen suddenly: I would feel an apprehension of the age and experience of the mountains, and realize that they had stood here silent and oblivious, as civilizations rose and fell. Against the backdrop of the Andes, it was impossible to ignore the fact that a human life was just a tiny blip in time, and I knew that if the mountains had minds, our lives would pass too quickly for them to notice. It struck me, though, that even the mountains were not eternal. If the earth lasts long enough, all these peaks will someday crumble to dust. So what is the significance of a single human life? Why do we struggle? Why do we endure such suffering and pain? What keeps us battling so desperately to live, when we could simply surrender, sink into the silence and the shadows, and know peace?

I had no answer to these questions, but when they troubled me too much, or in those moments when I thought I had finally found the limits of my strength, I would remind myself of my promise to my father. I would decide, as he did on that river in Argentina, to suffer a little longer. I would take one more step, then take another, and tell myself each brought me closer to my father, that each step I took was a step stolen back from death.

AT SOME POINT on the afternoon of December 18, I heard a sound in the distance ahead—a muffled wash of white noise that grew louder as I approached it, and I soon recognized it as the roar of rushing water. We were still stumbling over the rugged fields of rubble-strewn snow, but I quickened my pace, terrified that the sound was from some impassable torrent that would cut us off and seal our fate. I made my way down a gentle slope, then slid down a small, icy cliff. A gigantic mountain loomed in front of me. The valley we had been following led directly to the mountain's base and ended, but two smaller valleys split from it and disappeared as they wound around either side of the mountain.

This is the Y we saw from the summit, I thought. *We are on our way home, if we only have the strength to make it.*

I turned to my left, and walked around the short, curving ice cliff toward the mysterious roar. As I rounded the cliff, I found myself standing at the base of an ice wall some fifteen feet high. A thick jet of water, fed by tons of melting snow, was spouting from the wall, through a large crevice about five feet from the ground. The water splashed at my feet, then flowed swiftly across the ice and gravel and down into the valley ahead. To the human eye, the slope of the land here seemed gentle, but it was steep enough to give the water great momentum, and I could see a point, just a few hundred yards in the distance, where the cascading snowmelt rapidly broadened into a forceful stream.

"This is the birth of a river," I said to Roberto, when he'd reached me. "It will lead us out of here." We hiked ahead, following the river, certain that it would lead us down through the highlands and eventually to some civilized place. Snow, rocks, and grimy chunks of ice passed beneath my feet as I lumbered along, then suddenly the snowline ended as abruptly as the edge of a carpet, and at last we found ourselves trekking on dry ground. But our walk was no easier here than it was in the snowfields, because the floodplain on either side of the stream was littered with huge boulders, many taller than our heads, and we had to weave our way through these big rocks, or scale them, and hop from the top of one wobbly rock to another. It took us hours to cross the boulder fields, but eventually the terrain settled down and we were walking again on a more manageable landscape of loose rocks and rubble. The river beside us grew broader and stronger with every mile, until its roar drowned out all other sounds. I walked, as always, in a trance state, living from one labored step until the next, and as the miles crept by, the only fact of my existence, of my *universe,* was the small patch of difficult ground that would provide a base for my next footfall.

We walked until sunset that day, and when we rested, Roberto showed me a rock he'd picked up along the way.

"I'm keeping this as a souvenir for Laura," he said. Laura Surraco was Roberto's fiancée.

"She must be worried about you," I said.

"She is a wonderful girl. I miss her very much."

"I envy you, Roberto," I said. "I have never had a serious girlfriend. I've never been in love."

"Really?" he laughed. "All those girls you chased with Panchito? None of them ever stole your heart?"

"I guess I never gave any of them the chance," I said. "I have been thinking, somewhere out there is the girl I would marry. She's walking around, living her life. Maybe sometimes she wonders about the man she might marry, where he is, what he's doing right now. Would she ever guess he is in the mountains, trying to cross the Andes to get to her? If we don't make it, I'll never meet her. She'll never know me. She'll marry someone else, never guessing I ever existed."

"Don't worry," said Roberto, "we'll make it home and you will find someone. You'll make someone happy."

I smiled at Roberto's kindness, but found no comfort in his words. I knew that somewhere in the ordinary world, the woman I would have married was living her life, moving toward the point in time when we might have met and my future would have begun. Now I knew that when she reached that point, I would not be there. She would never know me. Our children would never be born. We would never make a home, or grow old together. The mountains had stolen these things from me; that was reality and I had begun to accept it. But still, still, I longed for the very things I knew I would never have—the love of a wife, a family of my own, a reunion with my grandmother and older sister, and always the embrace of my father. My ordeal had simplified my mind and whittled me down very close to the essence of what I was, and now I saw that this longing, this love and affection for the very idea of my life, was a deeper part of me than hopelessness or fear or pain or hunger. It seemed to live on beyond all reason. I wondered how durable it was. How much longer would it survive? And if it finally faded, would that be the moment my body failed? Or would it persist to my last conscious moment? Would I die longing for the life I couldn't have?

DECEMBER 19 WAS another fine day, the eighth perfect day in a row. We had hiked for several hours in the morning, and now, as I waited for Roberto to catch up with me, I examined the sole of my boot. It had torn out so many stitches that it flapped as I walked. I looked at the jagged rocks that littered the floor of the valley. *I wonder,* I thought, *will my shoe fail first, or will I?* We had left so many dangers behind us; we were no longer at risk of freezing to death, or of dying in a fall. It was a matter of simple endurance now, and of luck and time. We were walking ourselves to death, and hoping that we would stumble upon help before we used up all the life left in us.

Later that morning we spotted trees far ahead in the valley, and Roberto thought he saw something more.

"There," he said, squinting at the horizon. "I think I see cows."

My nearsightedness prevented me from seeing anything so far away, but I worried that Roberto, in his exhausted state, might be hallucinating. "It could be deer," I said. "Let's keep going."

A few hours later, Roberto bent over and picked something off the ground. When he showed it to me, I saw it was a rusted soup can.

"People have been here," he said.

I refused to let my hopes rise. "That could have been here for years," I said. "Or maybe it fell from a plane."

Roberto scowled and tossed the can away. "You stupid bastard," he said, "airplane windows don't open." Later we found a horseshoe, and then some piles of dung that Roberto insisted had come from a cow.

"Do you want to explain how cow shit might have fallen from a plane?" he asked.

"Keep walking," I said. "When we find a farmer, then I'll get excited."

As we trekked farther, we found more signs of human habitation: more cow droppings, horse dung, and tree stumps that still showed the marks of an ax. And finally, as we rounded a bend of the valley, we saw, a few hundred yards away, the small herd of cows Roberto had spotted that morning.

"I told you I saw cows," Roberto said. "There must be a farmhouse or something very close."

"But couldn't these cows be left here to graze on their own?" I said. "It is so high and desolate here. It's hard to believe anyone lives in a place like this."

"The proof is in front of your eyes," said Roberto. "We are saved. Tomorrow we will find the farmer who owns these cows."

When we camped that evening, Roberto's spirits were high, but I knew he could not stand many more hours in the mountains.

"My legs hurt so badly," he said, "and I feel so weak. Sometimes it takes all my strength to lift my foot and place it in front of me."

"Get some rest," I told him. "Maybe tomorrow we will find help."

THE NEXT MORNING was December 20, the ninth day of our trek. We started out early and found a good path beside the river. It had been worn smooth by cows or other grazing animals, and it was the first good footing we had felt on our journey. Roberto expected to find a peasant's hut at any moment, but as hours passed and we saw no more signs of life, he tired quickly and I had to wait more often than usual for him to rest. Still, we made good progress along the path until, in late morning, we reached a point where a boulder as large as a two-story house had tumbled into the stream. The massive rock blocked our path completely.

"We have to climb this," I said.

Roberto studied the rock, and saw a narrow ledge winding around the rock above the rushing waters of the river.

"I'll go that way," he said.

"It's too dangerous," I said. "One slip and you're in the river. We have to go over the top."

"I'm too weak to climb," he said. "I'll take my chances on the ledge." He eased his way onto the ledge and around the rock until I lost sight of him, then I started climbing. When I came down the far side of the rock, there was no sign of Roberto, even though the route he'd chosen was much shorter than mine. I waited, impatiently at first, and then with concern. When he finally appeared, he was staggering, doubled over, and clutching his stomach. All the color was drained from his face, and his eyes were narrowed in pain.

"What's wrong?" I asked.

"My gut is exploding," he grumbled. "It's diarrhea. Very bad. It hit while I was on the ledge"

"Can you walk?" I asked. "The path seems clear now."

Roberto shook his head. "I can't," he muttered. "It hurts too much."

He sank to the ground in misery. I was afraid that his sickness would drain the last of his energy, and I didn't want to leave him here.

"Come on," I said, "just a little farther—"

"No, please," he begged, "let me rest."

I looked to the horizon. A broad plateau rose in the distance. If we could scramble to the top of it, we would have a good vantage point to spot any huts or farms. "I'll carry your pack," I said, "but we have to keep moving. Let's make it to the top of that plateau, then we'll rest."

Before Roberto could answer, I took his pack and set off on the path, giving him no choice but to follow. He fell behind quickly, but I kept my eye on him. He was hunched over, limping, in great discomfort and suffering with every step. "Don't give up, Muscles," I whispered to myself, and I knew that he wouldn't. He was forcing himself forward now through stubbornness and the sheer power of his will. As I watched him, I knew I had been right in choosing him as my traveling companion.

We reached the base of the plateau by late afternoon, and helped each other up a steep path to the top, where we found ourselves looking down across a meadow of thick grass. There were trees and wildflowers and, to our left, the low stone walls of some mountain farmer's corral. We were high above the gorge of the river now, and the land fell away steeply down to the banks of the stream. Another steep slope rose on the far side of the river, which was about thirty-five yards wide at this point and flowing with torrential force. Roberto could barely walk anymore, so I helped him across the meadow to a small cluster of trees where we decided to camp.

"You rest," I said. "I'm going to explore a little. Maybe there's a farmhouse somewhere near."

Roberto nodded. He was very weak, and as he settled heavily on the soft turf, I knew he wouldn't be going any farther with me. I didn't want to think about what would happen if I had to leave him.

The afternoon was fading now, as I followed the winding path of the river gorge to see what lay ahead. I saw some cows grazing on the grassy slopes, and this raised my hopes, but after walking about three hundred yards, I saw exactly what I feared: another broad, swift river was flowing in from the left to join the river we had followed. We were cut off by the confluence of these two big streams. It didn't seem possible that we could cross either one. Barring a miracle, we had come to the end of our trail.

When I returned to Roberto, I told him about the river, and about the animals I'd seen. We were both very hungry. What little meat we had was going bad in the warm temperatures, and for a while we considered trying to kill and butcher one of the cows, but Roberto pointed out that this would probably not incline the cow's owner to help us. In any case, it was doubtful that we had the strength between us to catch and subdue such a large animal, and we quickly abandoned the idea. Darkness was beginning to fall now, and a chill was rising.

"I'm going to find some firewood," I said, but when I had walked only a few yards across the meadow, I heard Roberto shout.

"*Nando, I see a man!*"

"*What? What did you say?*"

"*There! Look! A man on a horse!*"

Roberto was pointing at the slope on the far side of the river gorge. I squinted into the evening shadows.

"I can't see anything."

"*Go! Run!*" Roberto shouted. "Go down to the river!"

Blindly, I stumbled down the slope toward the stream with Roberto correcting my course as I ran—"*Go right, no, I said right! No, too far! Go left!*"

I zigzagged down the slope, following Roberto's directions, but I saw no sign of a man on horseback. I turned to see Roberto staggering down the slope behind me.

"I swear I saw something," he said.

"It's dark over there," I replied. "Maybe it was the shadow of a rock." I took Roberto's arm and helped him back up the hill to the campsite, when we heard, above the roar of the river, the unmistakable sound of a human voice. We whirled around, and this time I saw him, too, a rider on horseback. He was shouting to us, but the noise of the river drowned out most of what he said. Then he turned his horse and disappeared into the shadows.

"Did you hear him?" shouted Roberto. "What did he say?"

"I only heard one word," I answered. "I heard him say *mañana*."

"We are saved," Roberto said.

I helped Roberto back up the slope to the campsite, then I built a fire and we lay down to sleep. For the first time since the crash, I felt real hope. I would live. I would see my father again, I was sure of it. Then my concern shifted to the ones we'd left behind. Obsessed with my own survival, I had barely thought of them since leaving the crash site nine days ago.

"I'm worried about the guys," I told Roberto. "Roy and Coche were so weak. I hope there's still time."

"Don't worry," said Roberto. "When the man comes back tomorrow, we'll make him understand there's not a second to lose."

The next morning, December 21, the tenth day of our journey, Roberto and I woke before dawn, and glanced across the river. Three men were sitting in the glow of a fire. I ran down the slope to the very lip of the gorge, then climbed down to the bank of the river. On the other side, one of the men, dressed in the work clothes of a hill-country peasant, did the same. I tried to shout, but the roar of the river drowned my words. I pointed to the sky, then I made gestures with my hand to indicate an airplane falling. The peasant just stared. I began running up and down the banks of the river, with my arms spread out like wings. The man turned away from me and shouted something to his friends. For a moment I panicked, thinking they would dismiss me as a lunatic and leave without helping. Instead, he took some paper from his pocket, scribbled on it, then tied the paper around a rock with some string and tossed it across the river. I retrieved it quickly, and when I unfolded the paper I saw this message:

There is a man coming later that I told him to go. Tell me what you want.

I searched my pockets for something to write with, but all I could find was the lipstick I'd found in my mother's luggage. I knew I couldn't write a legible note with that, so I gestured to him, making writing motions with my hands and shaking my head. He nodded, tied his pencil to another rock, and threw it to me. I took the pencil and began to write on the back of the peasant's note. I knew I had to choose the words precisely, to make him understand the urgency of our situation, and that we needed help without delay. My hands were shaking, but as the pencil touched the paper, I already knew what to say:

Vengo de un avión que cayó en los montanas . . .

. . . I come from a plane that fell into the mountains. I am Uruguayan. We have been walking for ten days. I have a friend up there who is injured. In the plane there are still fourteen injured people. We have to get out of here quickly and we don't know how. We don't have any food. We are weak. *When* are you going to come and fetch us? Please. We can't even walk. Where are we?

When I finished I turned the paper over, and I used the lipstick to scrawl, in bold red letters, *CUANDO VIENE?* ("When will you come?"). Wanting to save every precious second, I didn't take the time to sign my name. I wrapped the note around the rock just as the peasant had done and drew back my arm to throw the package across the river. But as I gauged the distance, and how much force would be required, I suddenly realized the extent of my physical weakness. I was not sure I had the strength in my arm to throw the rock so far. What if it fell short, into the water? Would the peasant lose patience with me and leave? Would he take the time to throw more paper? I summoned all my strength and hurled the rock with all the force I had. It bounced at the water's edge and rolled onto the bank. When the peasant read the message, he nodded and raised his open palms in a gesture that said, *Wait here. I understand.* Before leaving, he threw some bread to me. I took it to Roberto and we devoured it, then we waited for help to arrive.

Around 9:00 a.m., another man came, riding a mule, this time on the side of the river where we waited. He introduced himself as Armando Serda. He took some cheese from his pocket and gave it to us, then asked us to wait while he tended his sheep in the high pastures. A few hours later he returned. When he saw that Roberto could not walk, he helped him onto the mule, then he led us to a gentle stretch of the river where the stream could be forded. After thirty minutes or so on wooded mountain trails, we came into a clearing. I saw two crude wooden huts near the banks of the river. "Where are we?" I asked him, as we traveled.

"Los Maitenes," said Armando, referring to a mountainous region of the Chilean province of Colchagua, near the Azufre River. "We use these huts when we tend the flocks in the high pastures."

"We have friends still in the mountains," I said. "They are dying and we need to get help to them as soon as possible."

"Sergio has gone for help," Armando answered. Sergio Catalan, he explained, was the man on horseback who'd first spotted us the night before.

"How far is help?" I asked.

"The nearest police outpost is at Puente Negro," he answered. "About ten hours on horseback."

A second peasant came out of the larger hut, and Armando

introduced him as Enrique Gonzales. He led us to a campfire near the larger hut, where we sat on some stumps. Enrique brought us cheese and milk. Armando started cooking in a big pot on the campfire, and in moments he served us hot food—plates of beans, macaroni, bread. We ate everything he brought us, and he laughed as he refilled our plates again and again. After eating our fill, we were led to a second hut, where two beds were waiting. There were no mattresses, just some soft fleeces spread over the springs, but Roberto and I thanked Armando profusely, and in moments we were both sound asleep.

When we woke, it was early evening. Armando and Enrique had another meal waiting for us—more cheese and milk, a stew of meat and beans, plus sweet caramel *dulce de leche* spread on bread, and hot coffee.

"We're emptying your pantry," I joked, but the two peasants only laughed and urged us to eat more. After eating, we all relaxed together around the fire. Armando and Enrique listened in fascination as Roberto and I told the story of our ordeal, but we were soon interrupted by the sight of two Chilean policemen running up the trail to the hut, followed soon after by a patrol of ten more policemen on horseback. Riding with the police was Sergio Catalan. When he dismounted, Roberto and I rushed forward and embraced him. "There is no need to thank me," he said quietly, and as we hugged him he only whispered, "Thank God, thank God."

When the captain of the mounted police introduced himself, I explained that fourteen more survivors were waiting at the crash site. He asked for their names, but I refused to give them. "Some of them were near death when we left them," I explained. "I'm afraid some may have died. If you release their names, it will give their parents false hope, then they will have to lose their sons a second time."

The captain understood. "Where is the plane?" he asked. I looked at Roberto. It was clear the captain did not understand how difficult this rescue would be, but when we described our ten-day odyssey, and the approximate location of the crash site, he quickly realized his patrol could not reach the crash site on horseback.

"I'll send some men back to Puente Negro," he said, "and have them radio for a helicopter from Santiago."

"How long will that take?" I asked.

"They could be here tomorrow," he said, "if the weather is clear."

My concern for the survivors at the crash site was increasing with every passing moment, but we had no choice now except to wait. We talked for a while with Enrique and Armando, and some of the police. Then I went to bed. I spent a restless night in the sleeping hut, anxious for morning, but when I woke and went outside, I was distressed to see that a heavy fog had descended upon Los Maitenes.

"Do you think they can land in this?" I asked Roberto.

"Maybe it will burn off soon," he replied.

Enrique and Armando had breakfast waiting for us at the fire. Sergio and some of the policemen joined us, and as we were eating we heard the noise of an approaching crowd. Within seconds we were shocked to see a horde of reporters running up the dirt road toward the hut. They rushed forward when they spotted us.

"Are those the survivors?" they shouted. "Roberto? Fernando?" Now cameras were snapping, microphones were jabbed in our faces, and newspaper reporters were scribbling on notepads and shouting questions over one another's voices.

"How long did you trek?"

"Who else is alive?"

"How did you survive the cold? What did you eat?"

I looked at Roberto in amazement. "How did they find us," I muttered, "and how did they get here before the helicopters?"

We found ourselves surrounded by journalists from newspapers and television stations all over the world. Their unexpected arrival startled us, and we were rattled a little by the intensity of their questioning, but we tried our best to answer their inquiries, though we kept the more sensitive facts to ourselves. The captain of the mounted police allowed the interviews to continue for a while, then he took us aside.

"The fog is still heavy," he told us. "I don't think the helicopters will come today. I'm going to send you down to Puente Negro to wait for the rescue team to arrive. It might be easier for them to land there."

We nodded, and in moments Roberto and I were on horseback, following two of the mounted policemen down the trail, with the press in hot pursuit. Suddenly the entire noisy entourage came to a stop and gazed up at the overcast sky. There was commotion above us, the thunder of powerful engines and a roar of wind. The fog was still so thick that we couldn't see the helicopters land, but on horseback we followed the noise to a spot about four hundred yards away, a flat meadow near the huts, where three huge helicopters of the Chilean air force had just set down.

We dismounted from the horses as medics and crew members leaped out of the helicopters and came forward to examine us. Roberto needed their attention badly, but I refused to be examined. Instead, I sought out two of the helicopter pilots, Carlos Garcia and Jorge Massa, and tried to impress upon them the importance of leaving right away.

Commander Garcia shook his head. "There's no way we can fly in this fog," he said. "We have to wait for it to lift. In the meantime, what can you tell me about the location of the plane?"

Once again I described our trek through the Andes. Garcia gave me a skeptical frown, then retrieved a flight chart from the helicopter and spread it on the grass. "Do you think you can show me on the map?" he asked. He jabbed his finger at the chart and said, "We are here." I stared at the map for a moment, and once I got my bearings, it was easy to trace in reverse the route Roberto and I had followed.

"Here," I said, tapping the map where the valley ended at the foot of the peak I had christened Mount Seler. "They are on the far side of this mountain."

Massa and Garcia exchanged dubious glances.

"That's Argentina," Garcia said. "The High Andes. That's more than seventy miles from here."

"We have to hurry," I said. "Our friends are dying."

Massa frowned at Garcia. "He's confused," he said. "They couldn't have crossed the Andes on foot! Impossible!"

"Are you sure you understand this map?" Garcia asked me.

"I am sure of it," I said. "We came down this mountain, along this valley. Here is where the valley splits, and we followed this fork and it brought us here! The plane is lying there, just beyond this mountain, on a glacier above a wide valley that goes east."

Garcia nodded and folded the map. I was still not sure he believed me.

"When will you go for them?" I asked.

"As soon as the fog lifts, we will take off," he said, then he and Massa walked off with their heads together, and I knew they were discussing my account of the trek and how much of it they should believe.

Three hours later the fog still persisted, but it had thinned a little and the pilots now thought it was safe to fly. As the crews prepared for takeoff, Garcia approached me. "We're going to go now," he said. "But the location you showed us is in a very high and remote section of the Andes. Flying there will be very difficult, and with no landmarks, we will never find your friends in all those mountains. Do you think you can come with us, and guide us to the plane?"

I don't remember how I answered him, or if I answered him at all, but in seconds I felt arms all over me as I was lifted into the helicopter and strapped into a jumpseat in the cargo area. Someone slipped a seat of headphones over my ears, and positioned the tip of the small attached microphone close to my mouth. Three members of the Andean Rescue Corps climbed in beside me. The copilot sat in front of me, and Commander Garcia took the controls. As Garcia revved the engines, I looked out the window and saw Roberto, the only one who could understand how frightened I was to be flying back into the Andes. He didn't wave; we just exchanged glances. Then the helicopter lurched into the air and my stomach dropped as we banked hard and swooped off to the east and into the mountains. At first my earphones crackled with technical chatter as the pilot and mechanic began to set our course, then Garcia spoke to me.

"Okay, Nando," he said, "show us the way."

I guided them into the valley and we followed it across the Chilean border and into the Argentine Andes, with a second helicopter, piloted by commander Massa, close on our tail. The air was turbulent, and the helicopter danced and bobbed like a speedboat on rough water, but the flight was short—in less than twenty minutes we were hovering at the eastern end of the valley where the massive bulk of Mount Seler towered above us like the walls of a gigantic fortress.

"Holy Jesus," someone muttered.

Garcia let the helicopter hover as he gazed up to the mountain's snow-capped peak and down the black slopes plunging to the floor of the valley, several thousand feet below.

"Mother of God," he said, "you didn't come down this?"

"Yes," I said, "this is the way."

"Are you *sure?*" he said. "Are you *certain?*"

"I'm certain," I said. "They're on the other side."

Garcia looked at his copilot. "With so many people, we're heavy," the copilot said. "I don't know if we have the power to clear that mountain."

Garcia asked again. "Nando, are you absolutely certain this is the way?"

I barked into the microphone, "I am!"

Garcia nodded. "Hold on," he said. I felt the copter surge forward as the pilots gunned the engines. We raced at the face of the mountain, gathering speed, and then, slowly, the copter began to climb. As we flew closer to the mountains, we were battered by the swirling air rushing up from the slopes. Garcia fought for control as the helicopter lurched wildly from side to side. The engines screamed, the windshield rattled in its frame, and my seat shook so violently it blurred my vision. It seemed that every bolt and rivet in the aircraft was being pushed beyond its limits, and I was certain the aircraft would soon shake itself to bits. I had seen this kind of mechanical chaos before, in the moments just before the Fairchild slammed into a ridge, and seeing it again, I felt panic rising in my throat like vomit. Garcia and the copilot were barking commands so rapidly I couldn't tell who was speaking.

"The air is too thin! There's not enough lift."

"Come on, push it!"

"One hundred percent, one hundred ten . . ."

"Keep it level! Keep it level!"

I glanced at the rescue team, hoping for a sign from them that any of this was normal, but their faces were drawn and pale. Garcia continued to push the engines, battling for every foot of altitude, and finally he managed to force the copter above the mountain's summit, but no sooner had we cleared the top than the strong air currents streaming over the ridge threw us back violently, and Garcia had no choice but to let the copter fall away in a long, swooping circle to keep the craft from being dashed against the slopes. As we fell, I began to scream, and I kept screaming as we swung around and made one more assault on the summit, only to be pushed back in the same terrifying fashion.

"We can't make it over this mountain," Garcia announced. "We'll have to find a way around it. This is a life-threatening mission now, and I won't go forward unless everyone on board volunteers. I'll leave it to all of you. Shall we continue or go back?"

I exchanged glances with the others on board, then we turned to the captain and nodded. "Okay," he said, "but hold on, it will be rough going." My stomach pitched again as we banked to the right and flew over some lower peaks just south of Mount Seler. It was the only route open to us, but we were veering off the path Roberto and I had followed now, and I quickly lost my bearings over the unfamiliar landscape below.

"Which way?" Garcia demanded.

"I'm not sure . . . I'm all turned around . . ."

I scanned the horizon, searching frantically for a point of reference, terrified that my friends were now hopelessly lost. Everywhere I looked I saw repetition and sameness, just an endless ocean of white snow and black rock. . . . Then something in the jagged profile of one of the ridges caught my eye.

"Wait!" I shouted. "I know that mountain! I know where we are! Go down!"

As we dropped lower into the mountains, I realized that Garcia had found his way around the mountains that bordered the crash site to the south. We were above the valley that we had trekked through on our attempts to escape to the east, and climbing west toward the eastern face of Mount Seler.

"They must be up there," I said, pointing east.

"I don't see anything," said the pilot.

"Keep going!" I said. "They're on the glacier!"

"The wind is bad!" said the copilot. "I don't know if we can land here."

I stared at the slopes, and suddenly I spotted it, a faint dot in the snow. "I see the plane!" I shouted. "There, on the left."

Garcia scanned the slopes. "Where . . . I can't see anything. Wait, okay, I see it. Shut up now, everyone shut up!"

In moments we were circling high above the crash site, and my heart pounded as Garcia battled strong turbulence above the glacier, but my fears faded as I saw a line of tiny figures coming out of the fuselage. Even from that altitude I could make some of them out—I recognized Gustavo from his pilot's cap, Daniel, Pedro, Fito, Javier . . . There were others, running, waving. I tried to count them, but the lurching of the helicopter made it impossible. I could see no sign of Roy or Coche, the ones who worried me the most.

I heard Garcia's voice in the headphones, speaking to the rescue team. "The slope is too steep for a landing," he said. "I'm going to hover as low as I can. You'll have to jump out." Then he turned his attention to the dicey business of bringing the helicopter down safely in the swirling winds.

"Shit! This turbulence is bad. Keep it level."

"Watch the slope, we're too close!"

"Keep it level!"

"Easy now . . ."

He turned the copter so that one side faced up the slope, then eased it down until one of its skis just touched the snow. "Go!" he shouted. The rescuers threw open the sliding door, tossed their gear out onto the mountain, and jumped out beneath the whirling blades. I looked out and saw Daniel running toward us. He ducked under the blades and tried to dive into the helicopter, but he misjudged his leap and slammed his chest against one of the copter's skis.

"Carajo!" he shouted. "I think I broke my ribs."

"Don't kill yourself now!" I cried. Then I reached down and pulled him inside. Alvaro Mangino climbed in after him.

"That's all we can take," shouted Garcia. "We'll get the rest to-morrow. Now close the door!" I obeyed the captain's orders, and in seconds we were hovering above the crash site as the second heli-copter dropped down and more rescuers leaped out onto the mountain. I saw Carlitos, Pedro, and Eduardo climb into the wait-ing aircraft. Then I saw the emaciated figure of Coche Inciarte limping toward the copter.

"Coche is alive!" I said to Daniel. "How is Roy?"

"Alive," said Daniel, "but barely."

The flight back to Los Maitenes was just as harrowing as the ear-lier trip, but in less than twenty minutes we had landed safely in the meadow near the peasants' hut. As soon as the doors were opened,

Daniel and Alvaro were whisked away by the medics. In moments the second helicopter set down about thirty yards away, and I was there as the doors slid open. Coche fell out happily into my arms, then Eduardo and Carlitos. Amazed to see flowers and greenery again, some of them fell to their knees in the grass. Others embraced and rolled about on the ground in each other's arms. Carlitos wrapped his arms around me and wrestled me to the ground. "You bastard!" he cried. "You made it! You made it!" Then he reached into his pocket and drew out the little red shoe I had given him when I left the fuselage. He was beaming at me, his eyes lit with joy and his face only inches from mine.

"I'm happy to see you, Carlitos," I said, "but please, you aren't going to kiss me, are you?"

When the celebration ended, they brought us hot soup, cheese, and chocolates. While the medics examined the six new arrivals, I found Commander Garcia and asked when the rest of the survivors would be taken off the mountain. He explained that it would be too dangerous to fly into the mountains at night. Rescue would have to wait another day. But he assured me that the medics and the rescue workers who had stayed on the mountain would make sure all the boys were safe.

After we all were fed, we were loaded into the helicopters and flown to a military base near the town of San Fernando. Teams of doctors and nurses were there to help us into waiting ambulances. The ambulances left in a convoy, escorted by police on motorcycles, and in about ten minutes we had reached St. John of God hospital in San Fernando. Hospital personnel met us in the parking lot with gurneys. Some of the guys needed this help, but I told the nurses I would walk. After hiking across the Andes, I was not about to let them carry me the last few yards.

They led me to a small, clean room and began peeling off layers of filthy clothing from my body. They threw the dirty rags into a corner and I saw them lying there—the sweaters, jeans, and slacks that had been my second skin. It felt good to shed them, and put them in my past. I was taken into the bathroom and given a warm shower. I felt hands washing my hair and a soft cloth scrubbing the dirt from my skin. When the shower was over, they dried me with soft towels, and then I caught sight of myself in the bathroom's full-length mirror. My jaw dropped when I saw what I had become. Before the crash, I had been an athlete in training, but now there was not a trace of muscle anywhere on my frame. The bones of my ribs, hips, and shoulder blades showed through the skin, and my arms and legs had withered so close to the bone that my knees and elbows bulged like thick knots tied in a rope. The nurses steered me from the mirror and dressed me in a fresh hospital gown, then led me to a narrow bed and began to examine me, but I asked them to leave me alone for a while. When they'd all left, I quietly rejoiced in the comfort and cleanliness and peace of the pleasant little room. I lay back on the soft mattress, felt the smoothness of the crisp cotton sheets. Slowly I let it sink in: I was safe; I was going to go home. I drew a long breath and then slowly, richly, I exhaled. *Breathe once more,* we used to say on the mountain, to encourage each other in moments of despair. *As long as you breathe, you are alive.* In those days, each breath was almost an act of defiance. In my seventy-two days in the Andes, there had not been a single breath that wasn't taken in fear. Now, at last, I enjoyed the luxury of ordinary breathing. Again and again, I filled my lungs, then let the air out in long, unhurried exhalations, and with each breath I whispered to myself in amazement:

I am alive. I am alive. I am alive.

Suddenly my thoughts were disturbed by shouting outside my door, and what sounded like a scuffle in the hallway. "Calm down!" barked a firm male voice. "No one is allowed in here."

A woman's voice answered. "My brother is in there!" she shouted. "I have to see him! Please!"

I stepped into the hallway just in time to see my sister Graciela pushing past a group of hospital orderlies. I called her name, and she began to sob when she saw me. In seconds she was in my arms, and my heart swelled with love as I held her. With her was her husband, Juan, his eyes bright with tears, and for a moment the three of us embraced without a word. Then I looked up. At the end of the hallway, standing motionless in the thin fluorescent light, was the slim, bowed figure of my father. I walked to him and embraced him, then I hoisted him in my arms until his feet left the ground. "You see, Papá," I whispered as I set him down again, "I am still strong enough to lift you." He pressed himself against me, touching me, convincing himself that I was real. I held him for a long time, feeling his body tremble gently as he wept. For a while neither of us spoke. Then, with his head still pressed to my chest, he whispered, "Mami? Susy?"

I answered him with a gentle silence, and he sagged a little in my arms as he understood. A few moments later my sister came to us and led us back to my room. They gathered around my bed, and I told them the story of my life in the mountains. I described the crash, the cold, the fear, the long journey I had made with Roberto. I explained how my mother had died, and how I had comforted Susy. My father winced when I mentioned my sister, so I spared him the details of her suffering, thinking it was enough to tell him she was never alone and that she had died in my arms. Graciela wept softly as I spoke. She could not take her eyes off me. My father sat quietly beside my bed, listening, nodding, with a heartbreaking smile on his face. When I finished, there was a silence until my father found the strength to speak.

"How did you survive, Nando?" he asked, "So many weeks without food . . ."

I told him that we had eaten the flesh of those who didn't survive. The expression on his face didn't change.

"You did what you had to do," he said, his voice cracking with emotion. "I am happy to have you home."

There was so much I wanted to tell him, that I had thought of him every moment, that his love had been the guiding light that led me to safety. But there would be time for that later. Right now I wanted to treasure every moment of our reunion, bittersweet as it was. At first it was hard to convince myself that this moment, the moment I had dreamed of for so long, was real. My mind was moving slowly, and my emotions were oddly muted. I felt no sense of elation or triumph, just a gentle glow of safety and peace. There were no words to explain how I felt, so I simply sat in silence. After a while we heard sounds of celebration in the hallway as the families of the other survivors found their sons. My sister rose and closed the door, and in the privacy of my room, I shared with what was left of my family the simple miracle of being together again.

Chapter Ten

After

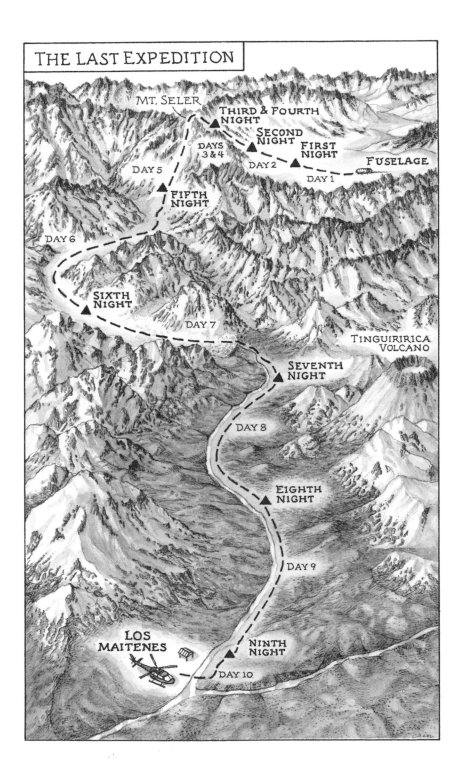

THE FOLLOWING DAY, December 23, the eight survivors who had been left on the mountain were flown to Santiago, where they were examined at a hospital known as the Posta Centrale. The doctors decided to hold Javier and Roy for observation—they were especially concerned about Roy, whose blood chemistry showed irregularities that could pose a threat to his heart—but the rest were released and moved to the Sheraton San Cristóbal Hotel, where many of them were joined by their families. The eight of us at St. John's hospital were moved to Santiago that same afternoon. Alvaro and Coche, the weakest in our group, were admitted to the Posta Centrale, while the rest of us were released and taken to the Sheraton to be reunited with our friends.

The atmosphere at the Sheraton, and throughout Santiago for that matter, was charged with an atmosphere of celebration and a sense of religious awe. The papers called our return "The Christmas Miracle," and many people were regarding us as almost mystical figures: young boys who had been saved by the direct intercession of God, living proof of His love. News of our survival was making headlines around the globe, and public interest was intense. The Sheraton's lobby and the streets outside the hotel were jammed, around the clock, with reporters and news crews waiting to pounce upon our every move. We could not go to a café for a snack, or have a quiet conversation with our families, without a horde of journalists poking microphones at us and firing flashbulbs in our faces.

On Christmas Eve, a party was arranged for us in a ballroom at the hotel. There was an air of joy and gratitude, as many of the survivors and their families gave thanks to God for saving us from death. "I told you we would be home for Christmas," Carlitos said to me, with the same smile of certainty he had shown in the mountains. "I told you God would not abandon us." I was happy for him, and for the others, but as I watched them sharing their joy with their loved ones, I realized that except for Javier, every one of my fellow survivors was returning to a life that was just as it had been before. Many of them had lost friends in the disaster, that was true, and all of them had endured an incredible nightmare, but now, for them, it was over. Their families were intact. They would be embraced again by their parents, brothers and sisters, girlfriends. Their worlds would begin again, and things would be just as they were before the crash interrupted their lives. But my world had been destroyed, and the party only underscored for me how much I had lost. I would never spend another Christmas with my mother, or with Susy. It was clear to me that my father had been shattered by the ordeal, and I wondered if he would ever again be the man I had known. I tried to share in the celebration that night, but I felt very alone, understanding that what was a triumph for the others was the beginning of a new and uncertain future for me.

After three days in Santiago, the circus atmosphere at the hotel became too much to bear, and my father moved us to a house in the Chilean beach resort of Viña del Mar. We spent three quiet days there, resting, driving around, lying in the sun. On the beach I felt like an oddity. My picture had been in all the papers, and with my long beard and my bones showing through my skin, it was easy to recognize me as a survivor. I couldn't walk far without being accosted by strangers, so I stayed close to the house, and spent many hours with my father. He didn't ask many questions about what happened to me in the mountains, and I sensed that he was still not yet ready to hear the details, but he was willing to share with me what his life had been like in the long weeks I was gone. He told me that at three-thirty in the afternoon of October 13, the very hour the plane had fallen from the sky, he was on his way to make a deposit at a bank near his office in Montevideo when, suddenly, something stopped him in his tracks.

"The door of the bank was only a few steps away," he told me, "but I couldn't make myself go any farther. It was so strange. I lost all interest in the bank. My stomach tightened. I just wanted to go home." In all his life, my father had missed work only a handful of times, but that day he forgot about the office and drove to our house in Carrasco. He poured himself a cup of *mate* and turned on the television, where special bulletins were reporting that a Uruguayan charter plane had been lost in the Andes. Not knowing about our unscheduled overnight stay in Mendoza, he calmed himself with the thought that we would have reached Santiago the previous afternoon. Still, a sense of dread haunted him as he watched the news. Then, about an hour after he had gotten home, there was a knock on the door.

"It was Colonel Jaume," my father explained, mentioning the name of a friend who was an officer in the Uruguayan air force. "He said, 'I have a car waiting. I want you to come with me. I'm afraid I have bad news . . .' " The colonel took my father to his house, where he confirmed the worst—the lost plane was, in fact, our flight. The next day my father was on a plane to Santiago, bound for a meeting with Chilean officials who would explain what they knew of the crash. His route took him above the Andes, and as he gazed down into the mountains below, he was chilled by the thought that his wife and children had fallen into such a merciless place. "In that moment," he told me, "I lost all hope. I knew I would never see any of you again."

The following weeks were as horrific as anything I had imagined for him in the mountains. He couldn't sleep or eat. He found no comfort in prayer or in the company of others. Many parents of other crash victims found ways to keep their hopes alive. Some of the mothers met regularly to pray for us. A group of the fathers, led by Carlitos's father, Carlos Paez-Villaro, had even mounted their own search efforts, hiring planes and helicopters to fly over the Andes in places where the authorities thought the Fairchild might have fallen. My father contributed money to these search efforts, though he was certain they were nothing but a waste of time. "When a plane falls into the Andes, it is lost forever," he said. "I knew we would be lucky if the mountains gave up even a small fragment of the wreckage."

With no hope to cling to, my father's emotional condition declined rapidly. He grew withdrawn and apathetic. He would sit alone, in silence, for hours, or wander aimlessly on the beach, with my dog, Jimmy, as his only companion. "Your mother was my strength," he told me. "I needed her so badly then, but she was gone, and without her I was lost." As days passed he grew increasingly apathetic and withdrawn, and more than once his grief led him to the edge of madness. "One day I was eating lunch with Lina," he said. "The house was so quiet. There were so many empty places at the table. I set down my fork and said, 'Mamá, I can't stay here.' Then I left the house and began to walk."

He walked the streets for hours, all through the afternoon and into the night. His mind was blank except for the unformed thought that he must keep moving, that through simple forward motion he might distance himself from his pain. Finally he found himself on the broad lawn of the Plaza Matriz, Montevideo's historic central square. In front of him rose the dark, ornate towers of the Catedral Metropolitana, built by Spanish colonists in 1740. My father was not a religious man, but something drew him into the church, a yearning for peace, or some small comfort he could cling to. He knelt and tried to pray, but he felt nothing. Slumping in the pew, he looked at his watch, and was shocked to see that he had been walking for more than ten hours. Fearing that he was losing his mind, he left the church and, in the darkness, made his way home.

"I told myself, 'I have to change everything,' " he said. Then, as if he could shed his pain by severing his physical connections to the past, my father began to dismantle his life. He sold his prized Mercedes and my mother's beloved Rover. He put the flat in Punta del Este on the market, and prepared to sell our house in Carrasco. He even tried to sell the businesses he had labored a lifetime to build, but Graciela and Juan caught wind of his plans and talked him out of his recklessness before too much damage had been done. "I didn't know what I was doing," he told me. "Sometimes I could think clearly, and others times I was absolutely *loco*. Nothing mattered to me in those days. Nothing made sense after the plane went down."

When my father heard that Roberto and I had been found in the mountains, he refused to believe it, but slowly he allowed himself to accept that it was true. On the morning of December 23, he boarded a charter flight, with Graciela and Juan and families of other victims of the crash, bound for Santiago. The names of the other survivors had not yet been released, and as my father flew over the Andes once again, he allowed his hopes to soar. "If anyone is alive," he told my sister, "it is because your mother got them out." Hours later he was in my arms, and I was letting him know that his hopes were false; my mother and sister had not survived.

"Papa," I said to him one day in Viña del Mar, "I am sorry I could not save Mami and Susy." He smiled sadly and took my arm. "When I was certain all of you were dead," he said, "I knew I would never recover from the loss. It was as if my house had burned to the ground, and I had lost everything I owned, forever. And now, to have you back, it's as if I have stumbled on something precious in the ashes. I feel I am reborn. My life can begin again. From now on, I will try not to feel sorry for what was taken from me, but to be happy for what was given back." He advised me to do the same. "The sun will come up tomorrow," he told me, "and the day after that, and the day after that. Don't let this be the most important thing that ever happens to you. Look forward," he said. "You will have a future. You will live a life."

We left Viña del Mar on December 30 in a plane bound for Montevideo. I was terrified to fly across the Andes again, but with the help of sedatives prescribed by a Chilean doctor, I made myself board the plane. When we arrived at our house in Carrasco, a crowd of friends and neighbors had gathered in the street to meet me. I shook hands and embraced them as I climbed the long set of steps from the sidewalk to the front door, where my grandmother Lina was waiting. I fell into her arms, and she hugged me with such force and bittersweet affection that I knew in her mind she was embracing Susy and my mother, too. We all stepped inside. Ahead of me, lying on the tile floor of the hallway, was my dog, Jimmy. He had been fast asleep, and now, hearing us enter, he opened his eyes wearily without lifting his big square head from his paws. He gave me a curious glance, then his ears perked and he sat up and cocked his head as if in disbelief. For a long moment he studied me, then, with a happy yelp, he launched himself toward me so fast that at first he ran in place as his paws scrabbled on the slippery tile. I hugged him as he leaped into my arms, and let him lick my face with his warm, wet tongue. Everyone laughed at Jimmy's happiness, and for me it was a fine welcome home.

Those first moments in the house were eerie for me. I was happy, and amazed, to be in my home again, but the rooms thundered with the absence of my mother and my sister. I walked to my old bedroom. Graciela had moved in with my father just after the crash, and her two-year-old son was using my room now. I saw that all my things were gone. In his tortured efforts to purge himself of his past, my father had gotten rid of all my things—my clothes, my books, my sports equipment and racing magazines, even the poster of Jackie Stewart that had hung on the wall for years. In the living room I saw my photograph on the mantel, arranged with photos of my mother and Susy in a somber memorial. I glanced out the window. Cars were passing on the street. Lights were coming on in other houses where people were going on with their lives. *This is how life would look if I had died,* I thought. *I did not leave a very big hole. The world has gone on without me.*

THOSE FIRST WEEKS at home were a kind of limbo for me. So much had changed, and I couldn't seem to find my way back into my life. With Guido and Panchito gone, I passed much of my time alone. I played with Jimmy and spent hours riding my motorcycle—my father had sold it in my absence, but the friend who had bought it returned it the moment he heard of our rescue. Sometimes I walked the streets, but I was recognized everywhere I went, and after a while it was easier to stay at home. When I did go out, I could not avoid reminders of what had happened to me. Once, at La Mascota, a neighborhood pizza parlor I had patronized since I was a child, the owner and waiter made a fuss about what an honor it was to have me there, and they refused to take my money. They meant well, I know, but it was a long time before I went back. On the sidewalk, strangers approached me to shake my hand, as if I were some kind of conquering hero who had brought honor to Uruguay by my exploits. In fact, our survival had become a matter of national pride. Our ordeal was being celebrated as a glorious adventure. People compared our accomplishments with the heroic achievements of the Uruguayan soccer team that had won the World Cup in 1950. Some people even went so far as to tell me that they envied me for my experience in the Andes, and wished they had been there with me. I didn't know how to explain to them that there was no glory in those mountains. It was all ugliness and fear and desperation, and the obscenity of watching so many innocent people die.

I was also shaken by the sensationalism with which many in the press covered the matter of what we had eaten to survive. Shortly after our rescue, officials of the Catholic Church announced that according to church doctrine we had committed no sin by eating the flesh of the dead. As Roberto had argued on the mountain, they told the world that the sin would have been to allow ourselves to die. More satisfying for me was the fact that many of the parents of the boys who died had publicly expressed their support for us, telling the world they understood and accepted what we had done to survive. I will always be grateful for the courage and generosity they showed in their support for us. Despite these gestures, many news reports focused on the matter of our diet, in reckless and exploitive ways. Some newspapers ran lurid headlines above grisly front-page photos, taken after our rescue by members of the Andean Rescue Corps, showing piles of bones near the fuselage, and human body parts scattered around on the snow. In the wake of this exploitative coverage, rumors began to rise, including one theory that the avalanche had never happened, and that we had actually killed the people who died in that disaster so we could use them as food.

Graciela and Juan were a great help to me in those days, but I missed Susy and my mother intensely. My father was my comrade in suffering, but, reeling from grief, he was just as lost as I was. I soon learned that in his loneliness he had sought comfort in the company of another woman, and he was seeing her still. I didn't blame him for this. I knew he was a man who needed a strong emotional center in his life, and that the death of my mother had taken from him a sense of completeness and balance he couldn't live without. Still, it was hard for me to see the two of them together so soon after the disaster, and just one more indication that my old life was gone forever. So, as summer approached, I decided I would escape Montevideo, and all the memories there, to spend some time alone at my father's flat in Punta del Este. Our family had summered there for years, ever since the days when Susy and I were small children playing on the beach. Everything was different now, of course. Everyone knew me, and wherever I went I was surrounded by gawkers, well-wishers, and strangers seeking autographs. At first I hid out in my flat, but as time passed, I must admit, part of me began to enjoy the attention—especially when I realized that so many attractive young women seemed determined to get to know me. I had always envied Panchito's effortless ability to attract the prettiest girls on the beach, and now these same girls were drawn just as powerfully to me. Were they attracted because of who I was, or what I had done? Or was it simply my new celebrity? I didn't care. For the first time in my life, girls found me fascinating—irresistible, in fact—and I did my best to make the most of it. For weeks on end I partied with one beautiful woman after another, sometimes with two or three in a single day, and always I kept my eye peeled for someone new. I became one of Punta del Este's most visible libertines, with my picture appearing often in the newspaper's society pages—Nando at one fancy party or another, lifting a glass, living the leisurely life of a full-time playboy, and always with a flashy girl or two on his arms.

This notoriety did not escape the attention of my fellow survivors, who were not happy with my behavior. For them the ordeal had been a transforming experience that had showed them the dignity of human life and had led them to commit themselves to living lives of morality and high principle. In their eyes, I was forgetting the lessons I had learned. At some point in the summer I was asked to judge a beauty contest at the beach, an offer I happily accepted. The news was announced in a local paper, which ran a photo of me smiling intensely, surrounded by half a dozen bikini-clad beauties. This was too much for the others, and out of respect for them I backed out of the deal. Still, I thought my friends were taking themselves a bit too seriously. After all, considering what we'd been through, didn't the world owe us a little fun? I told myself I was savoring life, making up for the time I'd lost on the mountain. But perhaps I was fooling myself. I think now that at the center of my soul there was a numbness, an emptiness, and I was trying to fill that emptiness with night after night of carousing. I was still denying the pain I had held inside me since the first days of the disaster. I was trying to find a safe way to *feel*.

One evening, at a Punta nightclub called 05, I was talking with my date and sipping a Coke, when reality ambushed me like a billy club to the head. I had spent so many nights at the same club with Panchito, and now, out of habit, I found myself waiting for him to walk through the door. I had thought of him so many times since our rescue, but that night, in that place, I felt his absence viscerally, as a pain in my gut, and I understood with brutal certainty that he was gone. The realization of that loss brought all my other losses to the surface, and for the first time since the Fairchild fell in the mountains, I began to cry. I bowed my head and sobbed so hard I could not control myself. My date kindly helped me home, and for hours I sat on the balcony of my flat, watching the ocean, alone with my thoughts. As I brooded on all the things that had been taken from me, my grief soon gave way to outrage. Why had this happened? Why was I made to suffer so much loss when so many others were allowed to live their lives happily? For hours I sat like this, cursing God or my luck, and torturing myself with possibilities: *If only the pilots had seen that ridge sooner. If only Panchito had taken a different seat. If only I hadn't invited my mother and sister to come along.* I thought of boys who had dropped out of the trip at the last moment, or had missed the plane and had to take a different flight. Why wasn't I spared, like those boys? Why was it *my* life that had to be destroyed?

As the hours passed and I sank deeper into these bitter thoughts, my anger grew so strong that I thought I would never forgive life for the way it had cheated me of a happy future. But then, sometime before dawn, as weariness softened my rage, I remembered the advice my father had given me at Viña del Mar: *You will have a future. You will live a life.*

And as I pondered his words, I saw the error I was making. I had been thinking of the disaster as a horrible mistake, as an unscripted deviation from the happy story of the life I had been promised. But now I began to understand that my ordeal in the Andes was not an interruption of my true destiny, or a perversion of what my life was *supposed* to be. It simply *was* my life, and the future that lay ahead was the only future available to me. To hide from this fact, or to live in bitterness and anger, would only keep me from living any genuine life at all. Before the crash, I took so much for granted, but the mountains showed me that life, any life, is a miracle. Now, miraculously, I had been granted a second chance to live. It was not the life I wanted or expected, but I understood that it was my duty now to live that life as richly and as hopefully as I could. I vowed to try. I would live with passion and curiosity. I would open myself to the possibilities of life. I would savor every moment, and I would try, every day, to become more human and more alive. To do any less, I understood, would be an insult to those who hadn't survived.

I made these vows with no expectation to be happy. I simply felt it was my obligation to make the most of the chance I had been given. So I opened myself to life, and, to my great fortune, my new life began to happen.

IN JANUARY OF 1973, some friends invited me to go with them to see the Argentine Formula One Grand Prix in Buenos Aires. At the time I was not eager to travel, but my time in the mountains hadn't dulled my passion for motor sports, and this was a chance to see the greatest drivers in the world, so I agreed to go. We hadn't been at the track long before the press caught wind of my presence, and soon I found myself surrounded by photographers. I let them snap their pictures, then we moved on. A few moments later I was surprised by an announcement on the track's PA system.

"Will Nando Parrado please report to the Tyrell F1 pit area . . ."

"It's probably some newspaper wanting an interview," I told my friends. "But that's the pit area for the Tyrell racing team. Let's go. It's a chance to see the cars up close."

When we arrived, the Tyrell pits were buzzing with activity. Some twenty mechanics in blue coveralls were busily attending to two beautiful grand prix racing cars. When I introduced myself, one of the mechanics took me by the arm and led me past the cars to a patch of asphalt at the rear of the pits, where a long motor home was parked. The mechanic opened the door for me and motioned me in, then went back to the pits. I climbed a small set of stairs and stepped inside the trailer. To my left, a slender, dark-haired man was sitting on a sofa, tugging bright gray fireproof racing coveralls over his legs. When he looked up, and I saw who he was, I gasped and stepped backward.

"You're Jackie Stewart!" I blurted.

"Yes, I am," he said, in the smooth Scottish accent I had heard on television a hundred times. "Are you Nando Parrado?"

I nodded dumbly.

"I heard you were here," he said, "and I asked them to find you." Then he told me that he had wanted to meet me since he'd heard the story of the Andes disaster. He was very impressed with what I'd done, he said, and he hoped I wouldn't mind talking with him about it.

"Yes," I stammered, "I'd be happy to . . ."

He smiled and looked me over. "Do you like racing?" he asked.

I drew a deep breath. Where should I begin? "I love it," I said, finally. "I have loved racing since I was a kid. You are my favorite driver. I've read your books. I know all your races, I have your poster in my room . . ." I don't know how long I rambled on like this, but I wanted him to understand that I was no mere fawning fan. I wanted him to know I had studied his techniques and that I respected his mastery of the sport—the virtuosity with which he pushed his car to the limits of physics without going over the top, how he balanced aggressiveness and grace, risk and control. I wanted him to see that I understood racing in my soul, and knew that good driving was more poetry than machismo.

Jackie smiled kindly as he finished dressing. "I have to qualify now," he said, "but stick around the pits and we'll talk when I come back." In less than an hour, Jackie returned. He showed me his car—he even let me sit behind the wheel—then he invited me to stay for his team's pre-race meeting. I listened in awe as Jackie discussed with his engineers and mechanics the last-minute adjustments they'd make to the car's engine and suspension to bring it into racing tune. After the meeting, Jackie and I talked for hours. He asked about the Andes, and I asked him about races and cars. After a while, it was not so mind-boggling to be with him. For all his fame and stature, he was a genuine, generous man, and as we got to know each other, I realized, in amazement, that my boyhood idol and I were becoming friends.

A few months later I accepted Jackie's invitation to visit him at his home in Switzerland, where I grew close to his family, and our friendship deepened. Jackie and I spent hours talking about cars and racing, and I tried to absorb everything he said. Finally, I confessed to him that I had dreamed of driving race cars since I was a child.

Jackie took my interest seriously, and encouraged me to do the same. In 1974, at Jackie's recommendation, I enrolled in the Jim Russell driving school at Snetterton in Great Britain. At the time, this was the premier racing school in the world, and its graduates— Emerson Fitipaldi among them—were racing at the top tracks around the globe. At the Russell school I trained in sleek Formula Fords—as spectacular a machine as any car I'd dreamed of as a kid—and proved to myself that I had what it takes to be an elite racer.

When classes ended, I went home to South America and spent the next two years racing motorcylces and stock cars in Uruguay, Argentina, and Chile. I enjoyed my share of victories, but I always dreamed of driving on the great tracks of Europe, and it didn't take long for that dream to come true. In 1973, at the Buenos Aires Grand Prix—the same race at which I'd met Jackie Stewart—I'd been introduced to Bernie Ecclestone, the British racing impresario who is now considered one of the founding fathers of modern Formula One racing. At the time, Bernie was already one of the most influential figures on the international racing scene, and the owner of the great Brabham racing team. Like Jackie, he recognized my passion for racing, and this became the basis of a strong friendship. Since then we had kept in touch, and he had followed my short racing career. In early 1977 I learned from Bernie that Alfa-Romeo's prestigious Autodelta racing team was looking for drivers. He offered to arrange an introduction for me, and a few weeks later I traveled to the Alpha-Romeo offices in Italy with three other South American drivers—Juan Zampa, Mario Marquez, and Eugene "Chippy" Breard. Our meetings with the Autodelta officials went well, and by May of 1977, Juan, Mario, Chippy, and I began driving as teammates in long-distance races on the European Touring Car Championship. I had made it happen, the life I'd dreamed of, racing fine cars against elite drivers at the greatest racetracks of the world. We did well, finishing second at Silverstone, in England, and at Zandvoort, in the Netherlands, and taking our first win at Pergusa, a very fast track in southern Italy. With each race I felt more confidence. I drove more smoothly, with more balance and precision and speed. I pushed the edge farther and farther, and proved to myself that even in competition with the very best, I could hold my own. And, little by little, I was realizing the dream I had as a boy—the dream of finding poetry in the power and precision of a fine machine.

It was an incredible year, filled with excitement, great challenges, interesting people, and glamorous travel. I was living a dream come true, and when we arrived in Belgium for a race at the Zolder racetrack in September, I had no reason to think it would end. But in the days before the race, as our team prepared the cars, I wandered into a VIP hospitality area hosted by Philip Morris, looking for a Coke, and was struck by a tall blonde in a red blazer and white slacks. She was standing with her back to me, but something about her stopped me in my tracks. Then she turned around and smiled.

"Nando?" she said.

"Veronique?" I stammered, "What are you doing here?"

I knew her. Her name was Veronique van Wassenhove, a Uruguayan by birth, whose parents had emigrated from Belgium. She was a striking girl, tall and willowy, with long hair and wide-set green eyes. I had met her three years earlier, in 1974, in Montevideo, when she was dating Gustavo Zerbino's younger brother, Rafael. Rafael had suffered a minor car crash just before a big party, and he'd called to ask me if I would pick up his date. I was on my way to the party with Roberto and his girlfriend Laura, so we stopped at Veronique's place to give her a lift. Rafael was supposed to meet us at the party, but he never showed up, so I became Veronique's date for the evening. She was only sixteen at the time, but she had an easy grace about her and a quiet sense of maturity that told me she had her feet planted firmly on the ground. I liked her right away. We had a wonderful time together, talking and dancing, and she impressed me more and more as the night wore on. But she was much too young for me, and besides, she was dating my friend, so I never thought of it as anything more than a casual evening. In the next few years I would see Veronique at the beach, or at clubs or parties, and we would always say hello. One afternoon my friends and I were in the audience at the annual Miss Punta del Este beauty pageant, a prestigious event that draws the loveliest women from all across South America, watching as one breathtaking woman after another appeared in elegant evening dresses. After a while, a tall blonde in a sleek blue dress took the stage. She moved differently than the others. Her stride was less studied and more naturally graceful. There was humor in her eyes, and while the others seemed to be working very hard to present their glossiest, most glamorous image, this one had an easy smile and an effortless bearing that told me she was really having fun. It was Veronique, of course. She had entered the contest at the last moment, urged by friends who thought it would help launch her modeling career. I chuckled as she passed by the judges' table. The other contestants had obviously spent much time and effort polishing their looks and outfits, down to the fancy shoes each of them wore. But as Veronique crossed the stage I saw, beneath the hem of her long gown, that she was barefoot. I was completely charmed, as were the judges, who, at the end of the evening, awarded her the crown.

Now, here she was in Belgium, a few years older, no longer with Rafael, and looking even lovelier than I remembered. She told me she was staying with her mother at their apartment in Brussels, that she had taken a temporary job in public relations here at the track, and that she was planning on going to London to study English, but my thoughts were too scattered to register much of what she said. I couldn't stop looking at her. I could barely breathe. I had wondered, since I was a boy, what it would be like when I first met the woman I would marry. How would I know her? Would I hear a thunderclap? See fireworks in my mind? Now I knew. It was nothing like that, there was only a firm, quiet voice of certainty whispering in my mind: *Veronique. Of course . . .*

It took no more than a second. I saw my future in her eyes. And I think she saw her future in mine. We spoke for a while, then she invited me to lunch on Monday at her family's apartment. I raced the next day and finished second, which was a miracle, because it rained heavily, and racing in the rain requires fierce concentration. But as I threw my car into turn after turn, and accelerated into the straightaways, I wasn't thinking about balance or traction or the importance of finding the most efficient line through a curve. My mind was on Monday, when I would see Veronique again. When Monday finally arrived, I found myself at lunch with Veronique and her mother at their elegant apartment on the Avenue Louis in Brussels. Veronique's mother was an impressively aristocratic woman who greeted me warmly but must have been wary of a twenty-seven-year-old race car driver calling on her nineteen-year-old daughter. I tried to be on my best behavior, but already I was madly in love, and it required all my effort to take my eyes off Veronique, and to remind myself there was anyone else in the room.

After lunch we took a day trip to Brugge, the romantic medieval city of canals and cathedrals. With each step we walked, I felt the connection between us growing stronger. When the afternoon had faded and it was time to take her home, I begged her to visit me in Milan.

"You're crazy!" she laughed. "My mother would kill me if I even asked."

"Come to Spain, then," I persisted. "I am racing next week at Jarama."

"Nando, I can't," she said. "But we will see each other soon."

I went back to my apartment in Milan on Tuesday, missing her terribly, but on Wednesday she surprised me with a call, saying she was on her way. There was nothing giddy or impulsive about her decision. She had thought things through carefully, and had made a conscious choice. We had spent just one day together in Belgium, but there was no question that there was something real between us. She was choosing her future now. Was I ready to do the same?

On Thursday night I met her at the Milan train station. She stepped off the train with only a backpack and a small duffel, looking very beautiful, and I fell in love with her all over again. Veronique came with me to Jarama, then we traveled to Morocco and vacationed there for a couple of weeks. I realized I was facing a great decision. I had proven to myself that I had the makings of a top-flight driver, but to make that dream come true would require an ever-increasing commitment to the sport of racing. Driving would have to be the center of my life, and that was not the sort of life, I knew, that would interest a woman like Veronique. Could I give up all my racing dreams, the dreams of a lifetime, just as they were about to come true? I knew that if we settled down together, it would be in Uruguay. Did I have the strength to trade the glamorous life I was living for long days toiling at my father's hardware stores, balancing books, filling orders, tracking shipments of nuts and bolts? In the end, there really was no question. The lessons I'd learned on the mountain prevented me from doing anything but choosing correctly; I would make a future with the woman I loved.

By the spring of 1978, my racing career was a memory, and Veronique and I had returned to Montevideo. In 1979 we were married. We moved into a small house in Carrasco and began to build a life together. Veronique found work as a model, and I discovered that I liked working at the hardware stores. Graciela and Juan had been working there for years, and together, with the guidance of my father, we built our business into the largest chain of hardware stores in the country.

As years passed, other opportunities presented themselves. In 1984 I was asked to produce and anchor a show about motor sports for National TV Channel 5 in Uruguay. I had never been in front of a camera before, but it was a chance to be part of the racing world again, so I jumped at the chance. In TV, I found a new passion that grew into a second career. Today, Veronique and I produce and host five programs for Uruguayan TV, including shows on travel, nature, fashion, and current events. We are involved in every aspect of producing these shows—we do the writing, editing, and direction; we even select the music. The broadcasting work satisfies my appetite for creativity, and our success in that field has led to other businesses, including a cable TV company. We worked hard to build all these enterprises, and we have been blessed many times over with success. But the greatest blessing of our lives by far has been the births of our two daughters.

Veronica was born in 1981. Until then, I had thought I could never love anything as much as I loved my wife, but when I gazed into my baby's face, I was struck senseless by my love for her. Just moments after her birth, she had become yet another treasure in my life, and I knew I would die for her without hesitation. From the start, I savored every moment of fatherhood. I loved changing her diapers, feeding her, bathing her, putting her to bed. Sometimes I would hold her, amazed by the sweetness and perfection of her little body, and realize that if I hadn't found my way out of the Andes, this beautiful little person would not exist. I felt a sudden, staggering sense of gratitude for the rich joys of my life—I had been given so much love and happiness—and I realized that every grueling step I had taken through that godforsaken wilderness was a step toward the tiny, precious miracle I held in my arms.

Two and a half years later my daughter Cecilia was born after only five and a half months of pregnancy. She weighed only two and three-quarters pounds, and spent the first two months of her life in intensive care. There were many nights when the doctors told us to prepare for the worst, that we should go home and pray, and each of those nights was another Andes for me. But Veronique spent hours at the hospital every day, caressing our baby, speaking to her softly, coaxing her back to life, and slowly Cecilia grew stronger. Now both my daughters are beautiful young girls in their early twenties, full of life and spirit, and ready to face the world on their own.

And as my daughters start out in life, my father enters his eighty-eighth year, still sound in mind and body. It is impossible to describe the closeness between us. In the many years since the Andes disaster, he has become more than a father to me; he is my closest and most intimate friend. We are bonded by our suffering and our losses, but also by a great sense of mutual respect and, of course, a deep, unquestioned love. I don't know if my father has ever understood how important he was to me when I was lost. I'll never forget what he told me, soon after I returned from the Andes. "I planned everything for you, Nando," he said. "For Mami and Susy and Graciela. Everything was taken care of. I had written the story of your lives like a book. But I did not plan for this to happen. I did not write this chapter."

I understood that this was an apology. For all his efforts to keep us safe and happy, he had not been able to protect us, and somewhere in his heart was the notion that he had somehow let us down. I wanted to write this book to tell him he was wrong. He did not fail me. He saved my life. He saved me by telling me stories when I was a boy, and those stories helped me find my strength in the mountains. He saved me by working so hard, by never giving in, and by teaching me, through his example, that anything is possible if you are willing to suffer. Mostly, he saved me with his love. He was never an openly affectionate man, but I never doubted his love when I was a boy. It was quiet love, but solid and deep and enduring. When I was in the mountains, stranded in the shadows of death, that love was like a safety line anchored in the world of the living. As long as I held on to that love, I was not lost, I was connected to my home and to my future, and in the end it was that strong cord of love that led me out of danger. When he thought that all of us were dead, my father despaired, and in his pain he gave up his hope for us. But it was not his hope that I needed. He saved me simply by being the father I love.

WHEN MY FELLOW survivors and I first returned from the mountains, our parents and teachers, worried that we'd been scarred by the horrors we'd faced, asked us to visit a therapist. As a group, we said no. We knew we had one another's support, and for me that has always been enough. But even now, people are curious about the psychological effects of such an ordeal, and I am often asked how I have dealt with the trauma. Do I suffer nightmares? Flashbacks? Have I struggled with survivor guilt? These people are always surprised and sometimes, I suspect, dubious, when I tell them that I have experienced none of those things. I have lived a happy life since the disaster. I have no guilt or resentments. I look forward to tomorrow, and I always expect the future to be good.

"But how is that possible?" they often ask. "How can you be at peace with life after what you suffered?" I tell them I am not at peace *in spite* of what I suffered, but *because* of it. The Andes took so much from me, I explain, but they also gave me the simple insight that has liberated me and illuminated my life: *Death is real, and death is very near.*

In the mountains, there was never a minute that I did not feel death at my side, but the moment I stood on the summit of the mountain, and saw nothing but towering peaks as far as the eye could see, was the moment all my doubts were swept away and the certainty of my own death became viscerally real. The realness of death stole my breath away, but at the same time I burned more brightly with life than I ever had before, and in the face of total hopelessness I felt a burst of joy. The realness of death was so clear and so potent that for a moment it burned away everything temporary and false. Death had shown its face, dark, predatory, invincible, and for a split second it seemed that beneath the fragile illusions of life, death was all there is. But then I saw that there was something in the world that was *not* death, something just as awesome and enduring and profound. There was love, the love in my heart, and for one incredible moment, as I felt this love swell—love for my father, for my future, for the simple wonder of being alive—death lost its power. In that moment, I stopped running from death. Instead, I made every step a step toward love, and that saved me. I have never stopped moving toward love. Life has blessed me with material success. I like fast cars, good wine, fine food. I love to travel. I have a beautiful house in Montevideo, and another one at the beach. I believe life should be enjoyed, but my experiences have taught me that without the love of my family and my friends, all the trappings of worldly success would ring hollow. I also know that I would be a happy man if all those trappings were taken from me, as long as I am close to the people I love.

I expect most people would like to think of themselves this way, but I know that if I had not suffered as I did, and had not been forced to stare death in the face, I would not treasure the simple, precious pleasures of my life as richly as I do. There are so many perfect moments in a day, and I don't want to miss a single one—the smiles of my daughters, my wife's embrace, a slobbering welcome from my new puppy, the company of an old friend, the feel of beach sand beneath my feet, and the warm Uruguayan sun on my face. These moments bring time to a stop for me. I savor them and let each one become a miniature eternity, and by living these small moments of my life so fully, I defy the shadow of death that hovers over all of us, I reaffirm my love and gratitude for all the gifts I've been given, and I fill myself more and more deeply with life.

In the years since the disaster, I often think of my friend Arturo Nogueira, and the conversations we had in the mountains about God. Many of my fellow survivors say they felt the personal presence of God in the mountains. He mercifully allowed us to survive, they believe, in answer to our prayers, and they are certain it was His hand that led us home. I deeply respect the faith of my friends, but, to be honest, as hard as I prayed for a miracle in the Andes, I never felt the personal presence of God. At least, I did not feel God as most people see Him. I did feel something larger than myself, something in the mountains and the glaciers and the glowing sky that, in rare moments, reassured me, and made me feel that the world was orderly and loving and good. If this was God, it was not God as a being or a spirit or some omnipotent, superhuman mind. It was not a God who would choose to save us or abandon us, or change in any way. It was simply a silence, a wholeness, an awe-inspiring simplicity. It seemed to reach me through my own feelings of love, and I have often thought that when we feel what we call love, we are really feeling our connection to this awesome presence. I feel this presence still when my mind quiets and I really pay attention. I don't pretend to understand what it is or what it wants from me. I don't *want* to understand these things. I have no interest in any God who *can* be understood, who speaks to us in one holy book or another, and who tinkers with our lives according to some divine plan, as if we were characters in a play. How can I make sense of a God who sets one religion above the rest, who answers one prayer and ignores another, who sends sixteen young men home and leaves twenty-nine others dead on a mountain?

There was a time when I wanted to know that God, but I realize now that what I really wanted was the comfort of certainty, the knowledge that *my* God was the *true* God, and that in the end He would reward me for my faithfulness. Now I understand that to be certain—about God, about anything—is impossible. I have lost my need to know. In those unforgettable conversations I had with Arturo as he lay dying, he told me the best way to find faith was by having the courage to doubt. I remember those words every day, and I doubt, and I hope, and in this crude way I try to grope my way toward truth. I still pray the prayers I learned as a child—Hail Marys, Our Fathers—but I don't imagine a wise, heavenly father listening patiently on the other end of the line. Instead, I imagine love, an ocean of love, the very source of love, and I imagine myself merging with it. I open myself to it, I try to direct that tide of love toward the people who are close to me, hoping to protect them and bind them to me forever and connect us all to whatever there is in the world that is eternal. This is a very private thing for me, and I don't try to analyze what it means. I simply like the way it makes me feel. When I pray this way, I feel as if I am connected to something good and whole and powerful. In the mountains, it was love that kept me connected to the world of the living. Courage or cleverness wouldn't have saved me. I had no expertise to draw on, so I relied upon the trust I felt in my love for my father and my future, and that trust led me home. Since then, it has led me to a deeper understanding of who I am and what it means to be human. Now I am convinced that if there is something divine in the universe, the only way I will find it is through the love I feel for my family and my friends, and through the simple wonder of being alive. I don't need any other wisdom or philosophy than this: My duty is to fill my time on earth with as much life as possible, to become a little more human every day, and to understand that we only become human when we love. I have tried to love my friends with a loyal and generous heart. I have loved my children with all my strength. And I have loved one woman with a love that has filled my life with meaning and joy. I have suffered great losses and have been blessed with great consolations, but whatever life may give me or take away, this is the simple wisdom that will always light my life: I have loved, passionately, fearlessly, with all my heart and all my soul, and I have been loved in return. For me, this is enough.

TWO YEARS AFTER the miracle in the Andes, my father and I returned to the crash site in the High Andes near Sosneado Mountain. A route had been discovered, passable only in summer, leading from the Argentine foothills to the glacier where the Fairchild lay. It's a grueling, three-day trip that begins with an eight-hour drive in off-road vehicles across the rugged terrain of the Andean foothills, then two and a half days on horseback. We forded a swift stream, then rode specially trained Andean horses along steep, narrow trails that wove up into the mountains above hair-raising drops to the rocky slopes below. We reached the base of the glacier at midday, then made our final climb to the gravesite on foot. The grave itself, built just after our rescue by air force members from Uruguay and Chile, sits on a rocky promontory jutting above the snow. Beneath the rocks lie Susy and my mother, along with the remains of the others who died here, all safely out of reach of the grinding glacier a few hundred feet away. It's a simple shrine, just a pile of stones and a small steel cross rising above the grave. My father brought flowers and a stainless-steel box containing the teddy bear Susy had slept with every night of her life. He placed these gifts on the grave, and we stood there quietly in the silence of the mountains. I remembered that silence so well, a constant and absolute absence of sound. On calm days you hear nothing but your own breathing, your own thoughts. My father's face was pale, and tears wet his cheeks as we shared this sad reunion, but I felt no pain or grief. I felt tranquillity in that place. There was no more fear there, or suffering, or struggle. The dead were at peace. The pure, perfect stillness of the mountains had returned.

It was a bright, clear spring day. My father turned to me with a sad smile. He looked at the glacier, at the black peaks above us, at the wide, savage Andean sky, and I know he was trying to imagine this place in the cold months of early spring. He glanced at the remains of the fuselage. Was he seeing young boys huddled inside? Frightened faces in the dark and the cold, listening to the howl of the wind and the rumble of distant avalanches, with nothing to depend on but each other? Did he imagine me in this hard place, so frightened, so impossibly far from home, and longing so desperately to be with him? My father didn't say. He only smiled tenderly, took me by the arm, and whispered, "Nando, now I understand . . ."

We stayed at the gravesite for an hour or so, then made our way back down to the horses. We never thought, for a moment, about moving the bodies of our loved ones to a cemetery in the civilized world. As we descended the mountain, the grandeur of the Andes thundered all around us—so silent, so massive, so perfect—and neither of us could imagine a more majestic shrine.

Epilogue

EACH YEAR FOR the last thirty-odd years the survivors of the Andes disaster have gathered with their families on December 22 to commemorate the day we were rescued from the mountain. We celebrate this date as our common birthday, because on this day all of us were reborn. But it was more than life that was given to us; each of us came down from the mountain with a new way of thinking, a deeper appreciation for the power of the human spirit, and a profound understanding of what a wonder it is—for us, for anyone— to be alive. The ability to be truly alive and aware, to savor each moment of life with presence and gratitude, this is the gift the Andes gave us. A stranger may not notice the special warmth with which my friends embrace their wives, or the tenderness with which they caress their children, but I do, because like them I know these things are marvels. After we were rescued from the mountains, the newspapers called our survival "The Miracle of the Andes." For me, the true miracle is that by living so long beneath the shadow of death, we learned in the most vivid and transforming way exactly what it means to be alive. This is the knowledge that bonds us all together, and while like all friends we have our share of conflicts and misunderstandings, and while life has led some of us far away from our home in Montevideo, we will never allow these bonds to be broken.

Even today, more than three decades after the disaster, I think of all these men as my brothers. But no one has been a better brother to me than Roberto Canessa, my partner in that long trek through the Andes. Several days into that journey, as we grew steadily weaker in the bleak terrain and hope seemed to fade with each step, Roberto pointed to the distinctive belt he was wearing. I recognized it as Panchito's. "I am wearing the belt I took from the body of your best friend," he said, "but I am your best friend now."

In that moment, neither of us trusted that we had any kind of future, but we did, and more than thirty years later I am proud to say that I am still best friends with Roberto, who has only grown more resourceful, more confident, and, yes, more hardheaded with the passage of time. These qualities, which made him such an important and difficult character in the mountains, have helped make him one of the most respected pediatric cardiologists in Uruguay and earned him a reputation as a man whose knowledge and skills are surpassed only by his ferocious determination to help his young patients. Most of the children Roberto treats are seriously ill, and it comes as no surprise to anyone who knows him that he will stop at nothing to help them. Once, for example, a good friend of his, who was head of cardiology at a hospital in New York, told Roberto that his hospital had a Doppler imaging machine they no longer needed. He offered it to Roberto, with the stipulation that Roberto would be responsible for transporting the machine to Uruguay. Roberto knew that such a machine would be a great help in treating his patients, and he also knew that his hospital in Montevideo could not afford such expensive technology. It took him only moments to make up his mind, and less than twenty-four hours later, Roberto was in New York taking possession of the equipment. With no clear plan for moving it, and no one to help him, Roberto loaded the bulky machine—it was the size of a small refrigerator—onto a handcart he had borrowed from the hospital's maintenance department and wheeled it into an elevator. Moments later he was on a busy sidewalk, trying to flag down passing trucks. He stood there waving for a very long time, as traffic sailed by. No one seemed to notice him, but finally he caught the attention of the driver of a pick-up truck who agreed, for a fee, to take Roberto and the machine to JFK airport.

Roberto faced more challenges when he arrived in Montevideo, where finicky customs officials refused to allow the machine into the country. Roberto, of course, would not be denied. He hailed a cab and went directly to the offices of the president of Uruguay, where he demanded a meeting with the leader of our country. Incredibly, his request was granted, and after he made his case to the president, airport customs officials were ordered to cut the red tape and allow the Doppler to enter the country. Roberto arranged for it to be taken to his hospital, where it was immediately put into service. Less than forty-eight hours had passed since Roberto had first heard about the machine, but it was already up and running and saving the lives of Uruguayan children.

Roberto has enjoyed a rich and peaceful personal life. Three years after our return from the Andes he married Laura Surraco, the girl he had missed so badly in the mountains, and this was a lucky thing for him, because she may be the only woman in Uruguay who could stand up to his stubbornness and harness his boundless energy. They have two sons and a daughter. I am godfather to his son Hilario, who is now a standout player for the Old Christians. Roberto, who has always been active in the affairs of the team, is now president of the Old Christians Club, a position he relishes because he loves the team and is convinced no one could guide it better. Of course, he feels this way about everything and believes he should have a say in all important matters, including the loftiest affairs of the Uruguayan state. In 1999, in fact, he grew so unhappy with the leadership of our government that he formed his own political party and ran for president of the country. His grassroots campaign drew only a small percentage of the vote, but, as always, he made his voice heard. I tease him mercilessly about his ego, but I would not have him any other way.

Gustavo Zerbino is another especially good friend, with whom I have grown very close over the years. He is a man of strong principles and straight talk, and when he speaks he makes his words count. I can't imagine a more dependable friend than Gustavo. In the Andes, he was always brave, smart, and steady, and if he hadn't burned himself out on that nearly fatal attempt to climb the mountain, he most certainly would have been one of our most trusted expeditionaries. But even before the disaster he was a loyal and protective ally who would never desert a teammate or a friend. I'll never forget how he came to my aid during a very tough rugby match, when an opposing player ambushed me from behind with an illegal punch to the back of the head. The blow stunned me. I never saw it coming, but Gustavo did. "It was Number 12," he said to me, as my head spun. "Don't worry," he whispered, "he's mine."

Moments later a "maul" formed, as players from each team locked in a shoving match to take possession of the ball. Suddenly, out of the tangle of bodies I saw Number 12 stagger, then topple backwards like a falling tree. Gustavo stepped over the fallen Number 12 and approached me. He gave me a matter-of-fact nod. All he said was, "Done."

Gustavo was an idealistic and compassionate young man who often worked with the Jesuits in the slums of Montevideo. Today, he shows the same concern for the welfare of others, and this makes him a strong and generous friend. Gustavo runs a large chemical company, is active in many community organizations, serves as the president of the Uruguayan Chemical Association, and is the vice-president of the Old Christians Rugby Club. He is divorced with four fine sons from his first marriage, and because he lives only blocks away, I see him and his family often.

Carlitos Paez, another of my favorite friends, remains as irreverent, as affectionate, and every bit as loveable as he was each day in the mountains. I love him for his creativity and his outrageous humor and for the warmth he has always shown my daughters, with whom he is especially close and who have been drawn to his magnetic personality since they were babies. Carlitos has faced more than his share of challenges in life. His first marriage ended after only two years, and he has been single ever since. About fifteen years ago he fell so deeply into an addiction to alcohol and drugs that we all knew something had to be done. One afternoon, Gustavo and I showed up at Carlitos's house. We told him we were taking him to a rehab hospital where he would stay until he had recovered completely. He was shocked by this confrontation, and at first he refused to budge, but we told him the decision was no longer his. All the arrangements had been made, we told him, and we let him see, in our faces, that there was no use in resisting. Happily, Carlitos recovered completely. He has been sober ever since, and now volunteers his time to counsel people who are battling substance abuse and addiction. Carlitos works as an executive at a public relations firm in Montevideo. He has such a passion for golf that he recently purchased a home that borders the fairway of a golf club. But his greatest passion these days is his granddaughter, Justine, the child of his daughter Gochi. His world revolves around this baby, and it is good to see the joy she brings him. Once, Carlitos wrote to me, "We continue to walk our paths with the certainty that life is worth living, that nothing is impossible if affection and solidarity exist, if we have the people willing to give a hand to [those who] need it." Carlitos has survived more than one ordeal in his life, but he has learned to find happiness, and I am always happy to be with him.

Alvaro Mangino was one of the youngest boys in the disaster, and perhaps because of this I always felt a special sense of protectiveness toward him while we were in the mountains. He has grown into a man of great common sense and inner calmness who has learned to put the ordeal behind him and, while learning much from the experience, has gone on to live his life. He has been married for many years to his wife, Margarita, and has raised four children. For many years he lived in Brazil, but he has recently returned to Montevideo, where he works for a heating and air conditioning company and serves on the board of the Old Christians. He is a loyal and steady friend, and I am happy to have him back close to home.

Alvaro is particularly close to another of my good friends, Coche Inciarte, who may be the calmest, gentlest, and most thoughtful of all the survivors. Coche has a naturally mild and peaceful nature; I can honestly say I have never heard him raise his voice. He speaks with great natural eloquence and sharp wit, but while he often jokes and teases, he has a deep emotional understanding of what we suffered, and he never hides the closeness he feels for the rest of us. Coche married his childhood sweetheart Soledad, who had thought she lost him in the mountains. Their reunion was a miracle for both of them, and Coche has never let himself forget what a wonder it is to have her and the three children they have raised.

For many years, Coche, a dairy farmer, was one of the largest producers of dairy products in Uruguay. He recently sold his holdings and retired to enjoy his family and to devote time to his great passion—painting. Coche, it turns out, is quite a talented artist. One of his paintings hangs in my office now and I think of him every time I see it, because his artwork reveals the same depth, gentleness, and dignity that make him such a great friend.

As one of the triumvirate of leaders known as "the cousins," Eduardo Strauch was an important figure in the mountains. His clear and deliberate thinking helped add stability and direction to our daily struggle to survive. He is much the same today as he was in the Andes: cool and collected, a man of few words, but always worth listening to. Eduardo and his wife, Laura, have five children. He is an accomplished architect in Montevideo who has built many fine homes and buildings there, including my first house.

Eduardo's cousin Daniel Fernandez still possesses the humor and charisma he used to ease the intense pressures and fears we faced in the wrecked fuselage. Daniel is a great storyteller and has the ability to truly capture the imagination of his audience when he speaks. Sparks always fly when Daniel, a member of the Blanco political party, and Roberto, a die-hard Colorado, discuss Uruguayan politics. They are both bull-headed, and each loves to incite the other. Their arguments inevitably end in a stalemate, but no matter how hot these discussions may grow they are always laced with humor, and the rest of us greatly enjoy the show. Daniel runs a successful computer and technology firm based in Montevideo. He and his wife, Amalia, have three wonderful kids.

I have always admired Pedro Algorta, the great friend of Arturo Nogueira, for his intelligence, keen wit, and independent thinking. I have not seen Pedro as much as I would like, because he lives in Argentina, where he works as the general manager of a large brewery and beverage manufacturer. But recently he bought a ranch in Uruguay, and I hope this will allow me to see him more often. He and his wife, Noel, have two daughters and a son, all of them studying or working abroad.

In the Andes, none of the survivors was as cool and collected as Bobby François. He was frightened as any of us, I am sure, but he seemed determined to face his destiny with a minimum of drama. "If we die, we die," he seemed to be saying. "Why waste energy over it?" He has lived his life with much the same attitude, and it has served him well. Bobby is a rancher, a lifestyle of slow and simple rhythms that suits him. He spends his days in the saddle, riding alone on the open range, tending herds under the broad skies of the Uruguayan plains. He has five children with his wife, Graciana. They spend half of their time on the ranch, the other half in Carrasco, where Bobby is especially close to Coche and Roy Harley.

Javier Methol, the only survivor other than me to lose a family member on the mountain, struggled to recover from Liliana's death, but he found strength in his strong Catholic faith and in the love of the four children he and Liliana shared. After grieving his lost wife for years, Javier met and married his second wife, Ana Maria, with whom he now has four more children! For many years he was an executive at a large tobacco company—a company that was founded by Panchito's family—but he is now happily retired.

Of all the survivors, Javier is most convinced that it was the hand of God that led us out of the mountains. Once he wrote to me: *God gave us life again in the mountain and made us brothers. When we considered that you were dead, He brought you back to life, so that afterwards together with Roberto you became His messengers in search of the salvation of all of us. I am so sure, that for some moments He carried you both in his arms . . .*

Javier and I have different ideas of God, and the role God played in our survival. Still, I respect the humility and sincerity of his faith and the way he has rebuilt his life after his devastating loss. Calm and even tempered, he is one of the stabilizing forces in our group, and I always feel a sense of peace when I am with him.

Antonio Vizintin, who bravely climbed the mountain with Roberto and me, has faced many challenges and difficulties in his life. His first marriage ended in divorce, and his second wife died tragically. He is now married for a third time, and we all pray that he has a happier future ahead. Tintin, as we still call him, has two children, a daughter and a son, both from his second marriage. He is a good father and has been successful in his work as an importer of chemicals and other supplies for the plastics industry. Tintin still lives in Carrasco, but he is a bit of a loner, and in recent years we have seen less of him than we'd like. Still, he will always be one of us, and we would like to see more of him, even though he allows his son, a fine rugby player, to play for the Old Boys Rugby Club, the Old Christians' longtime archrival.

Roy Harley is one of the survivors I think about very often. For more than thirty years I have been troubled by the way Roy was portrayed in previous accounts of the disaster, primarily in Piers Paul Read's magnificent book *Alive*. I've even been puzzled by the way I treated him, at times, in the mountains. It's true, Roy's emotions were fragile in the Andes, but it is also true that he was one of the youngest in our group, and that he hovered closer to death than any of the others who survived. The fact that he wore his emotions close to the surface does not mean he was weaker or more frightened than the rest of us. No one could have been more frightened than I was, and, in fact, I have realized in writing this book that it was my own fear that fueled the anger and frustration I felt toward Roy. *Alive* was based heavily on extensive interviews conducted with each of the survivors, and I regret that in those discussions we all may have drawn too simple a picture of Roy's particular struggle. But we were young men then, and things seemed much simpler. In *Miracle in the Andes,* I have tried to set the record straight: in my eyes, Roy Harley was no coward and no weakling. He was and always will be one of us, a survivor, a reliable friend, and an important part of our circle. Over the years he has proven himself again and again as a man of integrity and strength, and he is one of the guys I know I can always count on. Today Roy is a successful engineer working for a large manufacturer of paint. He lives in Montevideo with his wife, Cecilia—the sister of Roberto's wife, Laura—two lovely daughters and a son who is now playing for the Old Christians. Roy, a great advocate of physical fitness, has hardly aged, and the rest of us envy him for his flat stomach and firm muscles, because most of us have seen our muscles soften and our bellies grow.

Alfredo "Pancho" Delgado is another survivor for whom the record must be cleared. In *Alive*, Pancho comes across as a manipulative and dishonest character, who schemed behind our backs to increase his own comfort, often at the expense of others. There is no doubt that Pancho did these things, but in fact, so did we all. Each of us, at times, acted selfishly—trying to pilfer more than our share of food or cigarettes, to escape work, or to secure for ourselves the warmest clothes and the most comfortable sleeping places. None of us were saints. We survived not because we were perfect, but because the accumulated weight of our concern for each other far outweighed our natural self-interest. Why Pancho stood out in this regard is a puzzle. He had a keen wit and a natural eloquence, and perhaps we resented his talent for getting away with his transgressions. In any case, it is not right that Pancho has been singled out like this and has had to be burdened with this unfair reputation. The truth is that Pancho always was and always will be one of us and, like the others, he will always have my friendship, my trust, and my respect. Pancho, who lives close to me in Carrasco, is a prominent lawyer. He is married to his life-long sweetheart, Susana, with whom he has two sons and two daughters. His oldest son, Alfredo, is the captain of the Old Christians First XV.

Ramon "Moncho" Sabella, who has never married, is the confirmed bachelor in our group. Despite our constant efforts to introduce him to many suitable matches, he remains a happily single man-about-town, who swears he is simply having too much fun to ever settle down. When he is not partying on the beach at Punte del Este, or in the clubs of Montevideo, Moncho works in real estate development, and in a new venture, in partnership with fellow survivor Fito Strauch, to breed and raise ostriches. Moncho is a good friend, he still has a keen eye for beautiful women, and he is always fun to be around.

Fito Strauch was one of the most important guys on the mountain, and none of us, least of all me, has forgotten the many ways in which he contributed to our survival. Like Javier, Fito firmly believes that it was God's personal intervention on the mountain that saved us, and that we should live our lives as His messengers. Sometimes I feel that Fito is unhappy with me for the way I have lived my life; that I have minimized or even dismissed God's role in our rescue, and that I have not been faithful to the spiritual lessons of the ordeal. I tell him I am not sure how to spread God's message, because I am not sure what that message could be. Fito might say that the lesson of the Andes is that God saved us because He loves us. But did He not love my mother and sister and the twenty-nine others who died? What happened to us in the Andes transformed me in profound ways and gave me a deeper and more spiritual approach to life than I had before, but for me, the lesson of the mountains is that life is precious, and that it should be lived fully, from the heart and out of love. I don't want my life to be defined by what happened to me thirty years ago; I feel I am writing the script of my own life every day. For me, this is not a denial of the spiritual lessons we learned on the mountain, but the very fulfillment of those lessons.

Fito and I will probably never see eye to eye on this issue, but for me, this does not diminish the respect and friendship I feel for him, and when we meet we always embrace like brothers. Fito lives in the countryside where he owns and operates a cattle ranch. He has four children with his wife, Paula.

Sergio Catalan, the Chilean peasant who first spotted Roberto and me in the mountains, and whose quick and competent response led directly to our rescue and the salvation of fourteen other young lives, is not, technically, one of the survivors. But he is definitely part of our family, and we have kept in touch with him over the years, visiting him at his village in Chile, or flying him in to see us in Montevideo. He remains the same humble, gentle, and immensely dignified man who rode on horseback for ten hours to lead rescuers to us at Los Maitenes. He lives a simple life, spending weeks at a time in the mountain pastures, with only his dog for company, as he tends to his cattle and sheep. Sergio and his wife have raised nine children, and it impresses me that even on the modest means of a mountain herdsman, he has managed to send most of them to college and to see all of them established in good marriages and jobs.

In March of 2005, Sergio's wife, Virginia, called me to invite us to their fiftieth wedding anniversary. It would be a surprise for Sergio, she said. She would not tell him we were coming. We agreed, and the day before the celebration was to begin, Roberto, Gustavo, and I, along with our families, were driving up the narrow, rocky road leading to Sergio's village. The rugged, barren foothills of the Andes rose all around us as we steadily climbed, then someone spotted a figure on a horse. He was wearing the traditional garb of a Chilean cattleman—the short-waisted jacket, the pointed boots, the broad-brimmed hat.

"It's Sergio!" someone said.

We pulled over. Roberto, Gustavo, and I got out of the cars and walked toward the horseman. At first he was wary of us, just as he had been the first time we'd met, but when he saw Roberto and me his eyes widened and filled with tears. Before he could speak, I stepped forward. "Excuse me, good man," I said, "but we are lost again. Can you help us one more time?"

When I am together with my fellow survivors, we say in silence all that needs to be said about our time in the mountains, and, for many years, it was enough to know that these friends and my family understood what I went through. I had little interest in sharing my personal story with anyone outside our circle, and though I sometimes gave interviews to magazines and newspapers, or participated in documentaries commemorating various anniversaries of the disaster, I was always wary of sharing too much of myself with strangers. All the public needed to know, I believed, was covered, masterfully, in *Alive*. True, that book concentrated almost entirely on the factual events of our ordeal; no reader could have more than just the slightest understanding of my inner struggle or of the surging emotions that drove me to survive. But I did not care to reveal those things too deeply. Let the readers have the drama, the horror, and the adventure. I would keep the most intimate, most painful memories to myself.

As the years passed I was approached on more than one occasion by agents and publishers, asking me to retell the story from my own personal perspective. I always refused. Those people saw me as a hero, and I knew they wanted to celebrate the disaster as an inspirational story of triumph and perseverance. But they were missing the point. I was no hero. I was always frightened, always weak and confused, always hopeless. And thinking of the disaster—the rankness of our suffering, the obscene waste of so many innocent lives—conjured no sense of triumph or glory in my heart. Our story may have inspired millions of people around the world as a tale of the power of the human spirit, but for me those months in the mountains were days of heartbreak, horror, and irretrievable loss. The disaster was not something to be celebrated. It was something to be outlived, and I had tried my best to do just that, filling my life with the riches of friendship and family, so that all those broken parts of my life were buried beneath a lifetime's accumulation of happiness and love.

And I was content to have it that way. I don't mean to say I denied my past—even now, my memories of the Andes touch me every day. I only wanted to keep the sadness and suffering from shaping my future. I was following the advice my father gave me in the aftermath of our rescue. *Look forward, Nando,* he said. *Do not let this be the most important thing that ever happens to you.* I did not want to live my life as a survivor. I did not want the disaster to define my life. I took what lessons I could from the ordeal. I savored the friendships that grew out of it, and I always honored the memory of those who died. But I could not glorify or romanticize what had happened to us, and I certainly had no desire to rummage through those dark memories with the unflinching honesty it would take to write a book.

Why, then, after thirty-odd years, did I agree to write the account you now hold in your hands? The answer begins in 1991, with a call from a man named Juan Cintron. Cintron was organizing a conference for young business owners in Mexico City, and he had decided that my story would make a great motivational speech for the gathering, so he tracked me down by phone in Montevideo and asked me to deliver the keynote address. I had no desire to turn my experiences into a pep talk, so I politely refused. But Juan would not take no for an answer. He called me again and again, begging me to reconsider. Finally he flew to Montevideo to plead with me face-to-face. Impressed by his persistence and enthusiasm, I succumbed to his persuasion and agreed to give the talk.

In the following months I labored to craft the kind of speech Cintron wanted. He had asked me to mine the story for lessons that would hold the attention of ambitious young entrepreneurs looking for insights and ideas that would help them prosper—points about leadership, innovation, working in teams, and creative problem-solving. He had urged me to keep my presentation crisp and to the point. These were busy and impatient people, he said. Move too slowly and you will lose them. As I worked on the speech, as I tried to draw from so much misery and grief the kind of inspirational tidbits that might help an audience of strangers improve their bottom lines, I deeply regretted my decision to deliver the address. But there was no backing out now. Finally, the day arrived and I found myself on stage in Mexico City, standing in the spotlight, with the notes for my speech on the podium in front of me. I had been introduced, the polite applause had ended, and it was time for me to begin. I wanted to speak, but no matter how I tried, the words would not come to me. My heart was pounding, cold sweat was trickling beneath the collar of my shirt, and my hands were trembling. I stared at my notes. They made no sense. I began to shuffle the papers. People shifted in their seats. The awkward silence grew so loud it sounded like thunder, and just as panic was about to overwhelm me, I heard myself speak.

"I should not be here," I said, out of nowhere. "I should be dead on a glacier in the Andes."

And then, as if a floodgate had opened, I poured out my story, sparing no emotion and holding nothing back. I simply spoke from my heart. I walked them through all the important moments of the ordeal so that they experienced it all just as I had, the wild grief I felt when Susy died, the terror when we heard that the search had been canceled, and the horror of chewing the flesh of our dead friends. I placed them with us inside the fuselage on the night of the avalanche and in the grim days that followed. I led them up the mountain and showed them the devastating view from the summit, then I took them with Roberto and me on the trek, which we were certain would lead us to our deaths. I didn't say a word about creativity or teamwork or problem solving. I didn't mention the word *success*. Instead, I shared with them what I suddenly realized was the true lesson of my ordeal: It wasn't cleverness or courage or any kind of competence or savvy that saved us, it was nothing more than love, our love for each other, for our families, for the lives we wanted so desperately to live. Our suffering in the Andes had swept away everything trivial and unimportant. Each of us realized, with a clarity that is hard to describe, that the only crucial thing in life is the chance to love and be loved. In our families, in our futures, we already had everything we needed. The sixteen of us who were lucky enough to return to our lives will never forget this. No one should forget this.

I spoke for more than ninety minutes, though it seemed like only five, and when I finished the hall was filled with a thick silence. For several seconds, no one moved, then applause swelled and the audience rose to their feet. Afterwards, strangers with tears in their eyes came forward to embrace me. Some took me aside to tell me about hardships they had faced in their own lives, struggles with illness, bereavement, divorce, addiction. I felt such a powerful connection with those people. They were not simply understanding my story; they were making it their own. This filled me with a great sense of peace and purpose, and while I didn't completely understand these emotions at the time, I knew I wanted to feel that way again.

After the success of the Mexico City speech, I was asked to give talks around the world, but my daughters were still small and my business obligations were heavy, so I was able to accept only a few of these invitations. As years passed, and I found the time, I began to speak more frequently. Today, I address audiences all across the globe, although my responsibilities at home still force me to be very selective. And each time I speak I simply do what I did the first time: I tell my story and share the plain wisdom I have learned. Always, the result is the same, an outpouring of warmth, gratitude, and that powerful sense of connection. Once, after a talk, a young woman asked to speak with me. "A few years ago I was backing out of my driveway," she said. "I didn't know my two-year-old daughter was behind me. I backed the car over her, and she died. My life stopped at that moment. Since then I have not been able to eat, or sleep, or even think about anything but that moment. I have tortured myself with questions. Why was she there? Why didn't I see her? Why wasn't I more careful? And mostly, *Why did this happen?* Ever since that moment I have been paralyzed by guilt and grief, and the rest of my family has suffered. Your story shows me that I have been wrong. It's possible to live, even when you suffer. I know now that I have to go on. I have to live for my husband and my other children. Even with the pain I feel, I have to find the strength to do it. Your story makes me believe this is possible."

Speechless, I gathered her into my arms and embraced her. In that moment an unformed thought that had been hovering in my mind took on a razor sharp focus. I realized that *my* story is *her* story; it is the story of everyone who hears it. This woman never felt the blast of a subzero wind. She never staggered through a high-altitude blizzard or watched in horror as her body wasted from starvation. But could there be any doubt that in the ways that mattered most, she had suffered as much as I had? I'd always thought of my story as something unique, something so extreme and outrageous that only those who had been there could genuinely understand what we had been through. But in its essence—the essence of human emotion—it is the most familiar story in the world. We all, at times, face hopelessness and despair. We all experience grief, abandonment, and crushing loss. And all of us, sooner or later, will face the inevitable nearness of death. As I hugged that sad woman, a phrase formed on my lips. "We all have our own personal Andes," I told her.

Now, after more than ten years of public speaking, after watching my story resonate, time and time again, with thousands around the world, I understand that the connection I feel with my audiences is rooted in something deeper than their admiration for what I did to survive. They are seeing, in my story, their own struggles and fears made real against a surreal backdrop, on an epic scale. The story chills them but also encourages them, because they see that even in the face of the cruelest kind of suffering, and against all odds, an ordinary person can endure. It satisfies me deeply that so many can find strength and comfort in the things I have to say, but they have given me much in return. They have shown me that there is more to my story than grief and meaningless tragedy. By using my suffering as a source of inspiration and reassurance they have helped heal my wounded memories. I saw that my mother, my sister, and the others did not die in vain, and that our suffering really does add up to something important, to some kind of wisdom, that can touch the hearts of human beings across the planet.

My listeners touch me, too. I draw so much love and fulfillment from the connection I feel with them, as if we are joined in a human web of understanding, as if every person moved by my story enriches and enlarges my life. It amazes me that I am the same man who once disliked talking about the Andes, because now I have a passion to share my story with as many people as possible, and out of that passion came the desire to write this book. I began writing it, in my heart, several years ago, and finally the time felt right to put my thoughts on paper. It has been a remarkable experience—painful, joyful, humbling, surprising, and very rewarding. I have tried to be as truthful as possible in writing this, and now I offer it as a gift:

To my father, so that he could see, in unflinching detail, what I lived through, and how my love for him was the real power that saved me;

To my fellow survivors, so that they will know the love and respect I will always feel for them;

To my wife and my daughters, so that they can stand beside me in the mountains, day-by-day, and see that even though they were still just a part of my distant future, every step I took was a step closer to them;

And finally, to those with whom I am bonded by suffering and by the joys and disappointments of life—that is, to everyone who reads this. I am no wise man. Every day shows me how little I know about life, and how wrong I can be. But there are things I know to be true. I know I will die. And I know that the only sane response to such a horror is to love. Before he died, Arturo Nogueira, one of the bravest of us all, said time and again, "Even here, even as we suffer, life is still worth living. . . ." What he meant was that even when everything had been taken from us, we could still think of our loved ones, we could still hold them in our hearts and cherish them as the treasures of our lives. Like all of us, Arturo had discovered that this was all that mattered. My hope is that you who are reading this book will not wait so long to realize what treasures you have. In the Andes we lived heartbeat-to-heartbeat. Every second of life was a gift, glowing with purpose and meaning. I have tried to live that way ever since and it has filled my life with more blessings than I can count. I urge you to do the same. As we used to say in the mountains, "Breathe. Breathe again. With every breath, you are alive." After all these years, this is still the best advice I can give you: Savor your existence. Live every moment. Do not waste a breath.

A Note About the Photographs

IN THE WRECKAGE of the Fairchild we found an inexpensive camera with several unexposed frames on the roll. Some of the photographs reprinted in this book were taken with that camera. They show us in the Andes, as death was closing in and our hopes for rescue were rapidly fading. When I see these photographs today, I am amazed, because I see no trace of the terror and depression with which we all struggled. Instead, I see us lounging on the snow like college boys at the beach, or sunning ourselves on the glacier, in the seats we dragged out from the fuselage, like friends relaxing at a sidewalk café. In one photograph, three young men stand smiling, side by side, with the snow-packed slopes of the Andes rising in the distance. You might mistake them for poorly dressed tourists on a ski slope in the Alps or the Rockies. Only their shocking thinness hints that something is wrong.

I took some of those photographs myself, mostly on impulse, without much conscious thought, but each time I snapped the shutter I knew that the images I was capturing might outlive us all. The notion that we would vanish beneath the snow, and that our story would never be told, was horrific, and it comforted me to know that a record of our time in the mountains existed inside that little plastic Instamatic. Even if it lay undiscovered for decades, there was a chance that someday someone might find it. Then we would not vanish completely. The world would know that we had lived for a while, that we had fought to survive, and that despite all the hopelessness and fear, we still had the courage to smile for the camera.

Acknowledgments

I WOULD LIKE to express my gratitude to friends and colleagues, without whose contributions this book would not have been possible:

To my agents Stephanie Kip Rostan, Elizabeth Fisher, Daniel Greenberg, and Jim Levine for their wise counsel.

To my editor, Annik LaFarge, for her enthusiasm and expertise and for the passion and care with which she guided this book into being.

To Vince Rause, whose humor and skill made him a joy to work with, and whom I now can call my friend.

To Gail and Kelly Davis, who supported this book from the start and whose friendship I have always treasured.

To the late Mark McCormack, a great man and a great friend, who always encouraged me to tell my own personal story in a book. At last I have taken his advice.

To Jackie Stewart, his wife, Helen, and his sons, Paul and Mark, who have always made me feel like a part of their family. My friendship with Jackie has been a great blessing, and I am thankful to him for all the lessons he taught me about racing, about business, and about life.

To Bernie Ecclestone, who opened so many doors for me when I was young, and who, like Jackie, taught me so many things that have shaped who I am today. I am proud to claim him as a friend.

To my good friend Piers Paul Read, whose superb book *Alive* first revealed the story of the Andes disaster to the world, with honesty, sensitivity, and great power.

To all my teammates and friends who died in the crash. I have never forgotten them and have tried to live my life in their honor.

To my fifteen fellow survivors, my brothers for life, who are the only ones who can truly understand what we suffered. Without the loyalty and solidarity we showed one another, none of us would have made it out of the Andes.

To the Old Christians Rugby Club, and the Old Christians spirit, a spirit of unity and self-sacrifice, which bonded us and gave us the strength and common will to survive.

To my sister Graciela, who was a great comfort to me in the aftermath of the ordeal, and with whom I have grown closer and closer in all the years since.

To my wife, Veronique, and my daughters, Veronica and Cecilia, for their constant love and support, and for the patience with which they endured the long hours I spent working on this book. For me, they are the dearest things in the world.

To my sister Susy, whom I still miss as much as I did in the first moments after I lost her.

To my mother, Xenia, whose warmth, love, and wisdom gave me the strength I needed to endure the unendurable . . .

And to my father, Seler, who inspired me as a boy and who inspires me still. It was my love for him, and nothing else, that carried me out of the mountains, and every moment with him since has been a blessing.

—*Nando Parrado*

Acknowledgments

WHEN I WAS APPROACHED about the possibility of working with Nando Parrado on *Miracle in the Andes,* my first impulse was to wonder if such a book was necessary. Like millions of others, I had been fascinated and inspired by the saga of the 1972 Andes Disaster, but the 1973 bestseller *Alive* had told that story in such exhaustive detail, and with such definitive scope and power, that I wondered if there was any good reason to tell it again. I knew that if this new book was to find an audience it would have to explore dimensions of the story *Alive* had left unfathomed—dimensions of emotion and introspection, of the spirit and the heart. To simply retell the events of the ordeal would be pointless. We would have to put readers inside Nando's skull, let them gaze out through his eyes at the bleakness of the Andes, and force them to trudge hopelessly, in his battered rugby shoes, on the frozen slopes he was certain would be his grave. We would have to strand them, with Nando and his friends, in the lifeless cordillera, make them live through the cold, the fear, and the desolation. The story would have to be told from inside out, through the emotional filter of Nando's desperation, and it would not succeed unless Nando understood that the best story he had to tell was about more than a young man conquering the mountains; it was about an ordinary boy who loved life too dearly to be defeated by impossible odds.

I knew that telling such a story well would require sensitivity and courage. Nando would have to tear open old wounds. He would have to relive, with eyes wide open, moments of loss and horror few of us can imagine. Would he show me those moments? Would he drag his most personal and painful memories out into the daylight and spread them out for me to see? What kind of man was he? Was he tough? Was he honest? Did he have the emotional intelligence to understand how the ordeal had transformed him? And after thirty years of reflection, did he have anything useful to say about what it all might mean?

I didn't know Nando then, but I knew the kind of man he would have to be to write a book we could both be proud of, and I knew that such men are not always easy to find. If Nando was not that kind of guy, if he couldn't illuminate his story with meaningful insight and the bravest kind of candor, then the book would be superfluous, and working on it would be a tedious chore. The risks seemed high and caution told me to bow out before the project went any further, but some nagging intuition wouldn't let me walk away. I lost sleep wrestling with it: I mean, what if he *was* that kind of guy? In the end that intuition won out, and when Nando officially offered me the job I accepted, then flew to Uruguay to meet him. We sat in the living room of his oceanside house in Punta del Este and slowly got to know each other. I showed him pictures of my family. I met his wife and daughters. We played with his big black Labrador, Sasha, and at some point, when the moment seemed right, he began to talk about the Andes. It was summer in South America and through the picture window behind him I could see green waves washing the beach. But once Nando started talking I forgot about the beach and the waves and the sunshine, because I wasn't in Punta del Este anymore. I was at Nando's side in the snowbound cordillera. His voice was soft, expressive, and unhurried, and I remember that he smiled gently, even when remembering some horror. He recalled the moment when he buried his sister in the snow, and how snowflakes sparkled on her cheeks before her face was covered. He remembered the panic he felt when he heard the news that rescue efforts had been canceled, and how he had to restrain himself from bolting off blindly into the wild. I saw him lying under the crushing weight of the avalanche, tired of fighting, waiting to see what death was like, and at the summit of Mount Seler, where the cruel view devastated him so completely that for more than a minute he forgot to breathe. He covered it all—the longing for home, the constant terror, the vicious edge of high-altitude cold, the feel of human flesh between the teeth. Nando kept his eyes on me as he described these things, and there was a quiet urgency in his voice. He wanted me to understand. *The story has been told before,* he seemed to be saying, *but not this story, not my story . . .*

He spoke for more than an hour, then sat back on the sofa and fell silent. Before I could gather my wits to speak he smiled broadly and gave me a self-effacing shrug. "I don't know," he said softly, "do you think it is enough to make a book?" In that moment I felt like a fool for ever having doubted Nando's ability to deliver the goods. Instead, I found myself shaken by the sobering realization that it would take everything *I* had to do this story justice. From that moment on I have tried with all my heart to help Nando write a book that is worthy of his experience, and now I can say that working with him has been one of the richest and most rewarding experiences of my life. So my first order of business here is to express my gratitude to Nando Parrado. I thank him for his courage, his generosity, his vision, and his good humor, and for the great gift of his friendship. But mostly, I thank him for trusting me with his story. It is the best true story I have ever heard, and having the chance to help him tell it has been an unforgettable privilege.

I AM PRIVILEGED, also, to be associated with the exceptional cast of characters at the Levine/Greenberg agency, including Jim Levine, Dan Greenberg, Arielle Eckstut, Elizabeth Fisher, and especially Stephanie Kip Rostan, whose hard work set this ship in motion, and whose gentle persistence kept it from sailing without me.

Our editor, Annik LaFarge, brought a rare combination of brains and heart to the project, and I can't imagine this book without her. She began as our strongest advocate, became a trusted adviser, and ended as a friend. I thank her for her guidance and enthusiasm. Thanks also to Steve Ross, Amy Boorstein, Mary Choteborsky, Genoveva Llosa, Luke Dempsey, and the entire crew at Crown for embracing this book with such spirited expertise; to Ernesto and Roselle Trello who offered emotional support and office space in times of need; to Gail Davis, for her pioneering efforts to make this book happen; to Roy Harley, Coche Inciarte, Alvaro Mangino, and Gustavo Zerbino, for sharing their memories, and to Ed West, for his good counsel and irreverent wit, and for a friendship that spans almost forty years.

Finally, I thank my wife, Chris, who anchors our family with quiet strength and endless patience, and my daughter, Carmela, who is not patient or quiet at all, but who lives her life with such a sweet and graceful exuberance that my days are full of smiles. Both of them made many sacrifices as I worked on this book, and now I dedicate that work to them, with love.

—*Vince Rause*

About the Authors

NANDO PARRADO reluctantly gained worldwide fame as one of the young heroes of the 1972 Andes disaster. Today he is CEO of several businesses based in his native Uruguay, including a national hardware chain, advertising and marketing firms, and a television production company, for which he produces and hosts popular programs on travel, fashion, current events, and motor sports. Since 1991 he has been one of the most sought-after speakers on the international lecture circuit. A former race car driver and winner of the European Team Cup for Touring Car racing, he still enjoys racing cars, motorcycles, and speedboats. He lives in Montevideo, Uruguay, with his wife, Veronique, and their daughters, Veronica and Cecilia. Nando can be contacted at nando1@parrado.com

VINCE RAUSE is an author and magazine writer whose stories have appeared in *The New York Times Magazine*, the *Los Angeles Times Magazine*, *Readers' Digest*, *Sports Illustrated*, and many other national and regional publications. His last book, written with noted brain researcher Andrew Newberg, was *Why God Won't Go Away: Brain Science and the Biology of Belief*. He lives in Pittsburgh with his wife, Christine, and their daughter, Carmela.